Fodor's 99

Maui and Lāna'i

The complete guide, thoroughly up-to-date

Packed with details that will make your trip

The must-see sights, off and on the beaten path

What to see, what to skip

Mix-and-match vacation itineraries

City strolls, countryside adventures

Smart lodging and dining options

Essential local do's and taboos

Transportation tips, distances and directions

Key contacts, savvy travel tips

When to go, what to pack

Clear, accurate, easy-to-use maps

Books to read, videos to watch, background essays

Excerpted from *Fodor's Hawai'i '99*

Fodor's Travel Publications, Inc.
New York • Toronto • London • Sydney • Auckland
www.fodors.com

Fodor's Maui and Lāna'i

EDITOR: Anastasia Redmond Mills

Editorial Contributors: David Brown, Jennifer Crites, Betty Fullard-Leo, Linda Kephart, Jack London, Pablo Madera, Richard J. Pietschmann, Helayne Schiff, M.T. Schwartzman (Gold Guide editor), Marty Wentzel

Editorial Production: Linda K. Schmidt

Maps: David Lindroth, *cartographer*; Steven Amsterdam, *map editor*

Design: Fabrizio La Rocca, *creative director*; Guido Caroti, *associate art director*; Jolie Novak, *photo editor*

Production/Manufacturing: Rebecca Zeiler

Cover Photograph: Frank S. Balthis

Copyright

Special Sales

Fodor's Travel Publications are available at special discounts for bulk purchases for sales promotions or premiums. Special editions, including personalized covers, excerpts of existing guides, and corporate imprints, can be created in large quantities for special needs. For more information, contact your local bookseller or write to Special Markets, Fodor's Travel Publications, 201 East 50th Street, New York, NY 10022. Inquiries from Canada should be directed to your local Canadian bookseller or sent to Random House of Canada, Ltd., Marketing Department, 2775 Matheson Boulevard East, Mississauga, Ontario L4W 4P7. Inquiries from the United Kingdom should be sent to Fodor's Travel Publications, 20 Vauxhall Bridge Road, London SW1V 2SA, England.

PRINTED IN THE UNITED STATES OF AMERICA

10 9 8 7 6 5 4 3 2 1

CONTENTS

ON THE ROAD WITH FODOR'S

WHEN I PLAN A VACATION, the first thing I do is cast around among my friends and colleagues to find someone who's just been where I'm going. That's because there's no substitute for a recommendation from a good friend who knows your tastes, your budget, and your circumstances, someone who's just been there. Unfortunately, such friends are few and far between. So it's nice to know that there's *Fodor's Maui and Lāna'i*.

In the first place, this book won't stay home when you hit the road. It will accompany you every step of the way, steering you away from wrong turns and wrong choices and never expecting a thing in return. Most important of all, it's written and assiduously updated by the kind of people you *would* hit up for travel tips if you knew them. They're as choosy as your pickiest friend, except they've probably seen a lot more of Maui and Lāna'i. Will this be the vacation of your dreams? We hope so.

About Our Writers

Our success in helping to make your trip the best of all possible vacations is a credit to the hard work of our extraordinary writers.

Pablo Madera, our Maui updater, is a freelance journalist, jazz drummer, and ethnobotanist who has made Maui his home base for 25 years. When he's not pursuing research projects on various Pacific islands, he tries to keep up with banana production on his small farm, which is off the road to Hāna.

A 17-year Hawai'i resident, **Marty Wentzel** is a prolific freelance writer whose articles have appeared in publications around the world, including *American Way, Modern Bride,* and *ALOHA Magazine.* A specialist in the Hawai'i dining scene, she has coauthored cookbooks with two of the state's top chefs, Sam Choy and Roy Yamaguchi—but she's equally happy eating fresh mango on the beach at sunset. Marty updated the Lāna'i chapter and wrote the Close-Up on Hawaiian music.

Connections

We're pleased that the American Society of Travel Agents continues to endorse Fodor's as its guidebook of choice. ASTA is the world's largest and most influential travel trade association, operating in more than 170 countries, with 27,000 members pledged to adhere to a strict code of ethics reflecting the Society's motto, "Integrity in Travel." ASTA shares Fodor's devotion to providing smart, honest travel information and advice to travelers, and we've long recommended that our readers—even those who have guidebooks and traveling friends—consult ASTA member agents for the experience and professionalism they bring to your vacation planning.

On Fodor's Web site (www.fodors.com), check out the new Resource Center, an online companion to the Gold Guide section of this book, complete with useful hot links to related sites. In our forums, you can also get lively advice from other travelers and more great tips from Fodor's experts worldwide.

How to Use This Book

Organization

Up front is the **Gold Guide,** an easy-to-use section arranged alphabetically by topic. Under each listing you'll find tips and information that will help you accomplish what you need to in Hawai'i. You'll also find addresses and telephone numbers of organizations and companies that offer destination-related services and detailed information and publications.

The first chapter in the guide, Destination: Maui helps get you in the mood for your trip. New and Noteworthy cues you in on trends and happenings, What's Where gets you oriented, Pleasures and Pastimes describes the activities and sights that make Maui unique, Fodor's Choice showcases our top picks, and Festivals and Seasonal Events alerts you to special events you'll want to seek out.

The Exploring Maui chapter is divided into neighborhood sections; each recommends driving tour and lists neighborhood sights alphabetically, including sights that are off the beaten path. The remaining chapters are arranged in alphabetical order by subject.

At the end of the book you'll find Portraits, wonderful essays about Maui adventures, followed by recommended books and videos that use Maui as a backdrop. A brief introduction to the Hawaiian language follows, along with a glossary of common terms and menu items.

Icons and Symbols

★ Our special recommendations
✕ Restaurant
🏠 Lodging establishment
☺ Good for kids (rubber duck)
☞ Sends you to another section of the guide for more information
✉ Address
☎ Telephone number
☉ Opening and closing times
🎟 Admission prices (those we give apply to adults; substantially reduced fees are almost always available for children, students, and senior citizens)

Numbers in white and black circles ③ ❸ that appear on the maps, in the margins, and within the tours correspond to one another.

Dining and Lodging

The restaurants and lodgings we list are the cream of the crop in each price range. Price categories are as follows:

For restaurants:

CATEGORY	COST*
$$$$	over $60
$$$	$40–$60
$$	$20–$40
$	under $20

*per person for a three-course meal, excluding drinks, service, and 4.17% sales tax

For hotels:

CATEGORY	COST*
$$$$	over $200
$$$	$125–$200
$$	$75–$125
$	under $75

*All prices are for a standard double room, excluding 10.17% tax and service charges.

Credit Cards

The following abbreviations are used: **AE,** American Express; **D,** Discover; **DC,** Diners Club; **MC,** MasterCard; and **V,** Visa.

Don't Forget to Write

You can use this book in the confidence that all prices and opening times are based on information supplied to us at press time; Fodor's cannot accept responsibility for any errors. Time inevitably brings changes, so always confirm information when it matters—especially if you're making a detour to visit a specific place.

Were the restaurants we recommended as described? Did our hotel picks exceed your expectations? Did you find a museum we recommended a waste of time? Keeping a travel guide fresh and up-to-date is a big job, and we welcome your feedback, positive *and* negative. If you have complaints, we'll look into them and revise our entries when the facts warrant it. If you've discovered a special place that we haven't included, we'll pass the information along to our correspondents and have them check it out. So send us your thoughts via e-mail at editors@fodors.com (specifying the name of the book on the subject line) or on paper in care of the Maui editor at Fodor's, 201 East 50th Street, New York, New York 10022. In the meantime, have a wonderful trip!

Karen Cure
Editorial Director

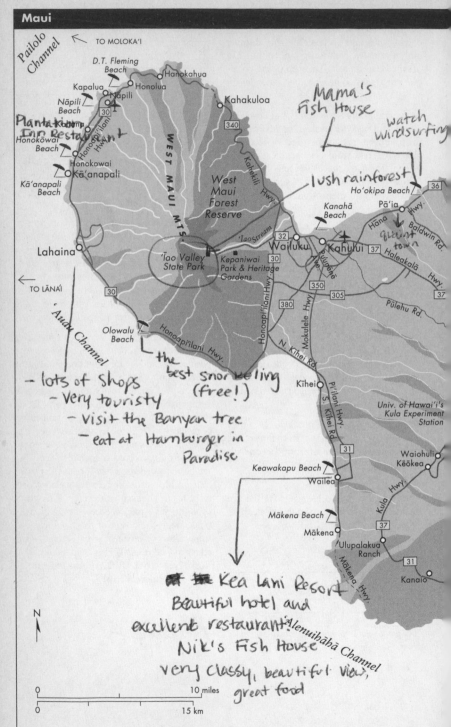

PACIFIC OCEAN

Ulumalu
Huelo
Kailua
365 Rd.
ROAD TO HANA
Beautiful
Curvy drive
360
Kaumahina State
Wayside Park
390
Kokomo
Honomanu
Valley
Ke'anae Arboretum
Makawao
Ke'anae Overlook
Wailua
Pukalani
Wailua Lookout
377
Waikāne
Falls
Nāhiku
Haleakalā
Crater Rd.
Kōolau
Forest
Reserve
360 Hāna Hwy
Wai'ānapanapa
State Park
37
Park
Headquarters
Visitor Center
Helani Gardens
Hāna Forest Reserve
Hāna
378
Kula Botanical
Gardens
Kaihalulu
Beach
Hamoa
Haleakalā
Haleakalā Visitor
Center
Haleakalā
National Park
Pu'u 'Ula'ula
Overlook
Mūolea
Kahikinui
Forest Reserve
Kīpahulu
31
Kaupō
'Alenuihāhā Channel
Pi'ilani Hwy
31

TO HAWAI'I

KAUA'I

Hā'ena

Wailua

Līhu'e

Waimea

Po'ipū

Pu'uwai

NI'IHAU

Kaua'i Channel

O'AHU

Kahuku

Hale'iwa

Kāne'ohe

Ma'kaha

Honolulu

Waikīkī

Kaiwi

PACIFIC OCEAN

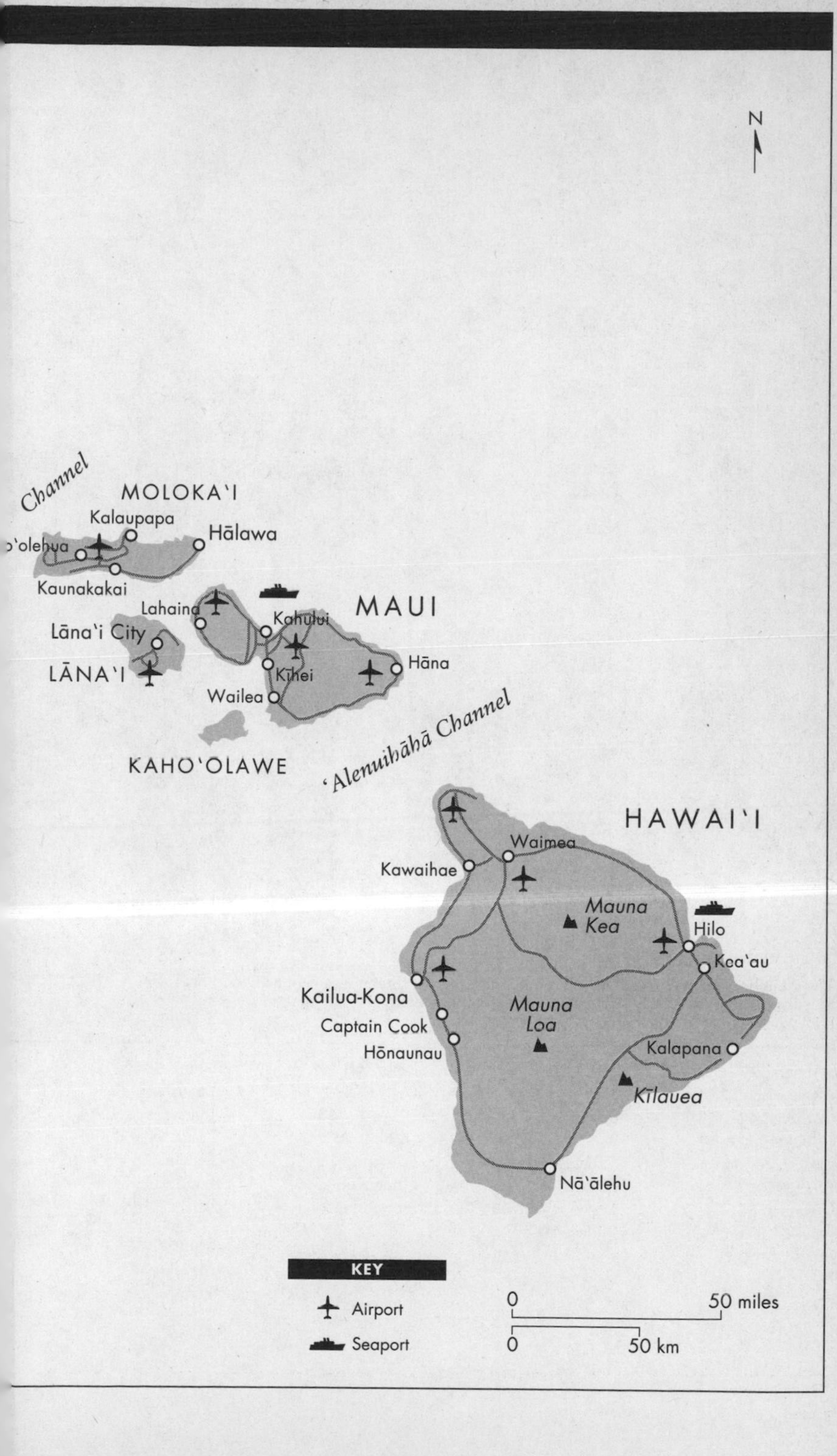

N

Channel

MOLOKA'I

Kalaupapa
Hālawa
ɔ'olehua
Kaunakakai

Lahaina
Kahului
MAUI
Lāna'i City
LĀNA'I
Kīhei
Hāna
Wailea

KAHO'OLAWE
'Alenuihāhā Channel

HAWAI'I

Waimea
Kawaihae
Mauna
Kea
Hilo
Kea'au

Kailua-Kona
Mauna
Loa
Captain Cook
Kalapana
Hōnaunau
Kīlauea

Nā'ālehu

KEY	
✈	Airport
⛴	Seaport

0   50 miles

0   50 km

World Time Zones

Numbers below vertical bands relate each zone to Greenwich Mean Time (0 hrs.).
Local times frequently differ from these general indications,
as indicated by light-face numbers on map.

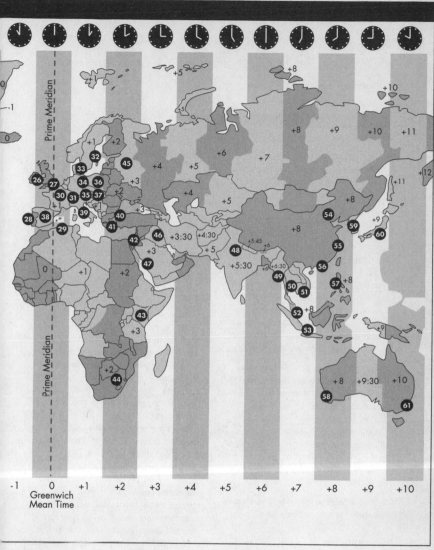

SMART TRAVEL TIPS A TO Z

Basic Information on Traveling in Maui, Savvy Tips to Make Your Trip a Breeze, and Companies and Organizations to Contact

AIR TRAVEL

BOOKING YOUR FLIGHT

Price is just one factor to consider when booking a flight: frequency of service and even a carrier's safety record are often just as important. Major airlines offer the greatest number of departures. Smaller airlines—including regional and no-frills airlines—usually have a limited number of flights daily. On the other hand, so-called low-cost airlines usually are cheaper, and their fares impose fewer restrictions, such as advance-purchase requirements. Safety-wise, low-cost carriers as a group have a good history—about equal to that of major carriers.

When you book, **look for nonstop flights** and **remember that "direct" flights stop at least once.** Try to **avoid connecting flights,** which require a change of plane. Two airlines may jointly operate a connecting flight, so ask if your airline operates every segment—you may find that your preferred carrier flies you only part of the way.

Ask your airline if it offers electronic ticketing, which eliminates all paperwork. There's no ticket to pick up or misplace. You go directly to the gate and give the agent your confirmation number. There's no worry about waiting on line at the airport while precious minutes tick by.

CARRIERS

➤ MAJOR AIRLINES: **American** (☎ 800/433–7300). **Delta** (☎ 800/221–1212). **Hawaiian** (☎ 800/367–5320). **United** (☎ 800/241–6522).

CONSOLIDATORS

Consolidators buy tickets for scheduled international flights at reduced rates from the airlines, then sell them at prices that beat the best fare available directly from the airlines, usually without restrictions. Sometimes you can even get your money back if you need to return the ticket. Carefully read the fine print detailing penalties for changes and cancellations, and **confirm your consolidator reservation with the airline.**

➤ CONSOLIDATORS: **Cheap Tickets** (☎ 800/377–1000). **Up & Away Travel** (☎ 212/889–2345). **Discount Travel Network** (☎ 800/576–1600). **Unitravel** (☎ 800/325–2222). **World Travel Network** (☎ 800/409–6753).

CUTTING COSTS

The least-expensive airfares to Maui are priced for round-trip travel and usually must be purchased in advance. It's smart to **call a number of airlines, and when you are quoted a good price, book it on the spot**—the same fare may not be available the next day. Airlines generally allow you to change your return date for a fee. If you don't use your ticket, you can apply the cost toward the purchase of a new ticket, again for a small charge. However, most low-fare tickets are nonrefundable. To get the lowest airfare, **check different routings.** Compare prices of flights to and from different airports if your destination or home city has more than one gateway. Also price off-peak flights, which may be significantly less expensive.

When flying within the U.S., **plan to stay over a Saturday night** and **travel during the middle of the week** to get the lowest fare. These low fares are usually priced for round-trip travel and are nonrefundable. You can, however, change your return date for a fee ($75 on most major airlines).

Travel agents, especially those who specialize in finding the lowest fares (☞ Discounts & Deals, *below*), can be especially helpful when booking a plane ticket. When you're quoted a price, **ask your agent if the price is**

likely to get any lower. Good agents know the seasonal fluctuations of airfares and can usually anticipate a sale or fare war. However, waiting can be risky: The fare could go *up* as seats become scarce, and you may wait so long that your preferred flight sells out. A wait-and-see strategy works best if your plans are flexible. If you must arrive and depart on certain dates, don't delay.

CHECK IN & BOARDING

Airlines routinely overbook planes, assuming that not everyone with a ticket will show up, but sometimes everyone does. When that happens, airlines ask for volunteers to give up their seats. In return these volunteers usually get a certificate for a free flight and are rebooked on the next flight out. If there are not enough volunteers, the airline must choose who will be denied boarding. The first to get bumped are passengers who checked in late and those flying on discounted tickets, so **get to the gate and check in as early as possible,** especially during peak periods.

Although the trend on international flights is to drop reconfirmation requirements, many airlines still ask you to reconfirm each leg of your international itinerary. Failure to do so may result in your reservation being canceled.

Always **bring a government-issued photo ID to the airport.** You may be asked to show it before you are allowed to check in.

ENJOYING THE FLIGHT

For more legroom, **request an emergency-aisle seat.** Don't sit in the row in front of the emergency aisle or in front of a bulkhead, where seats may not recline.

If you don't like airline food, **ask for special meals when booking.** These can be vegetarian, low-cholesterol, or kosher, for example.

FLYING TIMES

Flying time is about 10 hours from New York, 6 hours from Chicago, and 3 hours from Los Angeles.

HOW TO COMPLAIN

If your baggage goes astray or your flight goes awry, complain right away. Most carriers require that you **file a claim immediately.**

➤ AIRLINE COMPLAINTS: U.S. Department of Transportation **Aviation Consumer Protection Division** (✉ C-75, Room 4107, Washington, DC 20590, ☎ 202/366–2220). **Federal Aviation Administration Consumer Hotline** (☎ 800/322–7873).

LEI GREETINGS

For some visitors it's a rude awakening to get off a plane in Hawai'i with no lei to greet them. Some arrangement needs to be made in advance should you want such a welcome. If you've purchased a package tour, lei greetings are sometimes included; if friends are meeting you at the airport, they'll also know the island custom. If you're traveling independently, however, you can still receive a lei upon arrival by making arrangements with one of several companies. Greeters of Hawai'i operates statewide. Airport Flower & Fruit, based on Maui, also does a good job.

➤ LEI GREETERS: **Greeters of Hawai'i** (✉ Box 29638, Honolulu 96820, ☎ 800/366–8559) operates statewide. **Airport Flower & Fruit** (✉ Box 330039, Kahului 96733, ☎ 808/243–9367 or 800/922–9352).

AIRPORTS

Maui has two airports: **Kahului Airport,** in the island's central town of Kahului, and **Kapalua-West Maui Airport,** which is the easiest arrival point for visitors to West Maui (it saves about an hour's drive from the Kahului airport). The tiny town of **Hāna** in east Maui also has an airstrip, but it is only serviced by one commuter and one charter airline.

Kahului Airport is the only airport on Maui that has direct service from the mainland. Its chief disadvantage is its distance from the major resort destinations in West Maui and Wailea. It will take you about an hour, with traffic in your favor, to get to a hotel in West Maui and about 20 to 30 minutes to go to Wailea.

THE GOLD GUIDE / SMART TRAVEL TIPS

The best way to get from the airport to your destination is in your own rental car. You're going to need it for the rest of the trip, so you may as well get it right away. Most major car-rental companies have conveniently located desks at each airport (☞ Car Rentals, *below*).

➤ AIRPORT INFORMATION: **Kahului Airport** (☎ 808/872–3803). **Kapalua-West Maui Airport** (☎ 808/669–0228). **Hāna** airstrip (☎ 808/248–8208).

SHUTTLES

Most major hotels provide shuttle service from Kahului Airport; ask when booking your room if airport transfers are included in your rate.

➤ BUS/SHUTTLE: The **TransHawaiian Airporter Shuttle** (☎ 808/877–7308) leaves Kahului Airport on the half hour 9–4, bound for Kapalua, with stops in Lahaina and Kā'anapali; one-way fare is $13.

TAXIS

Maui has nearly two dozen taxi companies, and they make frequent passes through the airport. If you don't see a cab, you can call Yellow Cab or La Bella Taxi for islandwide service from the airport, or Kīhei Taxi if you're staying in the Kīhei, Wailea, or Mākena area. Charges from Kahului Airport to Kā'anapali run about $49; to Wailea, about $32; and to Lahaina, about $45.

➤ TAXIS: **La Bella Taxi** (☎ 808/242–8011). **Kīhei Taxi** (☎ 808/879–3000). **Yellow Cab** (☎ 808/877–7000).

BUS TRAVEL

Although Maui has no public transit system, both Akina Express and Speedy Shuttle offer private service around the island for $18–$36.

TransHawaiian Services operates a Maui Shopping Express, providing service between the island hubs of Wailea, Kahului, and Kapalua Mon.–Sat. 9:30 AM–7:30 PM and Sun. 9:30 AM–5 PM. One-way, round-trip, and all-day passes are available.

The Kā'anapali–Lahaina Shuttle runs daily from the Royal Lahaina Resort in Kā'anapali to the Wharf Cinema Center in Lahaina every half hour between 8 AM and 10:25 PM, with stops at all Kā'anapali hotels. The cost is $1. The double-decker West Maui Shopping Express ferries passengers to and from Kā'anapali, Kapalula, Honokōwai (Embassy Vacation Resort area) and Lahaina from 8AM to 10PM. The fare is $1. The Kā'anapali Trolley runs within the resort between 9 AM and 11 PM and stops automatically at all hotels and at condos when requested. It also goes to and from Lahaina at 55-minute intervals. It's free. All Kā'anapali hotels have copies of schedules, or you can call the Kā'anapali Beach Resort Association. The free Aston Hotels Shuttle in the Kā'anapali area runs from 8 PM to 6 PM for guests who want to go to the Whalers Village Shopping Center and Lahaina. You can get schedules at Aston hotel desks. The Wailea Shuttle and the Kapalua Shuttle run within their respective resorts and are free; schedules are available throughout each resort.

➤ BUSES: **Akina Express** (☎ 808/661–4567). **Kā'anapali Beach Resort Association** (☎ 808/661–3271). **Speedy Shuttle** (☎ 808/875–8070). **TransHawaiian Services** (☎ 808/877–7380)

BUSINESS HOURS

Banks on Maui are generally open Monday–Thursday 8:30–3, Friday 8:30–6.

Shops are usually open seven days a week, 9–5. Shopping centers tend to stay open later (until 9 on certain days).

CAMERAS & COMPUTERS

EQUIPMENT PRECAUTIONS

Always **keep your film, tape, or computer disks out of the sun.** Carry an extra supply of batteries, and **be prepared to turn on your camera, camcorder, or laptop** to prove to security personnel that the device is real. Always **ask for hand inspection of film,** which becomes clouded after successive exposure to airport X-ray machines, and **keep videotapes and computer disks away from metal detectors.**

TRAVEL PHOTOGRAPHY

➤ PHOTO HELP: **Kodak Information Center** (☎ 800/242–2424). *Kodak Guide to Shooting Great Travel Pictures,* available in bookstores or from Fodor's Travel Publications (☎ 800/533–6478; $16.50 plus $4 shipping).

CAR RENTAL

Rates in Maui begin at about $25 a day and $154 a week for an economy car with unlimited mileage, but special packages offered by hotels and interisland airlines may lower your cost. This does not include tax on car rentals, which is 4.16%. There is a $2 daily surcharge on all rental cars in Hawai'i.

Budget, Dollar, and National have courtesy phones at the Kapalua–West Maui Airport, while Hertz and Alamo are nearby. All the above plus Avis have desks at or near Maui's major airport in Kahului. If you fly into the Hāna Airport, you can call the local Dollar to pick you up, or if you have reserved a car from another company, the agent will usually know your arrival time and meet you.

➤ MAJOR AGENCIES: **Alamo** (☎ 800/327–9633, 0800/272–2000 in the U.K.). **Avis** (☎ 800/331–1212, 800/879–2847 in Canada, 008/225–533 in Australia). **Budget** (☎ 800/527–0700, 0800/181181 in the U.K.). **Dollar** (☎ 800/800–4000; 0990/565656 in the U.K., where it is known as Eurodollar). **Hertz** (☎ 800/654–3131, 800/263–0600 in Canada, 0345/555888 in the U.K., 03/9222–2523 in Australia, 03/358–6777 in New Zealand). **National InterRent** (☎ 800/227–7368; 0345/222525 in the U.K., where it is known as Europcar InterRent).

➤ LOCAL AGENCIES: **Roberts Tours** (☎ 808/523–9323) offers car rentals through package tours. **Thrifty Car Rental** (☎ 808/973–5188). **Rent-A-Jeep** (☎ 808/877–6626) will pick you up at Kahului Airport.

CUTTING COSTS

To get the best deal, **book through a travel agent who is willing to shop around.** When pricing cars, **ask about the location of the rental lot.** Some off-airport locations offer lower rates, and their lots are only minutes from the terminal via complimentary shuttle. You also may want to **price local car-rental companies,** whose rates may be lower still, although their service and maintenance may not be as good as those of a name-brand agency. Remember to ask about required deposits, cancellation penalties, and drop-off charges if you're planning to pick up the car in one city and leave it in another.

Also **ask your travel agent about a company's customer-service record.** How has the company responded to late plane arrivals and vehicle mishaps? Are there often lines at the rental counter? If you're traveling during a holiday period, does a confirmed reservation guarantee you a car?

Be sure to **look into wholesalers,** companies that do not own fleets but rent in bulk from those that do and often offer better rates than traditional car-rental operations. Prices are best during off-peak periods.

➤ RENTAL WHOLESALERS: **Auto Europe** (☎ 207/842–2000 or 800/223–5555, FAX 800–235–6321). **Kemwel Holiday Autos** (☎ 914/835–5555 or 800/678–0678, FAX 914/835–5126).

INSURANCE

When driving a rented car you are generally responsible for any damage to or loss of the vehicle. You also are liable for any property damage or personal injury that you may cause while driving. Before you rent, **see what coverage you already have** under the terms of your personal auto-insurance policy and credit cards.

For about $15 to $20 per day, rental companies sell protection, known as a collision- or loss-damage waiver (CDW or LDW), that eliminates your liability for damage to the car; it's always optional and should never be automatically added to your bill.

In most states you don't need a CDW if you have personal auto insurance or other liability insurance. However, **make sure you have enough coverage to pay for the car.** If you do not have auto insurance or an umbrella policy that covers damage to third parties, purchasing liability insurance and a CDW or LDW is highly recommended.

REQUIREMENTS

In Hawai'i you must be 21 to rent a car, and rates may be higher if you're under 25. You'll pay extra for child seats (about $3 per day), which are compulsory for children under five, and for additional drivers (about $2 per day). Non-U.S. residents will need a reservation voucher, a passport, a driver's license, and a travel policy that covers each driver, in order to pick up a car.

SURCHARGES

Before you pick up a car in one city and leave it in another, **ask about drop-off charges or one-way service fees,** which can be substantial. Note, too, that some rental agencies charge extra if you return the car before the time specified in your contract. To avoid a hefty refueling fee, **fill the tank just before you turn in the car,** but be aware that gas stations near the rental outlet may overcharge.

CAR TRAVEL

Maui, the second-largest island in the state of Hawai'i, with 729 square miles, has some 120 miles of coastline, not all of which is accessible. Less than one-quarter of its landmass is inhabited. To see the island your best bet is a car; there is no reliable public transportation.

Maui has several major roads. Highway 30, the Honoapi'ilani Highway, goes from Wailuku in Central Maui around the south of the West Maui mountains and up the west coast past Lahaina, Kā'anapali, and Kapalua. The road from the Pu'unēnē to Kīhei, Wailea, and Mākena is called Highway 311, or the Mokulele Highway. When you reach Kīhei, you can take Kīhei Road to reach all the lodgings in that town, or you can bypass them on Highway 31 (the Pi'ilani Highway) if you're staying in Wailea or Mākena. The latter road is the best on the island in terms of driving because it is wide and sparsely traveled. Another main thoroughfare is

the Haleakalā Highway (numbered 37, 377, and 378 at different points), which goes between Kahului and Haleakalā. Most of the island's roads have two lanes.

If you're going to attempt the dirt roads between Kapalua and Wailuku or from Hāna to Mākena, you'll need a four-wheel-drive vehicle. Be forewarned: Car-rental companies prohibit travel off the pavement, so if you break down, you're on your own for repairs. The only other difficult road on Maui is the Hāna Highway, which runs 56 miles between Kahului and Hāna and includes more twists and turns than a person can count. Take it slow and you should have no problems.

Asking for directions will almost always produce a helpful explanation from the locals, but you should be prepared for an island term or two. Instead of using compass directions, Hawai'i residents refer to places as being either mauka (toward the mountains) or makai (toward the ocean).

AUTO CLUBS

➤ IN AUSTRALIA: **Australian Automobile Association** (☎ 06/247–7311).

➤ IN CANADA: **Canadian Automobile Association** (CAA, ☎ 613/247–0117).

➤ IN NEW ZEALAND: **New Zealand Automobile Association** (☎ 09/377–4660).

➤ IN THE U.K.: **Automobile Association** (AA, ☎ 0990/500–600), **Royal Automobile Club** (RAC, ☎ 0990/722–722 for membership, 0345/121–345 for insurance).

➤ IN THE U.S.: **American Automobile Association** (☎ 800/564–6222).

EMERGENCY SERVICES

➤ AAA SERVICE: The two AAA companies that offer 24-hour island-wide service are **D & D Towing and Recovery** (✉ Box 1937, Wailuku, 96732, ☎ 808/871–1185) and **Wrecx and Company Towing** (✉ Kihei, 96758, ☎ 808/874–1920). They will travel anywhere on Maui with a tow truck.

CHILDREN & TRAVEL

CHILDREN IN MAUI

Be sure to plan ahead and **involve your youngsters** as you outline your trip. When packing, include things to keep them busy en route. On sightseeing days try to schedule activities of special interest to your children. If you are renting a car don't forget to **arrange for a car seat** when you reserve. Most hotels in Maui allow children under a certain age to stay in their parents' room at no extra charge, but others charge them as extra adults; be sure to **ask about the cutoff age for children's discounts.**

FLYING

If your children are two or older, **ask about children's airfares.** As a general rule, infants under two not occupying a seat fly at greatly reduced fares or even for free.

In general the adult baggage allowance applies to children paying half or more of the adult fare.

Experts agree that it's a good idea to use safety seats aloft for children weighing less than 40 pounds. Airlines, however, can set their own policies: U.S. carriers allow FAA-approved models but usually require that you buy a ticket, even if your child would otherwise ride free, since the seats must be strapped into regular seats. Airline rules vary, so it's important to **check your airline's policy about using safety seats during takeoff and landing.** Safety seats cannot obstruct the movement of other passengers in the row, so get an appropriate seat assignment as early as possible.

When making your reservation, **request children's meals or a free-standing bassinet** if you need them; the latter are available only to those seated at the bulkhead, where there's enough legroom. Remember, however, that bulkhead seats may not have their own overhead bins, and there's no storage space in front of you—a major inconvenience.

GROUP TRAVEL

When planning to take your kids on a tour, look for companies that specialize in family travel.

➤ FAMILY-FRIENDLY TOUR OPERATORS: **Families Welcome!** (✉ 92 N. Main St., Ashland, OR 97520, ☎ 541/482–6121 or 800/326–0724, FAX 541/482–0660). **Rascals in Paradise** (✉ 650 5th St., Suite 505, San Francisco, CA 94107, ☎ 415/978–9800 or 800/872–7225, FAX 415/442–0289).

CONSUMER PROTECTION

Whenever possible, **pay with a major credit card** so you can cancel payment or get reimbursed if there's a problem, provided that you can provide documentation. This is the best way to pay, whether you're buying travel arrangements before your trip or shopping at your destination.

If you're doing business with a particular company for the first time, **contact your local Better Business Bureau and the attorney general's offices** in your state and the company's home state, as well. Have any complaints been filed?

Finally, if you're buying a package or tour, always **consider travel insurance** that includes default coverage (☞ Insurance, *below*).

➤ LOCAL BBBs: **Council of Better Business Bureaus** (✉ 4200 Wilson Blvd., Suite 800, Arlington, VA 22203, ☎ 703/276–0100, FAX 703/525–8277). **Better Business Bureau** (✉ 1600 Kapi'olani Blvd., Ste. 201, Honolulu, HI 96814, ☎ 808/536–6956).

CRUISE TRAVEL

No regularly scheduled American ships steam between the Mainland and Maui. Although foreign-owned vessels often ply the Pacific, the Jones Act of 1896 prohibits them from carrying passengers between two U.S. ports unless the ships first stop at an intervening foreign port or carry the passengers to a foreign destination. What that means to those wishing for the relaxing ways of ship travel is that they can book with one of the major lines passing through Honolulu, but if they wish to sail on to Kahului, they'll need to book another passage, with American Hawai'i Cruises.

Approaching the Valley Isle from the deck of a ship is a great orientation. If a cruise is an option that appeals to you, you can book passage through American Hawai'i Cruises, which offers seven-day interisland cruises departing from Honolulu on the SS Constitution and the SS Independence. Ask about the company's seven-day cruise-resort combination packages.

➤ CRUISE LINES: **American Hawai'i Cruises** (✉ 2 North Riverside Plaza, Chicago IL 60606, ☎ 312/466–6000 or 800/765–7000).

CUSTOMS & DUTIES

When shopping, **keep receipts** for all of your purchases. Upon reentering the country, **be ready to show customs officials what you've bought.** If you feel a duty is incorrect, appeal the assessment. If you object to the way your clearance was handled, get the inspector's badge number. In either case, first ask to see a supervisor, then write to the appropriate authorities, beginning with the port director at your point of entry.

IN MAUI

Plants and plant products are subject to regulation by the Department of Agriculture, both on entering and leaving Hawai'i. Pineapples and coconuts with the packer's agricultural inspection stamp pass freely; papayas must be treated, inspected, and stamped. All other fruits are banned for export to the U.S. mainland. Flowers pass except for gardenia, rose leaves, jade vine, and mauna loa. Also banned are insects, snails; soil; and coffee, cotton, cacti, sugarcane, and all berry plants.

Leave dogs and other pets at home. A strict 120-day quarantine is imposed to keep out rabies, which is nonexistent in Hawai'i. Many other animals (including iguanas and snakes of any kind) are not allowed at all because non-native escapees can harm the Islands' delicate ecosystems.

➤ INFORMATION: **Animal Quarantine Station, Department of Agriculture** (✉ State of Hawai'i, 99–951 Hālawa Valley Rd., 'Aiea, O'ahu, HI 96701, ☎ 808/483–7171).

IN AUSTRALIA

Australia residents who are 18 or older may bring back $A400 worth of souvenirs and gifts (including jewelry), 250 cigarettes or 250 grams of tobacco, and 1,125 ml of alcohol (including wine, beer, and spirits). Residents under 18 may bring back $A200 worth of goods.

➤ INFORMATION: **Australian Customs Service** (Regional Director, ✉ Box 8, Sydney, NSW 2001, ☎ 02/9213–2000, FAX 02/9213–4000).

IN CANADA

Canadian residents who have been out of Canada for at least 7 days may bring in C$500 worth of goods duty-free. If you've been away less than 7 days but more than 48 hours, the duty-free allowance drops to C$200; if your trip lasts 24–48 hours, the allowance is C$50. You may not pool allowances with family members. Goods claimed under the C$500 exemption may follow you by mail; those claimed under the lesser exemptions must accompany you. Alcohol and tobacco products may be included in the 7-day and 48-hour exemptions but not in the 24-hour exemption. If you meet the age requirements of the province or territory through which you reenter Canada, you may bring in, duty-free, 1.14 liters (40 imperial ounces) of wine or liquor *or* 24 12-ounce cans or bottles of beer or ale. If you are 16 or older you may bring in, duty-free, 200 cigarettes and 50 cigars.

You may send an unlimited number of gifts worth up to C$60 each duty-free to Canada. Label the package UNSOLICITED GIFT—VALUE UNDER $60. Alcohol and tobacco are excluded.

➤ INFORMATION: **Revenue Canada** (✉ 2265 St. Laurent Blvd. S, Ottawa, Ontario K1G 4K3, ☎ 613/993–0534, 800/461–9999 in Canada).

IN NEW ZEALAND

Although greeted with a "Haere Mai" ("Welcome to New Zealand"), homeward-bound residents with goods to declare must present themselves for inspection. If you're 17 or older, you may bring back $700 worth of souvenirs and gifts. Your duty-free allowance also includes 4.5 liters of wine or beer; one 1,125-ml bottle of spirits; and either 200 cigarettes, 250 grams of tobacco,

50 cigars, or a combo of all three up to 250 grams.

➤ INFORMATION: **New Zealand Customs** (✉ Custom House, ✉ 50 Anzac Ave., Box 29, Auckland, New Zealand, ☎ 09/359–6655, ☎ 09/309–2978).

IN THE U.K.

From countries outside the EU, including the United States, you may import, duty-free, 200 cigarettes or 50 cigars; 1 liter of spirits or 2 liters of fortified or sparkling wine or liqueurs; 2 liters of still table wine; 60 milliliters of perfume; 250 milliliters of toilet water; plus £136 worth of other goods, including gifts and souvenirs.

➤ INFORMATION: **HM Customs and Excise** (✉ Dorset House, ✉ Stamford St., London SE1 9NG, ☎ 0171/202–4227).

IN THE U.S.

Non-U.S. residents ages 21 and older may import into the United States 200 cigarettes or 50 cigars or 2 kilograms of tobacco, 1 liter of alcohol, and gifts worth $100. Prohibited items include meat products, seeds, plants, and fruits.

➤ INFORMATION: **U.S. Customs Service** (Inquiries, ✉ Box 7407, Washington, DC 20044, ☎ 202/927–6724; complaints, Office of Regulations and Rulings, ✉ 1301 Constitution Ave. NW, Washington, DC 20229; registration of equipment, Resource Management, ✉ 1301 Constitution Ave. NW, Washington DC 20229, ☎ 202/927–0540).

DISABILITIES & ACCESSIBILITY

ACCESS IN MAUI

The Society for the Advancement of Travel for the Handicapped has named Hawai'i the most accessible vacation spot for the disabled; the number of ramped visitor areas and specially equipped lodgings in the state attests to its desire to make everyone feel welcome.

➤ LOCAL RESOURCES: The **Commission on Persons with Disabilities** (✉ 919 Ala Moana Blvd., Room 101, Honolulu 96814, ☎ 808/586–8121; ✉ 54 High St., Wailuku 96793,

☎ 808/984–8219) has information concerning accessibility on the Islands; it also publishes helpful travelers' guides that list support services on the Islands for disabled visitors.

MAKING RESERVATIONS

When discussing accessibility with an operator or reservations agent, **ask hard questions.** Are there any stairs, inside *or* out? Are there grab bars next to the toilet *and* in the shower/tub? How wide is the doorway to the room? To the bathroom? For the most extensive facilities meeting the latest legal specifications, **opt for newer accommodations,** which are more likely to have been designed with access in mind. Older buildings or ships may have more limited facilities. Be sure to **discuss your needs before booking.**

TRANSPORTATION

Those who prefer to do their own driving may rent hand-controlled cars from Avis (☞ Car Rentals, *above*), which suggests a one-month advance reservation. Hertz (☞ Car Rentals, *above*) also rents left- or right-hand controlled cars at no additional charge. A three-day notice is required, and an additional $25 deposit is required from customers renting on a cash basis. You can use the windshield card from your own state to park in spaces reserved for people with disabilities.

➤ COMPLAINTS: **Disability Rights Section** (✉ U.S. Department of Justice, Civil Rights Division, ✉ Box 66738, Washington, DC 20035–6738, ☎ 202/514–0301 or 800/514–0301, TTY 202/514–0383 or 800/514–0383, FAX 202/307–1198) for general complaints. **Aviation Consumer Protection Division** (☞ Air Travel, *above*) for airline-related problems. **Civil Rights Office** (✉ U.S. Department of Transportation, Departmental Office of Civil Rights, S-30, ✉ 400 7th St. SW, Room 10215, Washington, DC, 20590, ☎ 202/366–4648, FAX 202/366–9371) for problems with surface transportation.

TRAVEL AGENCIES & TOUR OPERATORS

As a whole, the travel industry has become more aware of the needs of

THE GOLD GUIDE / SMART TRAVEL TIPS

THE GOLD GUIDE / SMART TRAVEL TIPS

travelers with disabilities. In the U.S., the Americans with Disabilities Act requires that travel firms serve the needs of all travelers. Note, though, that some agencies and operators specialize in making travel arrangements for individuals and groups with disabilities.

➤ TRAVELERS WITH MOBILITY PROBLEMS: **Access Adventures** (✉ 206 Chestnut Ridge Rd., Rochester, NY 14624, ☎ 716/889–9096), run by a former physical-rehabilitation counselor. **Accessible Journeys** (✉ 35 W. Sellers Ave., Ridley Park, PA 19078, ☎ 610/521–0339 or 800/846–4537, FAX 610/521–6959), for escorted tours exclusively for travelers with mobility impairments. **Accessible Vans of Hawaii, Activity and Travel Agency** (✉ 186 Mehani Circle, Kihei, HI 96753, ☎ 808/879–5521 or 800/303–3750, FAX 808/879–0649). CareVacations (✉ 5019 49th Ave., Suite 102, Leduc, Alberta T9E 6T5, ☎ 403/986–6404, 800/648–1116 in Canada) has group tours and is especially helpful with cruise vacations. **Flying Wheels Travel** (✉ 143 W. Bridge St., Box 382, Owatonna, MN 55060, ☎ 507/451–5005 or 800/535–6790, FAX 507/451–1685), a travel agency specializing in customized tours and itineraries worldwide. **Hinsdale Travel Service** (✉ 201 E. Ogden Ave., Suite 100, Hinsdale, IL 60521, ☎ 630/325–1335), a travel agency that benefits from the advice of wheelchair traveler Janice Perkins.

➤ TRAVELERS WITH DEVELOPMENTAL DISABILITIES: **Sprout** (✉ 893 Amsterdam Ave., New York, NY 10025, ☎ 212/222–9575 or 888/222–9575, FAX 212/222–9768).

DISCOUNTS & DEALS

Be a smart shopper and **compare all your options** before making any choice. A plane ticket bought with a promotional coupon may not be cheaper than the least expensive fare from a discount ticket agency. For high-price travel purchases, such as packages or tours, keep in mind that what you get is just as important as what you save. Just because something is cheap doesn't mean it's a bargain.

CLUBS & COUPONS

Many companies sell discounts in the form of travel clubs and coupon books, but these cost money. You must use participating advertisers to get a deal, and only after you recoup the initial membership cost or book price do you begin to save. If you plan to use the club or coupons frequently, you may save considerably. Before signing up, find out what discounts you get for free.

➤ DISCOUNT CLUBS: **Entertainment Travel Editions** (✉ 2125 Butterfield Rd., Troy, MI 48084, ☎ 800/445–4137; $20–$51, depending on destination). **Great American Traveler** (✉ Box 27965, Salt Lake City, UT 84127, ☎ 801/974–3033 or 800/548–2812; $49.95 per year). **Moment's Notice Discount Travel Club** (✉ 7301 New Utrecht Ave., Brooklyn, NY 11204, ☎ 718/234–6295; $25 per year, single or family). **Privilege Card International** (✉ 237 E. Front St., Youngstown, OH 44503, ☎ 330/746–5211 or 800/236–9732; $74.95 per year). **Sears's Mature Outlook** (✉ Box 9390, Des Moines, IA 50306, ☎ 800/336–6330; $19.95 per year). **Travelers Advantage** (✉ CUC Travel Service, ✉ 3033 S. Parker Rd., Suite 1000, Aurora, CO 80014, ☎ 800/548–1116 or 800/648–4037; $59.95 per year, single or family). **Worldwide Discount Travel Club** (✉ 1674 Meridian Ave., Miami Beach, FL 33139, ☎ 305/534–2082; $50 per year family, $40 single).

CREDIT-CARD BENEFITS

When you use your credit card to make travel purchases you may get free travel-accident insurance, collision-damage insurance, and medical or legal assistance, depending on the card and the bank that issued it. American Express, MasterCard, and Visa provide one or more of these services, so **get a copy of your credit card's travel-benefits policy.** If you are a member of an auto club, always **ask hotel and car-rental reservations agents about auto-club discounts.** Some clubs offer additional discounts on tours, cruises, and admission to attractions.

DISCOUNT RESERVATIONS

To save money, **look into discount-reservations services** with toll-free numbers, which use their buying power to get a better price on hotels, airline tickets, even car rentals. When booking a room, always **call the hotel's local toll-free number** (if one is available) rather than the central reservations number—you'll often get a better price. Always ask about special packages or corporate rates.

➤ AIRLINE TICKETS: ☎ **800/FLY–4–LESS.** ☎ **800/FLY–ASAP.**

➤ HOTEL ROOMS: **Players Express Vacations** (☎ 800/458–6161). **RMC Travel** (☎ 800/245–5738).

PACKAGE DEALS

Packages and guided tours can save you money, but don't confuse the two. When you buy a package, your travel remains independent, just as though you had planned and booked the trip yourself. Fly/drive packages, which combine airfare and car rental, are often a good deal.

EMERGENCIES

➤ DOCTORS: **Doctors on Call** (✉ Hyatt Regency Maui-Nāpili Tower, Suite 100, Kā'anapali, ☎ 808/667–7676) serves patients in West Maui. A walk-in clinic at Whalers Village, **West Maui Healthcare Center** (✉ 2435 Kā'anapali Pkwy., Suite H-7, Kā'anapali, ☎ 808/667–9721) also serves West Maui. The clinic is open daily 8 AM–10 PM. **Kīhei Clinic** (✉ 2349 S. Kīhei Rd., Suite D, Kīhei, ☎ 808/879–1440) serves walk-in clients in Central Maui, Kīhei, and Wailea. All of the above groups are geared toward working with visitors.

➤ EMERGENCIES: **Police, fire, or ambulance,** ☎ 911.

➤ HOSPITALS: **Hāna Community Health Center** (✉ Box 807, Hāna Hwy., Hāna, ☎ 808/248–8294). **Kula Hospital** (✉ 204 Kula Hwy., Kula, ☎ 808/878–1221). **Maui Memorial Hospital** (✉ 221 Mahalani St., Wailuku, ☎ 808/244–9056).

➤ OTHERS: **Coast Guard Rescue Center** (☎ 808/244–5256). **Suicide and Crisis Center Help Line** (☎ 808/244–7407).

➤ PHARMACIES: Maui doesn't have any 24-hour pharmacies, but there are several where you can get prescrip-

tions filled during daylight hours. The least expensive are the island's three **Longs Drug Stores** (✉ Maui Mall, 70 Ka'ahumanu Ave., Kahului, ☎ 808/877–0068; ✉ Lahaina Cannery Shopping Center, Honoapi'ilani Hwy., ☎ 808/667–4390; (✉ Longs Shopping Center, 1215 S. Kīhei Rd., Kīhei, ☎ 808/879–2259; all open weekdays 8AM–10 PM, Saturday 8 AM–9 PM, Sunday 8–7).

GAY & LESBIAN TRAVEL

➤ GAY- AND LESBIAN-FRIENDLY TOUR OPERATORS: **Toto Tours** (✉ 1326 W. Albion Ave., Suite 3W, Chicago, IL 60626, ☎ 773/274–8686 or 800/565–1241, FAX 773/274–8695), for groups.

➤ GAY- AND LESBIAN-FRIENDLY TRAVEL AGENCIES: **Corniche Travel** (✉ 8721 Sunset Blvd., Suite 200, West Hollywood, CA 90069, ☎ 310/854–6000 or 800/429–8747, FAX 310/659–7441). **Islanders Kennedy Travel** (✉ 183 W. 10th St., New York, NY 10014, ☎ 212/242–3222 or 800/988–1181, FAX 212/929–8530). **Now Voyager** (✉ 4406 18th St., San Francisco, CA 94114, ☎ 415/626–1169 or 800/255–6951, FAX 415/626–8626). **Yellowbrick Road** (✉ 1500 W. Balmoral Ave., Chicago, IL 60640, ☎ 773/561–1800 or 800/642–2488, FAX 773/561–4497). **Skylink Travel and Tour** (✉ 3577 Moorland Ave., Santa Rosa, CA 95407, ☎ 707/585–8355 or 800/225–5759, FAX 707/584–5637), serving lesbian travelers.

➤ LOCAL RESOURCES: *Island Lifestyles,* put out by Island Publishing (✉ Box 11840, Honolulu 96828 ☎ 808/737–6400) is a monthly magazine ($3 per copy, $24 for 12 issues) covering news and entertainment in Hawai'i. For $4 an issue, Island Publishing also sells *The Pages,* a directory of gay and gay-supportive business organizations and services. **Pacific Ocean Holidays** (✉ Box 88245, Honolulu 96830, ☎ 808/923–2400 or 800/735–6600) not only arranges independent travel in the Islands, but publishes the **Pocket Guide to Hawai'i,** distributed free in the state at gay-operated venues and available for $5 by mail. Their Web site is www.gayhawaii.com.

A few small hotels and some bed-and-breakfasts in Hawai'i are favored by gay and lesbian visitors. A computerized Gay Community listing compiled by **GLEA** (Gay & Lesbian Education Advocacy Foundation) can be accessed by phone, ☎ 808/532–9000.

GROCERS

Three major supermarkets are open 24 hours a day. **Safeway,** at the Lahaina Cannery Shopping Center (✉ Honoapi'ilani Hwy., Lahaina, ☎ 808/667–4392), serves West Maui, while **Foodland,** in the Kīhei Town Center (✉ 1881 S. Kīhei Rd., Kīhei, ☎ 808/879–9350), and **Safeway** (✉ 170 E. Kamehameha Ave., Kahului, ☎ 808/877–3377) serve Kīhei and Wailea.

HEALTH

MEDICAL PLANS

No one plans to get sick while traveling, but it happens, so **consider signing up with a medical-assistance company.** Members get doctor referrals, emergency evacuation or repatriation, 24-hour telephone hot lines for medical consultation, cash for emergencies, and other personal and legal assistance. Coverage varies by plan, so **review the benefits of each carefully.**

➤ MEDICAL-ASSISTANCE COMPANIES: **International SOS Assistance** (✉ 8 Neshaminy Interplex, Suite 207, Trevose, PA 19053, ☎ 215/245–4707 or 800/523–6586, FAX 215/244–9617; ✉ 12 Chemin Riantbosson, 1217 Meyrin 1, Geneva, Switzerland, ☎ 4122/785–6464, FAX 4122/785–6424; ✉ 10 Anson Rd., 14-07/08 International Plaza, Singapore, 079903, ☎ 65/226–3936, FAX 65/226–3937).

HOLIDAYS

Major national holidays include: New Year's Day (Jan. 1); Martin Luther King, Jr. Day (third Mon. in Jan.); President's Day (third Mon. in Feb.); Memorial Day (last Mon. in May); Independence Day (July 4); Labor Day (first Mon. in Sept.); Thanksgiving Day (fourth Thurs. in Nov.); Christmas Eve and Day (Dec. 24–25); and New Year's Eve (Dec. 31).

INSURANCE

Travel insurance is the best way to **protect yourself against financial loss.** The most useful plan is a comprehensive policy that includes coverage for trip cancellation and interruption, default, trip delay, and medical expenses (with a waiver for preexisting conditions).

Without insurance, you will lose all or most of your money if you cancel your trip, regardless of the reason. Default insurance covers you if your tour operator, airline, or cruise line goes out of business. Trip-delay covers unforeseen expenses that you may incur due to bad weather or mechanical delays. It's important to compare the fine print regarding trip-delay coverage when comparing policies.

For overseas travel, one of the most important components of travel insurance is its medical coverage. Supplemental health insurance will pick up the cost of your medical bills should you get sick or injured while traveling. Residents of the United Kingdom can buy an annual travel-insurance policy valid for most vacations taken during the year in which the coverage is purchased. If you are pregnant or have a pre-existing condition, make sure you're covered. British citizens should buy extra medical coverage when traveling overseas, according to the Association of British Insurers. Australian travelers should buy travel insurance, including extra medical coverage, whenever they go abroad, according to the Insurance Council of Australia.

Always **buy travel insurance directly from the insurance company;** if you buy it from a cruise line, airline, or tour operator that goes out of business you probably will not be covered for the agency or operator's default, a major risk. Before you make any purchase, **review your existing health and home-owner's policies** to find out whether they cover expenses incurred while traveling.

➤ TRAVEL INSURERS: In the U.S., **Access America** (✉ 6600 W. Broad St., Richmond, VA 23230, ☎ 804/285–3300 or 800/284–8300). **Travel Guard International** (✉ 1145 Clark St., Stevens Point, WI 54481, ☎ 715/345–0505 or 800/826–1300). In Canada, **Mutual of Omaha** (✉ Travel

Division, ✉ 500 University Ave., Toronto, Ontario M5G 1V8, ☎ 416/598–4083, 800/268–8825 in Canada).

➤ INSURANCE INFORMATION: In the U.K., **Association of British Insurers** (✉ 51 Gresham St., London EC2V 7HQ, ☎ 0171/600–3333). In Australia, the **Insurance Council of Australia** (☎ 613/9614–1077, FAX 613/9614–7924).

LIMOUSINES

Arthur's Limousine Service (✉ Box 11865, Lahaina 96761, ☎ 800/345–4667) provides a chauffeured super-stretch Lincoln complete with bar, two TVs, and two sunroofs for $85 per hour. Arthur's fleet also includes less grandiose Lincoln Town Cars, for $65 per hour with a two-hour minimum.

LODGING

APARTMENT & VILLA RENTALS

If you want a home base that's roomy enough for a family and comes with cooking facilities, **consider a furnished rental.** These can save you money, especially if you're traveling with a large group of people. Home-exchange directories list rentals (often second homes owned by prospective house swappers), and some services search for a house or apartment for you (even a castle if that's your fancy) and handle the paperwork. Some send an illustrated catalog; others send photographs only of specific properties, sometimes at a charge. Up-front registration fees may apply.

➤ RENTAL AGENTS: **Europa-Let/Tropical Inn-Let** (✉ 92 N. Main St., Ashland, OR 97520, ☎ 541/482–5806 or 800/462–4486, FAX 541/482–0660). **Hometours International** (✉ Box 11503, Knoxville, TN 37939, ☎ 423/690–8484 or 800/367–4668). **Property Rentals International** (✉ 1008 Mansfield Crossing Rd., Richmond, VA 23236, ☎ 804/378–6054 or 800/220–3332, FAX 804/379–2073). **Rental Directories International** (✉ 2044 Rittenhouse Sq., Philadelphia, PA 19103, ☎ 215/985–4001, FAX 215/985–0323). **Rent-a-Home International** (✉ 7200 34th Ave. NW, Seattle, WA 98117, ☎ 206/789–9377 or 800/488–7368, FAX 206/789–9379). **Vacation Home Rentals Worldwide** (✉ 235

Kensington Ave., Norwood, NJ 07648, ☎ 201/767–9393 or 800/633–3284, FAX 201/767–5510). **Hideaways International** (✉ 767 Islington St., Portsmouth, NH 03801, ☎ 603/430–4433 or 800/843–4433, FAX 603/430–4444; membership $99) is a club for travelers who arrange rentals among themselves.

➤ HOUSES IN MAUI: By writing to the following management companies in Hawai'i, you can get more information on specific houses, including brochures with photographs and details of the types of properties. Try: **Premier Maui Properties** (✉ Box 1959, Kīhei, Maui 96753, ☎ 800/359–6284); **Windsurfing West Ltd.** (✉ Box 1359, Haiku, Maui 96708, ☎ 800/782–6105).

B&BS

Maui has quite a few bed-and-breakfasts and many have separate guest quarters, which allows privacy while still giving you a chance to get to know your hosts. Rates range from $35 a night to more than $150.

➤ RESERVATION SERVICES: **Bed & Breakfast Honolulu** (✉ 3242 Kā'ohinani Dr., Honolulu 96817, ☎ 808/595–3298 or 800/288–4666) has statewide listings, with about 50 B&Bs; on Maui. **Affordable Accommodations** (✉ 2825 Kanhale St., Kīhei 96753, ☎ 808/879–7865 or 888/333–9747) has listings for about 35 B&Bs; on Maui. **Bed & Breakfast Hawaii** (✉ Box 449, Kapa'a, Kaua'i 96746, ☎ 808/822–7771 or 800/733–1632) is headquartered on Kaua'i and has listings throughout the state. It handles about 35 B&Bs; on Maui; a directory is available for $12.95.

CONDOMINIUMS

Maui has condos you can rent through central booking agents. Most agents represent more than one condo complex, so be specific about what kind of price, space, facilities, and amenities you want.

➤ RENTAL AGENTS: **Aston Hotels & Resorts** (✉ 2155 Kalākaua Ave., Suite 500, Honolulu 96815, ☎ 800/922–7866). **Marc Resorts Hawai'i** (✉ 2155 Kalākaua Ave., Suite 706, Honolulu 96815, ☎ 800/535–0085).

Destination Resorts (⊠ 3750 Wailea Alanui Dr., Wailea, Maui 96753, ☎ 800/367–5246). Hawaiian Apartment Leasing Enterprises (⊠ 479 Ocean Ave., #B, Laguna Beach, CA 92651, ☎ 714/497–4253 or 800/854–8843). Hawaiian Resorts, Inc. (⊠ 1270 Ala Moana Blvd., Honolulu 96814, ☎ 800/367–7040 or, in Canada, 800/877–7331). Kīhei Maui Vacations (⊠ Box 1055, Kīhei, 96753, ☎ 808/879–7581 or 800/541–6284).

HOME EXCHANGES

If you would like to exchange your home for someone else's, **join a home-exchange organization,** which will send you its updated listings of available exchanges for a year and will include your own listing in at least one of them. It's up to you to make specific arrangements.

➤ EXCHANGE CLUBS: **HomeLink International** (⊠ Box 650, Key West, FL 33041, ☎ 305/294–7766 or 800/638–3841, FAX 305/294–1148; $83 per year).

HOSTELS

No matter what your age, you can **save on lodging costs by staying at hostels.** In some 5,000 locations in more than 70 countries around the world, Hostelling International (HI), the umbrella group for a number of national youth hostel associations, offers single-sex, dorm-style beds and, at many hostels, "couples" rooms and family accommodations. Membership in any HI national hostel association, open to travelers of all ages, allows you to stay in HI-affiliated hostels at member rates (one-year membership is about $25 for adults; hostels run about $10–$25 per night). Members also have priority if the hostel is full; they're eligible for discounts around the world, even on rail and bus travel in some countries.

➤ HOSTEL ORGANIZATIONS: **Hostelling International—American Youth Hostels** (⊠ 733 15th St. NW, Suite 840, Washington, DC 20005, ☎ 202/783–6161, FAX 202/783–6171). **Hostelling International—Canada** (⊠ 400-205 Catherine St., Ottawa, Ontario K2P 1C3, ☎ 613/237–7884, FAX 613/237–7868). **Youth Hostel Association of**

England and Wales (⊠ Trevelyan House, ⊠ 8 St. Stephen's Hill, St. Albans, Hertfordshire AL1 2DY, ☎ 01727/855215 or 01727/845047, FAX 01727/844126); membership in the U.S. $25, in Canada C$26.75, in the U.K. £9.30).

MONEY

CREDIT & DEBIT CARDS

Should you use a credit card or a debit card when traveling? Both have benefits. A credit card allows you to delay payment and gives you certain rights as a consumer (☞ Consumer Protection, *above*). A debit card, also known as a check card, deducts funds directly from your checking account and helps you stay within your budget. When you want to rent a car, though, you may still need an old-fashioned credit card. Although you can always *pay* for your car with a debit card, some agencies will not allow you to *reserve* a car with a debit card.

Otherwise, the two types of plastic are virtually the same. Both will get you cash advances at ATMs worldwide if your card is properly programmed with your personal identification number (PIN). Both offer excellent, wholesale exchange rates. And both protect you against unauthorized use if the card is lost or stolen. Your liability is limited to $50, as long as you report the card missing.

➤ ATM LOCATIONS: **Cirrus** (☎ 800/424–7787). **Plus** (☎ 800/843–7587) for locations in the U.S. and Canada, or visit your local bank.

➤ REPORTING LOST CARDS: To report lost or stolen credit cards, call the following toll-free numbers: **American Express** (☎ 800/327–2177); **Discover Card** (☎ 800/347–2683); **Diners Club** (☎ 800/234–6377); **Master Card** (☎ 800/307–7309); and **Visa** (☎ 800/847–2911).

EXCHANGING MONEY

For the most favorable rates, **change money through banks.** Although fees charged for ATM transactions may be higher abroad than at home, Cirrus and Plus exchange rates are excellent, because they are based on wholesale rates offered only by major banks.

You won't do as well at exchange booths in airports or rail and bus stations, in hotels, in restaurants, or in stores, although you may find their hours more convenient. To avoid lines at airport exchange booths, **get a bit of local currency before you leave home.**

➤ EXCHANGE SERVICES: **Chase Currency To Go** (☎ 800/935–9935; 935–9935 in NY, NJ, and CT). **International Currency Express** (☎ 888/842–0880 on the East Coast, 888/278–6628 on the West Coast). **Thomas Cook Currency Services** (☎ 800/287–7362 for telephone orders and retail locations).

TRAVELER'S CHECKS

Do you need traveler's checks? It depends on where you're headed. If you're going to rural areas and small towns, go with cash; traveler's checks are best used in cities. Lost or stolen checks can usually be replaced within 24 hours. To ensure a speedy refund, buy your own traveler's checks— don't let someone else pay for them: irregularities like this can cause delays. The person who bought the checks should make the call to request a refund.

MOPEDS/MOTORCYCLES

Mopeds from **A&B; Moped Rental** (⌧ 3481 Lower Honoapi'ilani Hwy., Lahaina, ☎ 808/669–0027) go for about $10/day, and are for local on-road use only. Be especially careful navigating the roads on Maui, since there are no designated bicycle or moped lanes.

NATIONAL PARKS

Look into discount passes to **save money on park entrance fees.** The Golden Eagle Pass ($50) gets you and your companions free admission to all parks for one year. (Camping and parking are extra). Both the Golden Age Passport ($10), for those 62 and older, and the Golden Access Passport (free), for travelers with disabilities, entitle holders to free entry to all national parks, plus 50% off fees for the use of many park facilities and services. You must show proof of age and of U.S. citizenship or permanent residency (such as a U.S. passport,

driver's license, or birth certificate) and, if requesting Golden Access, proof of disability. All three passes are available at all national park entrances where entrance fees are charged. Golden Eagle and Golden Access passes are also available by mail.

➤ PASSES BY MAIL: **National Park Service** (⌧ National Capitol Area Office, ⌧ 1100 Ohio Dr. SW, Washington, DC 20242).

PACKING

LUGGAGE

How many carry-on bags you can bring with you is up to the airline. Most allow two, but the limit is often reduced to one on certain flights. Gate agents will take excess baggage—including bags they deem oversize—from you as you board and add it to checked luggage. To avoid this situation, make sure that everything you carry aboard will fit under your seat. Also, get to the gate early, and request a seat at the back of the plane; you'll probably board first, while the overhead bins are still empty. Since big, bulky baggage attracts the attention of gate agents and flight attendants on a busy flight, make sure your carry-on is really a carry-on. Finally, a carry-on that's long and narrow is more likely to remain unnoticed than one that's wide and squarish.

If you are flying internationally, note that baggage allowances may be determined not by piece but by weight—generally 88 pounds (40 kilograms) in first class, 66 pounds (30 kilograms) in business class, and 44 pounds (20 kilograms) in economy.

Airline liability for baggage is limited to $1,250 per person on flights within the United States. On international flights it amounts to $9.07 per pound or $20 per kilogram for checked baggage (roughly $640 per 70-pound bag) and $400 per passenger for unchecked baggage. You can buy additional coverage at check-in for about $10 per $1,000 of coverage, but it excludes a rather extensive list of items, shown on your airline ticket.

Before departure, **itemize your bags' contents** and their worth, and label

THE GOLD GUIDE / SMART TRAVEL TIPS

the bags with your name, address, and phone number. (If you use your home address, cover it so that potential thieves can't see it readily.) Inside each bag, **pack a copy of your itinerary.** At check-in, **make sure that each bag is correctly tagged** with the destination airport's three-letter code. If your bags arrive damaged or fail to arrive at all, file a written report with the airline before leaving the airport.

PACKING LIST

You can pack lightly because Maui is casual. Bare feet, bathing suits, and comfortable, informal clothing are the norm. In the Hawaiian Islands there's a saying that when a man wears a suit during the day he's either going for a loan or he's a lawyer trying a case. Only a few upscale restaurants require a jacket for dinner, and none requires a tie.

If you don't own a *pareu,* buy one in Maui. It's simply a length (about 1½ yards long) of light cotton in a tropical motif that can be worn as a beach wrap, a skirt, or a dozen other wrap-up fashions. You can even tie it up as a handbag or sit on it at the beach.Bring a bathing suit and sunscreen with a sun-protection factor (SPF) of 15 or higher. It's best to put on sunscreen when you get up in the morning. Don't forget to reapply it periodically during the day, since perspiration can wash it away. Hats and sunglasses offer important sun protection, too. All the above are easy to find in island shops.

In your carry-on luggage **bring an extra pair of eyeglasses or contact lenses** and **enough of any medication you take** to last the entire trip. You may also want your doctor to write a spare prescription using the drug's generic name, since brand names may vary from country to country. **Never put prescription drugs or valuables in luggage to be checked.** To avoid customs delays, carry medications in their original packaging. And don't forget to copy down and carry addresses of offices that handle refunds of lost traveler's checks.

PASSPORTS & VISAS

When traveling internationally, **carry a passport even if you don't need one** (it's always the best form of I.D.), and make **two photocopies of the data page** (one for someone at home and another for you, carried separately from your passport). If you lose your passport, promptly call the nearest embassy or consulate and the local police.

➤ U.K. CITIZENS: **U.S. Embassy Visa Information Line** (☎ 01891/200–290; calls cost 49p per minute, 39p per minute cheap rate), for U.S. visa information. **U.S. Embassy Visa Branch** (✉ 5 Upper Grosvenor St., London W1A 2JB), for U.S. visa information; send a self-addressed, stamped envelope. Write the **U.S. Consulate General** (✉ Queen's House, ✉ Queen St., Belfast BTI 6EO) if you live in Northern Ireland.

PASSPORT OFFICES

The best time to apply for a passport or to renew is during the fall and winter. Before any trip, be sure to check your passport's expiration date and, if necessary, renew it as soon as possible. (Some countries won't allow you to enter on a passport that's due to expire in six months or less.)

➤ AUSTRALIAN CITIZENS: **Australian Passport Office** (☎ 131–232).

➤ NEW ZEALAND CITIZENS: **New Zealand Passport Office** (☎ 04/494–0700 for information on how to apply, 0800/727–776 for information on applications already submitted).

➤ U.K. CITIZENS: **London Passport Office** (☎ 0990/21010), for fees and documentation requirements and to request an emergency passport.

SENIOR-CITIZEN TRAVEL

To qualify for age-related discounts, **mention your senior-citizen status up front** when booking hotel reservations (not when checking out) and before you're seated in restaurants (not when paying the bill). Note that discounts may be limited to certain menus, days, or hours. When renting a car, **ask about promotional car-rental discounts,** which can be cheaper than senior-citizen rates.

➤ EDUCATIONAL PROGRAMS: **Elderhostel** (✉ 75 Federal St., 3rd floor, Boston, MA 02110, ☎ 617/426–8056).

SIGHTSEEING TOURS

AIR TOURS

Circle Island Tour: Helicopter companies handle this in different ways. Some have fancy names, such as Ultimate Experience or Circle Island Deluxe. Some go for two hours or more. Cost: about $185–$200.

Hāna/Haleakalā Crater Tour: This takes about 90 minutes to travel inside the volcano, then down to the Hawaiian village of Hāna. Some companies stop in secluded areas for refreshments, but local residents have had moderate success in getting this stopped. Cost: about $130.

West Maui Tour: Generally a 30-minute helicopter ride over Kā'anapali and Lahaina. Frankly, this is not a very exciting helicopter tour. Cost: about $70–$95.

➤ AERIAL TOURS: The best Maui operators include **Blue Hawaiian Helicopters** (✉ Kahului Heliport, Hanger 105, Kahului 96732, ☎ 808/871–8844), **Hawai'i Helicopters** (✉ Kahului Heliport, Hangar 106, Kahului 96732, ☎ 808/877–3900 or 800/367–7095 from the Mainland), **Maui Helicopters** (✉ Kahalui Heliport, Hangar 110, Kahului 96732, ☎ 808/877–7005), and **Kenai Helicopters** (✉ Box 4118, Kailua–Kona 96745, ☎ 808/882–1852 or 800/622–3144).

ART TOURS

Customized tours are available that take creative types into artists' homes for tea and conversation. The cost can be upwards of $150.

➤ ART TOURS: **Maui Art Tours** (✉ Box 1058, Makawao 96768, ☎ 808/572–7132). A free guided tour of the **Hyatt Regency Maui's** art collection and gardens (✉ 200 Nokea Kai Dr., Kā'anapali, ☎ 808/661–1234) starts at 11AM on Monday, Wednesday and Friday.

ASTRONOMY TOURS

Take a star-studded trip with an astronomer that may lead you to Haleakalā's summit to view the sunset and stars.

➤ ASTRONOMY TOURS: Take a stargazing trip with **Tours of the Stars** (✉ Hyatt Regency Maui's Lahaina

Tower, 200 Nohea Kai Dr., Kā'anapali, 96761, ☎ 808/661–1234, ext. 4727).

BICYCLE TOURS

Some companies will put you on a bicycle at the top of Haleakalā and let you coast down. Safety precautions are top priority, so riders wear helmets and receive training in appropriate bicycle-bell ringing. If you did the Haleakalā downhill on your last visit to Maui, you might want to try some of the new bicycle adventure tours offered by Cruiser Bob.

➤ BICYCLE TOURS: **Maui Downhill Bicycle Safaris** (✉ 199 Dairy Rd., Kahului 96732, ☎ 808/871–2155 or 800/535–2453) and **Maui Mountain Cruisers** (✉ Box 1356, Makawao 96768, ☎ 808/871–6014 or 800/232–6284) offer bike tours.

HIKING TOURS

Hiking in Maui can be a short five-hour outing or a week-long trek. Some tours are specially designed for photography enthusiasts.

➤ HIKING TOURS: **Crater Bound** (✉ Box 265, Kula 96790, ☎ 808/878–1743) specializes in treks into Haleakalā's craters, with tents and gear carried in ahead of the hikers, on pack horses. **Hike Maui** (✉ Box 330969, Kahului 96733, ☎ 808/879–5270) is owned by naturalist Ken Schmitt, who guides some 50 different hikes himself. Maui-Anne's **Island Photography Tours** (✉ Box 2250, Kīhei 96753, ☎ 808/874–3797) offers hiking trips with a focus on photography.

HORSEBACK TOURS

At least two companies on Maui now offer horseback riding that's far more appealing than the typical hour-long trudge over a boring trail with 50 other horses. Some tours traverse ocean cliffs on Maui's north shore, along the slopes of Haleakalā, as they pass by streams, through rain forests, and near waterfalls.

➤ HORSEBACK TOURS: Mauian Frank Levinson started **Adventures on Horseback** (✉ Box 1419, Makawao 96768, ☎ 808/242–7445) a few years back with five-hour outings into secluded parts of Maui. **Charley's Trail Rides & Pack Trips** (✉ c/o

Kaupō Store, Kaupō 96713, ☎ 808/248–8209) requires a hardy physical nature, as the overnighters go from Kaupō—a tiny village nearly 20 miles past Hāna—up the slopes of Haleakalā to the crater.

HUNTING TOURS

Maui has a year-round hunting season, so hunting tours are always available.

➤ HUNTING TOURS: **Hunting Adventures of Maui** (✉ Box 1745, Kaupakulua Rd., Ha'ikū 96708, ☎ 808/572–8214). This is a guided excursion on more than 100,000 acres of private ranch land on Maui, a "fair chase" hunt for Spanish mountain goats and wild boar.

LAND TOURS

Circle Island Tour: This is a big island to tour in one day, so several companies combine various sections of it—either Haleakalā, 'Īao Needle, and Central Maui, or West Maui and its environs. Some stops include the historical sections of the county seat of Wailuku, while others focus on some of the best snorkeling spots. Call a selection of companies to find the tour that suits you. The cost is usually $50–$80 for adults, half that for children.

Haleakalā Sunrise Tour: This tour starts before dawn so that visitors get a chance to actually make it to the top of the dormant volcano before the sun peeks over the horizon. Some companies throw in champagne to greet the sunrise. Cost of the six-hour tour starts at $50.

Haleakalā/Upcountry Tour: Usually a half-day excursion, this tour is offered in several versions by different companies. The trip often includes stops at a protea farm and at Tedeschi Vineyards and Winery, the only place in Hawai'i where wine is made. Cost: about $55 adults, $35 children.

Hāna Tour: This tour is almost always done in a van, as the winding road to Hāna just doesn't provide a comfortable ride in bigger buses. Of late, Hāna has so many of these one-day tours that it seems as if there are more vans than cars on the road. Still, it's a more relaxing way to do the drive than behind the wheel of your own car. Guides decide where you stop for photos. Cost: $70–$120.

➤ LAND TOURS: **Polynesian Adventure Tours** (✉ 273 Dairy Rd., Kahului 96732, ☎ 800/622–3011 or 808/877–4242) and **Roberts Hawai'i Tours** (✉ Box 247, Kahului 96732, ☎ 808/871–6226) both offer full schedules of a variety of tours. **Trans-Hawaiian Services** (✉ 720 Iwilei Rd., Suite 101, Honolulu 96817, ☎ 800/533–8765) is one of the island's largest tour operators.

PERSONAL GUIDES

Local guides are available to give you a personal tour of the island. Transportation may be in your own vehicle, and can be tailored to your particular interests.

➤ PERSONAL GUIDES: **Rent-a-Local** (✉ 333 Dairy Rd., Kahului 96732, ☎ 808/877–4042 or 800/228–6284). This is the best way to see Maui through the eyes of the locals. **Temptation Tours** (✉ 211 'Āhinahina Pl., Kula 96790, ☎ 808/877–8888) specializes in full-day exclusive tours to Haleakalā and Hāna.

WALKING TOURS

Walking-tour maps are available for interested visitors. These are all sights you could find yourself, but the maps are usually free, and it makes the walk easier.

➤ WALKING TOURS: The **Lahaina Restoration Foundation** (✉ Baldwin Home, 696 Front St., Lahaina, ☎ 808/661–3262) has published a walking-tour map for interested visitors. These are all sights you could find yourself, but the map is free, and it makes the walk easier.

➤ WHALE-WATCHING TOURS: **Pacific Whale Foundation** (✉ Kealia Beach Plaza, 101 N. Kīhei Rd., Kīhei, 96753, ☎ 808/879–8811) is the most experienced outfitter. For more information, see the Close-Up in the Outdoor Activities, Beaches, and Sports chapter.

STUDENT TRAVEL

TRAVEL AGENCIES

➤ STUDENT I.D.s & SERVICES: **Council on International Educational Ex-**

change (⊠ CIEE, ⊠ 205 E. 42nd St., 14th floor, New York, NY 10017, ☎ 212/822–2600 or 888/268–6245, FAX 212/822–2699), for mail orders only, in the United States. **Travel Cuts** (⊠ 187 College St., Toronto, Ontario M5T 1P7, ☎ 416/979–2406 or 800/ 667–2887) in Canada.

➤ STUDENT TOURS: **Contiki Holidays** (⊠ 300 Plaza Alicante, Suite 900, Garden Grove, CA 92840, ☎ 714/ 740–0808 or 800/266–8454, FAX 714/ 740–2034).

TAXES

Sales tax is 4.17% in Maui. A $2/day surcharge and sales tax are added to all car-rental charges. A 6% lodging tax, as well as sales tax, is added to hotel bills.

TAXIS

For short hops between hotels and restaurants, this can be a convenient way to go, but you'll have to call ahead. Even busy West Maui doesn't have curbside taxi service. Airport Shuttle and Yellow Cab of Maui both service the entire island, but you'd be smart to consider using them just for the areas where they're located. Ali'i Cab specializes in West Maui, while Kīhei Taxi serves Central Maui.

➤ CAB COMPANIES: **Airport Shuttle** (⊠ 2580 Kekaa Dr., Lahaina, ☎ 808/ 667–2605). **Yellow Cab of Maui** (⊠ Kahului Airport, ☎ 808/877–7000). **Ali'i Cab** (⊠ 475 Kū'ai Pl., Lahaina, ☎ 808/661–3688). **Kīhei Taxi** (⊠ Kīhei, ☎ 808/879–3000).

TELEPHONES

COUNTRY CODES

The country code for the United States is 1.

LOCAL CALLS

All Hawaiian island telephones have the area code 808; this area code must be used for interisland calls, as well as calls from other area codes. Many toll-free 800 numbers for hotels and other establishments may not be dialed from within the Islands. For facilities that have both an 808 phone number and an 800 number, use the 808 number once you arrive in Hawai'i. Include the area code when dialing if you are phoning to a different island.

LONG-DISTANCE CALLS

Competitive long-distance carriers make calling within the United States relatively convenient and let you avoid hotel surcharges. By dialing an 800 number, you can get connected to the long-distance company of your choice.

➤ LONG-DISTANCE CARRIERS: **AT&T** (☎ 800/225–5288). **MCI** (☎ 800/ 888–8000). **Sprint** (☎ 800/366– 2255).

TOUR OPERATORS

Buying a prepackaged tour or independent vacation can make your trip to Maui less expensive and more hassle-free. Because everything is prearranged, you'll spend less time planning.

Operators that handle several hundred thousand travelers per year can use their purchasing power to give you a good price. Their high volume may also indicate financial stability. But some small companies provide more personalized service; because they tend to specialize, they may also be more knowledgeable about a given area.

BOOKING WITH AN AGENT

Travel agents are excellent resources. In fact, large operators accept bookings made only through travel agents. But it's a good idea to **collect brochures from several agencies,** because some agents' suggestions may be influenced by relationships with tour and package firms that reward them for volume sales. If you have a special interest, **find an agent with expertise in that area**; ASTA (☞ Travel Agencies, *below*) has a database of specialists worldwide.

Make sure your travel agent knows the accommodations and other services. Ask about the hotel's location, room size, beds, and whether it has a pool, room service, or programs for children, if you care about these. Has your agent been there in person or sent others you can contact?

Do some homework on your own, too: Local tourism boards can provide information about lesser-known and small-niche operators, some of which may sell only direct.

THE GOLD GUIDE / SMART TRAVEL TIPS

BUYER BEWARE

Each year consumers are stranded or lose their money when tour operators—even very large ones with excellent reputations—go out of business. So **check out the operator.** Find out how long the company has been in business, and ask several travel agents about its reputation. If the package or tour you are considering is priced lower than in your wildest dreams, **be skeptical.** Try to **book with a company that has a consumer-protection program.** If the operator has such a program, you'll find information about it in the company's brochure. If the operator you are considering does not offer some kind of consumer protection, then ask for references from satisfied customers.

In the U.S., members of the National Tour Association and United States Tour Operators Association are required to set aside funds to cover your payments and travel arrangements in case the company defaults. It's also a good idea to choose a company that participates in the American Society of Travel Agent's Tour Operator Program (TOP). This gives you a forum if there are any disputes between you and your tour operator; ASTA will act as mediator.

➤ TOUR-OPERATOR RECOMMENDATIONS: **American Society of Travel Agents** (☞ Travel Agencies, *below*). **National Tour Association** (✉ NTA, ✉ 546 E. Main St., Lexington, KY 40508, ☎ 606/226–4444 or 800/755–8687). **United States Tour Operators Association** (✉ USTOA, ✉ 342 Madison Ave., Suite 1522, New York, NY 10173, ☎ 212/599–6599 or 800/468–7862, FAX 212/599–6744).

COSTS

The more your package or tour includes, the better you can predict the ultimate cost of your vacation. Make sure you know exactly what is covered, and **beware of hidden costs.** Are taxes, tips, and service charges included? Transfers and baggage handling? Entertainment and excursions? These can add up.

Prices for packages and tours are usually quoted per person, based on two sharing a room. If traveling solo, you may be required to pay the full double-occupancy rate. Some operators eliminate this surcharge if you agree to be matched with a roommate of the same sex, even if one is not found by departure time.

GROUP TOURS

Among companies that sell tours to Maui and Lanai, the following have a proven reputation and offer plenty of options. The classifications used below represent different price categories, and you'll probably encounter these terms when talking to a travel agent or tour operator. The key difference is usually in accommodations, which run from budget to better, and better-yet to best.

➤ DELUXE: **Globus** (✉ 5301 S. Federal Circle, Littleton, CO 80123-2980, ☎ 800/221–0090 or 303/797–2800, FAX 303/795–0962). **Maupintour** (✉ 1515 St. Andrews Dr., Lawrence, KS 66047, ☎ 785/843–1211 or 800/255–4266, FAX 785/843–8351). **Tauck Tours** (✉ Box 5027, 276 Post Rd. W, Westport, CT 06881, ☎ 203/226–6911 or 800/468–2825, FAX 203/221–6866).

➤ FIRST-CLASS: **Caravan Tours** (✉ 401 N. Michigan Ave., Chicago, IL 60611, ☎ 312/321–9800 or 800/227–2826). **Collette Tours** (✉ 162 Middle St., Pawtucket, RI 02860, ☎ 401/728–3805 or 800/340–5158, FAX 401/728–4745). **Gadabout Tours** (✉ 700 E. Tahquitz Canyon Way, Palm Springs, CA 92262, ☎ 619/325–5556 or 800/952–5068). **Mayflower Tours** (✉ Box 490, 1225 Warren Ave., Downers Grove, IL 60515, ☎ 708/960–3430 or 800/323–7064).

➤ BUDGET: **Cosmos** (☞ Globus, *above*).

PACKAGES

Like group tours, independent vacation packages are available from major tour operators and airlines. The companies listed below offer vacation packages in a broad price range.

➤ AIR/HOTEL/CAR: **American Airlines Vacations** (☎ 800/321–2121). **Continental Vacations** (☎ 800/634–5555).

Delta Vacations (☎ 800/872–7786). Haddon Holidays (✉ 1120 Executive Plaza, No. 400, Mt. Laurel, NJ 08054, ☎ 609/273–8778 or 800/257–7488). Pleasant Hawaiian Holidays (✉ 2404 Townsgate Rd., Westlake Village, CA 91361, ☎ 818/991–3390 or 800/242–9244). TWA Getaway Vacations (☎ 800/438–2929). United Vacations (☎ 800/328–6877).

➤ FLY/DRIVE: Delta Vacations (☎ 800/872–7786).

➤ FROM THE U.K.: Hawaiian Travel Centre (✉ Meridian House, 42 Upper Berkeley St., London W1H 8AB, ☎ 0171/304–5730, FAX 0171/224–9184). Hawaiian Dream (✉ 1–7 Station Chambers, High St. N, London E6 1JE, ☎ 0181/552–1201). Jetsave (✉ Sussex House, London Rd., East Grinstead, West Sussex RH19 1LD, ☎ 01342/327–711). Kuoni Travel (✉ Kuoni House, Dorking, Surrey RH5 4AZ, ☎ 01306/740–500). Many Hawai'i packages include stopovers in California or other mainland destinations.

THEME TRIPS

➤ BICYCLING: Backroads (✉ 801 Cedar St., Berkeley, CA 94710-1800, ☎ 510/527–1555 or 800/462–2848, FAX 510/527–1444).

➤ FISHING: Fishing International (✉ Box 2132, Santa Rosa, CA 95405, ☎ 800/950–4242). Rod & Reel Adventures (✉ 566 Thomson Ln., Copperopolis, CA 95228, ☎ 209/785–0444, FAX 209/785–0447).

➤ HIKING/WALKING: American Wilderness Experience (✉ Box 1486, Boulder, CO 80306, ☎ 303/444–2622 or 800/444–0099, FAX 303/444–3999). Country Walkers (✉ Box 180, Waterbury, VT 05676-0180, ☎ 802/244–1387 or 800/464–9255, FAX 802/244–5661). Walking the World (✉ Box 1186, Fort Collins, CO 80522, ☎ 970/498–0500 or 800/340–9255, FAX 970/498–9100) specializes in tours for ages 50 and older.

➤ LEARNING: Earthwatch (✉ Box 9104, 680 Mount Auburn St., Watertown, MA 02272, ☎ 617/926–8200 or 800/776–0188, FAX 617/926–8532) for research expeditions. Nature Expeditions International (✉ 6400 E. El Dorado Cir. #210, Tucson, AZ 85715, ☎ 520/721–6712 or 800/869–0639). Victor Emanuel Nature Tours (✉ Box 33008, Austin, TX 78764, ☎ 512/328–5221 or 800/328–8368, FAX 512/328–2919).

➤ SPAS: Spa-Finders (✉ 91 Fifth Ave., Suite 301, New York, NY 10003-3039, ☎ 212/924–6800 or 800/255–7727).

➤ SINGLES AND YOUNG ADULTS: Contiki Holidays (✉ 300 Plaza Alicante, Suite 900, Garden Grove, CA 92840, ☎ 714/740–0808 or 800/266–8454, FAX 714/740–0818).

TRAVEL AGENCIES

A good travel agent puts your needs first. Look for an agency that has been in business at least five years, emphasizes customer service, and has someone on staff who specializes in your destination. In addition, **make sure the agency belongs to a professional trade organization,** such as ASTA in the United States. If your travel agency is also acting as your tour operator, *see* Buyer Beware in Tour Operators, *above*).

➤ LOCAL AGENT REFERRALS: American Society of Travel Agents (ASTA, ☎ 800/965–2782 24-hr hot line, FAX 703/684–8319). Association of Canadian Travel Agents (✉ Suite 201, 1729 Bank St., Ottawa, Ontario K1V 7Z5, ☎ 613/521–0474, FAX 613/521–0805). Association of British Travel Agents (✉ 55–57 Newman St., London W1P 4AH, ☎ 0171/637–2444, FAX 0171/637–0713). Australian Federation of Travel Agents (☎ 02/9264–3299). Travel Agents' Association of New Zealand (☎ 04/499–0104).

TRAVEL GEAR

Travel catalogs specialize in useful items, such as compact alarm clocks and travel irons, that can **save space when packing.**

➤ CATALOGS: Magellan's (☎ 800/962–4943, FAX 805/568–5406). Orvis Travel (☎ 800/541–3541, FAX 540/343–7053). TravelSmith (☎ 800/950–1600, FAX 800/950–1656).

FOR RELATED INFO ON THE WEB VISIT **WWW.FODORS.COM /RESOURCE**

THE GOLD GUIDE / SMART TRAVEL TIPS

THE GOLD GUIDE / SMART TRAVEL TIPS

U.S. GOVERNMENT

Government agencies can be an excellent source of inexpensive travel information. When planning your trip, **find out what government materials are available.**

➤ PAMPHLETS: **Consumer Information Center** (✉ Consumer Information Catalogue, Pueblo, CO 81009, ☎ 719/948–3334 or 888/878–3256) for a free catalog that includes travel titles.

VISITOR INFORMATION

➤ HAWAI'I VISITORS BUREAU (HVB): In the U.S.: ✉ 350 5th Ave., Suite 1827, New York, NY 10118, ☎ 212/947–0717 or 800/525–6284, FAX 212/947–0725. In the U.K.: ✉ Box 208, Sunbury, Middlesex, TW16 5RJ, ☎ 0181/941–4009. Send a £2 check or postal order for an information pack.

➤ IN MAUI: ✉ 1727 Wili Pa Loop, Wailuku, HI 96793, ☎ 808/244–3530, ☎ 808/244–1337.

WHEN TO GO

A few years back, Hawai'i narrowly missed its chance to be voted the country's best place to live. The reason? The climate was too perfect. Although Upcountry Maui temperatures can drop to as low as 40°F on a chilly night and standing at the peak of Haleakalā is almost always a downright frigid experience, Maui's balmy weather is a boon to year-round vacationing.

Remember, too, this rule of island climatology: The mountains in the island's center stop the rain clouds, which tend to move east to west. These conditions create a wet, cooler climate on the eastern side of the island and leave the western side hot and dry. You'll find the best weather in the West Maui destinations of Kā'anapali and Kapalua and Central Maui's Wailea Resort. Temperatures year-round at the beaches average about 75°F; Upcountry is about 10° cooler. East Maui gets more than 70 inches of rain in an average year; West Maui gets no more than 15.

The island's peak tourist seasons fall between December 15 and Easter and during the summer. At these times, Maui will be more crowded and more expensive. You'll find escalated prices especially in the midwinter season.

CLIMATE

The following are average maximum and minimum temperatures for certain areas of Maui:

KĀ'ANAPALI

Jan.	79F	26C	May	81F	27C	Sept.	85F	29C
	65	18		67	19		70	21
Feb.	77F	25C	June	83F	28C	Oct.	85F	29C
	63	17		68	20		70	21
Mar.	79F	26C	July	85F	29C	Nov.	83F	28C
	67	19		72	22		68	20
Apr.	81F	27C	Aug.	85F	29C	Dec.	79F	26C
	65	18		72	22		67	19

LAHAINA

Jan.	85F	29C	May	86F	30C	Sept.	88F	31C
	61	16		63	17		70	21
Feb.	83F	28C	June	88F	31C	Oct.	88F	31C
	59	15		65	18		68	20
Mar.	85F	29C	July	88F	31C	Nov.	86F	30C
	63	17		65	18		67	19
Apr.	85F	29C	Aug.	88F	31C	Dec.	83F	28C
	63	17		68	20		65	18

➤ FORECASTS: **Weather Channel Connection** (☎ 900/932–8437), 95¢ per minute from a Touch-Tone phone.

1 Destination: Maui and Lāna`i

WELCOME TO THE VALLEY ISLE

MAUI, SAY THE LOCALS, *nō ka 'oi* it's the best, the most, the top of the heap. To those who know Maui well, there's good reason for the superlatives. Maui magic weaves a spell over the 2.2 million people who visit its shores each year and leaves them wanting more. Often visitors decide to return for good.

In many ways Maui, the second-largest island in the Hawaiian chain, comes by its admirable reputation honestly. The island's 729 square mi contain Haleakalā, a 10,023-ft dormant volcano whose misty summit beckons the adventurous; several villages where Hawaiian is still spoken; more millionaires per capita than nearly anywhere else in the world; three major resort destinations that have set new standards for luxury; Lahaina, an old whaling port that still serves as one of the island's commercial crossroads; and more than 80,000 residents who work, play, and live on what they fondly call the Valley Isle.

Maui residents have had a bit to do with their island's success story. In the mid-1970s, savvy marketers saw a way to improve the island's economy through tourism and started advertising and promoting their "Valley Isle" separately from the rest of the state. They nicknamed West Maui "the Golf Coast," luring heavyweight tournaments that, in turn, brought more visitors. They went after the upscale tourist—hotels were renovated to accommodate a clientele that would pay more for the best. Condominiums on Maui were also refurbished—the word condo no longer meant second-best accommodations. Maui's visitor count swelled, putting it far ahead of that of the other Neighbor Islands.

That quick growth has led to its share of problems. During the busy seasons—from Christmas to Easter and then again during the summer—West Maui can be overly crowded. Although the County of Maui has successfully widened the two-lane road that connects Lahaina and Kāʻanapali, the stop-and-go traffic during rush

hour reminds some visitors of what they left at home. It's not that residents aren't trying to do something about it—the Kapalua-West Maui Airport, with its free shuttle to and from Kāʻanapali, has alleviated some of the heavy traffic between Kahului and Lahaina.

The explosion of visitors seeking out the Valley Isle has also created a large number of businesses looking to make a fast buck from the high-spending vacationers. Lahaina could easily be called the T-shirt capital of the Pacific (in close competition with Waikīkī), and the island has nearly as many art galleries and cruise-boat companies as T-shirts. As in other popular travel destinations, the opportunity to make money from visitors has produced its fair share of schlock.

But then consider Maui's natural resources. Geologists claim that Maui was created between 1 and 2 million years ago by the eruption of two volcanoes, Puʻu kukui and Haleakalā, the former extinct and the latter now dormant; a low central isthmus formed between them and joined them into West and East Maui. The resulting depression between the two is what gives Maui its nickname, the Valley Isle. West Maui's 5,788-ft Puʻu kukui was the first volcano to form, a distinction that gives the area's mountainous topography a more weathered look. Rainbows seem to grow wild over this terrain as gentle mists move quietly from one end of the long mountain chain to the other. Sugarcane gives the rocky region its life, with its green stalks moving in the trade winds born near the summit.

The Valley Isle's second volcano is the 10,023-ft Haleakalā, a mountain so enormous that its lava filled in the gap between the two volcanoes. You can't miss Haleakalā, whose name means House of the Sun, a spectacle that rises to the east, often hiding in the clouds that cover its peak. To Hawaiians, Haleakalā is holy, and it's easy to see why. It's a mammoth mountain, and if you hike its slopes or peer into one of its craters, you'll witness an impressive variety of nature: desertlike terrain butted up against tropical forests;

dew-dripping ferns a few steps from the surface of the moon; spiked, alien plants poking their heads out of the soil right near the most elegant and fragrant flowers.

In fact, the island's volcanic history gives Maui much of its beauty. Rich red soil lines the roads around the island—*becoming* the roads in some parts. That same earth has provided fertile sowing grounds for the sugarcane that has for years covered the island's hills. As the deep blue of ocean and sky mingle with the red and green of Maui's land, it looks as if an artist has been busy painting the scenery. Indeed, visual artists love Maui. Maybe it's the natural inspiration; maybe it's the slower pace, so conducive to creativity.

Farmers also appreciate the Valley Isle. On the slopes of Haleakalā, the volcanic miracle has wrought agricultural wonders, luring those with a penchant for peat moss to plant and watch the lush results. Sweetly scented flowers bloom large and healthy, destined to adorn a happy brow or become a lovely lei. Grapes cultivated on Haleakalā's slopes ripen evenly and deliciously, and are then pressed for wine and champagne. Horses graze languidly on rolling meadows of the best Upcountry grasses, while jacaranda trees dot the hillsides with spurts of luscious lavender. On the eastern slopes of the volcano, lavish rains turn the soil into a jungle.

Maui had no indigenous plants or animals because of its volcanic origins. Birds brought some of the life that would inhabit Maui, as did the waves that washed upon its newly formed shores. Then in about AD 800, Polynesians began to arrive on Maui's shores. They had journeyed from the Marquesas and Society Islands, braving rough waters in their canoes as they navigated by the stars across thousands of miles. These first residents brought animals, such as pigs and chickens, as well as plants, such as breadfruit, yams, coconuts, and bananas.

Not until 1778, when Captain James Cook made his second voyage to the Hawaiian Islands, did the Mauians receive their first visitor. Months earlier, Cook had landed on Kaua'i and Ni'ihau; he had made friends with the Polynesians and left behind bartered goods, as well as dread white man's diseases. When he got to Maui, Cook was surprised to find that the venereal disease running rampant on his ships had preceded him there. Shortly after, Cook pushed on to the Big Island.

Before leaving, however, Cook anchored his ship off the northeast coast of Maui while he hosted Kalani'ōpu'u, the aging chief of the Big Island, who spent a night on the Englishman's HMS *Resolution*. At the time, the Hawaiian Islands were rife with divided kingdoms waging war one against another, and the elderly Kalani'ōpu'u was certainly plotting against Maui's principal chief, Kahekili. How much Cook figured into these strategy sessions is unknown, but the records show that Kalani'ōpu'u was accompanied by his young warrior nephew, Kamehameha.

PERHAPS IT WAS THE experience off Maui's coast that eventually fired Kamehameha's ambition to rule more than a tiny section of one island. Kamehameha witnessed that Cook was master of his destiny, and the callow youth, no doubt, wanted the same thing. Years of battle followed as the young chief fought for the right to dominate the Islands. Finally, in 1794, Kamehameha defeated Maui's chief, thereby gaining the Valley Isle as well as its smaller neighboring islands of Moloka'i and Lāna'i. The following year he conquered the Big Island and O'ahu. Kaua'i wouldn't knuckle under, but in 1810 it was won over diplomatically. Kamehameha had earned the right to be king of all the Islands. He was called Kamehameha I, or Kamehameha the Great, and the kingdom's headquarters were in Lahaina, on Maui. The site of the king's Lahaina palace is between the Pioneer Inn and the ocean; the palace itself is long gone, however.

The great king had 21 wives during his lifetime, and the two most notable hailed from Maui. Queen Keōpūolani was Kamehameha's "sacred" wife, the daughter of a traditional brother-sister union that was considered so powerful that Keōpūolani was assured of producing honorable heirs for her husband. Historians believe she was the first Christian convert; she was extremely supportive of the missionaries who came to Hawai'i. Preceded in death by her royal spouse, Queen Keōpūolani is buried in the Waine'e/Waiola Cemetery (on Waine'e Street in Lahaina), next to her second husband, Hawaiian chief Hoapili, who was governor of Maui.

Kamehameha's favorite wife, Ka'ahumanu, also came from Maui. She was tall, statuesque, and politically astute. In fact, after her husband's death in 1819, Queen Ka'ahumanu named herself Hawai'i's first regent when Keōpūolani's eldest son, Liholiho, took the throne; she even continued that role when Liholiho's brother Kau'ikea'ōuli succeeded him. Ka'ahumanu was so powerful that she was instrumental in banning the *kapu* system, the Hawaiian set of rules and standards that had been in force for generations. It was she who insisted that the king move from the Brick Palace in Lahaina to another home in Honolulu.

Not long after Captain Cook landed on Maui, others arrived to take up residence. Missionaries who came from the eastern United States thought Mauians were heathens who needed to be saved, and they diligently tried to convert the residents. The missionaries' job was made even more challenging by the almost simultaneous arrival of whalers from New England. Soon Lahaina developed into the area's most important whaling port, and with the new industry came a lusty lifestyle that included more diseases, wild revelry, and additional motivation for the missionaries to continue their quest.

In 1840 Kau'ikea'ōuli, as King Kamehameha III, moved his monarchic capital to Honolulu, but Lahaina continued to be an important city for trade, education, and hearty living. Many of the buildings used during this era still exist in Lahaina and are open to visitors. The Spring House, now located in the Wharf Shopping Center on Front Street, once protected a freshwater source for the missionaries, while the Seamen's Hospital, also on Front Street, was converted by the U.S. government from a royal party residence to a medical facility for sailors.

Along with missionaries and whalers, other new settlers began to come to Maui. The most notable arrivals were businessmen, who viewed the Islands as a place to buy cheap land—or, better yet, to get it for free by befriending a member of the royal family. To the most astute entrepreneurs, sugar, which grew wild on Maui, looked like a good bet for cultivation, and when the Civil War knocked out sugar supplies in the South, the Hawaiian plantations boomed. By the late 1800s, "King Sugar" had become the new ruler in the Islands.

SOME OF THE MOST prominent leaders in the sugar industry were the grown children of missionaries. On Maui two of the most important businessmen were Samuel Alexander and Henry Baldwin, who joined forces in a sugar dynasty eventually called Alexander & Baldwin. A&B, as it came to be known, was a charter member of Hawai'i's Big Five—the five giant corporations that controlled the Islands economically and politically well into the 20th century. Although the power and influence of the Big Five have waned dramatically in the past few years with the increase of takeovers and buyouts, Alexander & Baldwin remains both Maui's largest private landholder and its largest private employer. The company developed the sunny Wailea Resort and owned it until 1990, as well as all of the island's sugar operations and macadamia-nut farms.

It wasn't until the early 1960s—only a few years after Hawai'i became a state in 1959—that tourism took root on Maui in a major way. That was when Amfac Inc. opened its major resort destination in West Maui, calling it Kā'anapali. It soon became Hawai'i's second most popular resort area after Waikīkī and was the first to have a master plan. The Royal Lahaina, which opened in 1962, was the first lodging to break ground in the Kā'anapali Resort, which now contains six deluxe hotels and at least a dozen condominiums.

North of Kā'anapali, Maui Land & Pineapple entered into the tourism arena in the mid-1970s when it broke ground for the Kapalua Resort with its 194-room Kapalua Bay Hotel, joined in 1992 by the Ritz-Carlton's 550-room showplace.

Tourism now accounts for about half of all jobs on the Valley Isle. Beginning in the mid-1800s, the dwindling indigenous population—those Hawaiians whose descendants came from the Marquesas and the Society Islands—were reinforced by labor from Japan, China, Portugal, and the Philippines, so that today's Maui has become a heady stew of ethnicity and culture.

The Valley Isle is full of people ready to share the friendly aloha spirit. If you take the drive to Hāna, around dozens of hairpin curves, across bridges, and past waterfalls, you'll find plenty of folks who still speak the Hawaiian language. Or if you relax on the wharf in historic Lahaina, you can watch transplanted Californians have a great time surfing; most of them find West Maui the best place in the world for working and living. All these residents love their island and will gladly help you have a good time.

By all means, make the effort to meet some locals. Although a fantastic time can be had simply by relaxing on the silky-soft, white-sand beaches, the wonder of Maui is that much, much more awaits your discovery. Don't be surprised if quite a few of your fantasies are actually fulfilled. The Valley Isle hates to let anyone down.

WHAT'S WHERE

West Maui

The extinct volcano Pu'u kukui formed Maui's smaller, western land mass; its balmy leeward shore attracted Kamehameha I, who chose Lahaina for the first capital of his kingdom after he united the Hawaiian Islands. Later years brought missionaries, whalers, and sugar plantations to West Maui, making it an area rich in history. Two of the island's premier resorts, Kā'anapali and Kapalua, line the coast north of Lahaina.

Central Maui

The isthmus connecting West Maui and East Maui is home to Kahului, Maui's deepwater port, and Wailuku, the county seat. Some historic churches and homes, some of them housing museums, can be found here, as well as the island's largest shopping mall, Ka'ahumanu Center, just minutes from the main airport in Kahului.

Haleakalā and Upcountry

The dormant Haleakalā volcano beckons the eye from every place on Maui. Not surprisingly, the summit and its surrounding crater have views unlike any others on earth. Ranches, nurseries, farms, and a winery on the mountain's fertile slopes give the region an agricultural flavor, neatly encapsulated in the cowboy town of Makawao.

The Road to Hāna

One of the most famous drives in the world, the twisting, turning 55-mi road from Kahului to the tiny eastern shore town of Hāna delights the senses with photoworthy waterfalls and bridges, ginger- and plumeria-scented mists, and fascinating birdsongs. Turn off the radio and the air-conditioner, open the windows, drive slowly, and stop often to take it all in.

Wailea and Kīhei

Stretching along the western shore of East Maui are the family-friendly condos of Kīhei and, farther south, the grande luxe hotels and condos of Wailea, Maui's newest major resort. In addition to five perfect crescent beaches, Wailea has grass- and hard-surface tennis courts, and three (count 'em) first-class golf courses.

PLEASURES AND PASTIMES

Beaches

Enjoy the west coast's family-friendly playgrounds, watch daredevil surfers on the north shore, or contemplate the natural beauty of the sands around Hāna. The choice is yours, but you can't go home and tell your friends you went to Maui and never visited a beach. For swimming, sunning, and people-watching, as well as convenient parking and amenities, the resort beaches of Wailea and Kā'anapali can't be beat.

Hawaiian Culture and History

It would be a shame to leave Maui without learning at least a little about the island's history. Take time to visit the Hāna Cultural Center if you drive to the eastern shore town. Tour the Sugar Museum and the Bailey House near Wailuku. Chat with the well-informed guides at the Baldwin Home in Lahaina. You may even want to take one of the programs more and more hotels are offering that focus on

Hawaiian culture, including lessons in lei-making, hula, Hawaiian language or music. They're fun, and they'll enrich your enjoyment of what you see and hear as you travel around Maui.

Hiking

Hiking on Maui can be an easy stroll through a botanical garden, a walk along paved and guard-railed paths in 'Iao Valley State Park, or a pack trip into Haleakalā Crater. There's something to suit nearly every age and inclination, from the rugged outdoors-lover to the urbanite who hails cabs for exercise.

Water Sports

Surfing, snorkeling, scuba-diving, sailing, and fishing can be enjoyed year-round on Maui, and lessons are available for almost any water sport you'd like to try. Experienced divers will want to take one of the many snorkel or scuba cruises to the most exotic and challenging offshore dive sites, but Maui's shores offer plenty of colorful and unusual sea-life specimens to delight the underwater eye. If you've never surfed but have always wanted to try, the gentle waters of Lahaina Harbor are a great place to learn, and, yes, you can learn in a single half-day lesson.

NEW AND NOTEWORTHY

The island's biggest news—and a must-see for all visitors—is the new Maui Ocean Center, a world-class aquarium focusing on the marine life and ocean ecology of the Pacific. Its main attraction is a 2.5-million-liter open-ocean tank with a walk-through acrylic tunnel. The Reef Building simulates a walk down into a reef, level by level, from the shoreline to the sea floor. The 5-acre marine park, on the Honoapi'ilani Highway at Ma'alaea Harbor, is the cornerstone of several proposed projects that could turn sleepy Ma'alaea into a magnet for Maui's visitors.

The famous Road to Hāna has been spruced up—just as many twists and kinks as ever, but the roadway surface is as smooth as it's been in decades. The State Highways Division is still scratching its head over a bad stretch of cliffside road that has crumbled to one lane in the Ke'anae area. Some officials have proposed the unthinkable—closing the road entirely for up to nine months. It's not clear yet what action will be taken. Till then, drivers can count on a good road not only into Hāna but all the way around East Maui on the belt road. There's still one rather irritating 4-mi rocky stretch in Kaupo, but passenger cars will have no trouble on this spectacular "back side" two-lane route.

Visitors to Hāna can take a two-hour guided tour of Kahanu Garden and Pi'ilani-hale Heiau, the largest pre-discovery monument in the state. The temple dates to the 16th century; it's surrounded by a federally funded botanic research facility specializing in the ethnobotany of the Pacific. For years this remarkable place was closed to the public, in part because the Hawaiian guardians preferred it that way. They've opened it now to visitors who respect the site's sacred significance—and who call ahead for an appointment.

The old Courthouse in Lahaina is slated to emerge in January 1999 from a one-year restoration to its 1925 configuration. Besides government offices, the renewed Courthouse will have changing displays on Lahaina and Maui history, and its former tenant, the Lahaina Arts Society, will (probably) return. The Lahaina Visitors Center, formerly in the Courthouse, will relocate to a new building on Front Street just mauka of the town library.

After 23 years of planning and development, the Maui community now has its version of Central Park—the 110-acre Keōpūolani Park in Kahului. Named for the Maui queen who played a pivotal role in Hawaiian history, the park comprises seven ball fields, a picnic area, a 2-mi walking trail, a botanical garden, and a children's zoo—all wheelchair accessible and landscaped mainly with native plants.

FODOR'S CHOICE

No two people will agree on what makes a perfect vacation, but it's fun and helpful to know what others think. We hope you'll have a chance to experience some of Fodor's Choices yourself while visiting Maui. For more information about each entry, refer to the appropriate chapters in this guidebook.

Beaches

★ **Hāna Beach.** Though it's not easy to get to, if you want an idea of what Old Hawai'i was like, head for Hāna Beach, or stay at the Hotel Hāna-Maui, and ride the free shuttle.

★ **Ho'okipa Beach.** This is the place to watch world-class windsurfing, but not the place to try to learn the sport yourself.

★ **Kapalua Beach.** This stretch of resort sand is so well-kept, you almost think the sand won't get into your suit here.

★ **Little Mākena Beach.** Although nude sunbathing is illegal on Maui, Little Mākena is best-known for attracting people in search of that all-over tan.

★ **Nāpili Beach.** This sparkling white beach forms a secluded cove tailor-made for honeymooners.

Drives

★ **Coming down Mt. Haleakalā.** We recommend that you try to drive to Haleakalā's summit without stopping, to arrive as early as possible, but take your time coming down; the countryside is lovely, and the views are amazing.

★ **From Lahaina to Mā'alaea.** The road along the northwest shore offers plenty of good stopping places from which to watch for whales wintering off Maui's coast.

★ **The road to Hāna.** This trip is all about the drive, not the destination. If you're pressed for time and can't make it all the way to Hāna, at least try and make it halfway. This drive—crossing bridges and passing waterfalls—is one you won't forget, especially if you bring your camera along.

Hotels

★ **Four Seasons Resort.** A spectacular setting and impeccable service, plus the beaches, golf, and tennis of Wailea, make this one of Hawai'i's top-rated hotels. $$$$

★ **Hotel Hāna-Maui.** The fabled eastern shore hideaway of the rich and famous is about as far from the madding crowd as you can get on Maui. $$$$

★ **Kea Lani Hotel Suites & Villas.** A family-friendly resort with peaceful enclaves for the grown-ups and three terrific restaurants, this property offers celebrities privacy right in Wailea. $$$$

★ **Kula Lodge.** This Upcountry chalet is completely un-tropical, but cozy and romantic, and a great place to start a trip up Haleakalā. $$–$$$

★ **Lahaina Hotel.** This tiny (12 rooms), antiques-filled gem of a hotel is smack-dab in the heart of Lahaina. $$

Restaurants

★ **Gerard's.** Chef-owner Gerard Reversade serves French cuisine at this celebrity favorite; the menu changes daily according to the freshest foods available. $$$–$$$$

★ **David Paul's Lahaina Grill.** An innovative menu that changes seasonally, late-afternoon wine tastings, and a loyal clientele from the nearby art galleries keep this popular place growing. $$–$$$$

★ **Hāli'imaile General Store.** This out-of-the-way, one-time camp store just can't stop drawing crowds, and rave reviews, for chef-owner Beverly Gannon's great food. $$–$$$

★ **Trattoria Ha'ikū.** A country-style Italian dinner house brings white linens to the jungle and serves locally produced foods in a 1920s building, formerly a lunchroom for pineapple cannery workers. $$–$$$

Sights

★ **Haleakalā.** You couldn't miss seeing it if you tried, but take the drive to see it up close.

★ **Ho'okipa Beach.** The north shore windsurfers here will earn your respect.

★ **'Īao Needle.** You don't have to be a nature-lover to find this rock formation, and the surrounding park, awe inspiring.

★ **Lahaina Historic District.** The town is funky and fun, as painless an education as you'll find.

★ **Sunsets.** Of course.

FESTIVALS AND SEASONAL EVENTS

WINTER

Dec.➤ **Bodhi Day** (☎ 808/ 522–9200), the traditional Buddhist Day of Enlightenment, is celebrated at temples throughout the island. Visitors are welcome at the services. **Nā Mele O Maui** (☎ 808/661– 3271): The first week of December, this Hawaiiana festival at Ka'anapali features arts and crafts. Schoolchildren compete in Hawaiian song and hula performances. **Christmas:** The hotels outdo one another in extravagant exhibits and events, such as Santa arriving by outrigger canoe.

Jan.➤ **Hula Bowl Game** (☎ 808/947–4141): This annual college all-star football classic, which moved to Maui in 1998, is followed by a Hawaiian-style concert. **Celebration of Whales** (☎ 808/ 874–8000): Scientists and conservationists convene at the the Four Seasons Resort Wailea for a week of lectures, videos, and whale-watch outings. Visitors are welcome.

Feb.–Mar.➤ **Cherry Blossom Festival:** This popular celebration of all things Japanese includes a run, cultural displays, cooking demonstrations, music, and the inevitable queen pageant and coronation ball.

SPRING

Mar.➤ **Prince Kūhiō Day** (☎ 808/822–5521): March 26, a local holiday, honors Prince Kuhio, a member of Congress who might have been king if Hawai'i had not become a U.S. territory and later a state. **Celebration of the Arts** (☎ 808/669–6200): For three days the Ritz-Carlton Kapalua pays tribute to Hawai'i's culture with hula and chanting demonstrations, art workshops, a lu'au, and Hawaiian music and dance concerts—most activities are free. **Art Maui** (☎ 808/874–1319): The best of a wide variety of media is shown at this prestigious annual event, held at the Maui Arts & Cultural Center in Kahului. **Buddha Day:** Flower pageants are staged at temples to celebrate the birth of the Buddha.

May➤ **Lei Day:** The annual flower-filled celebration on the first day of May includes music, hula, food, as well as lots of flower garlands on exhibit and for sale, some of them exquisite masterpieces. **Barrio Festival:** This cultural celebration is organized by the Binha Filipino Community. **Junior World Wave Sailing Championships:** Competitors under age 18 come from 15 countries to race the challenging surf at Ho'okipa Beach.

SUMMER

June➤ **King Kamehameha Day** (☎ 808/586–0333): Kamehameha united the islands and became Hawai'i's first king. Festivities on June 12 include parades and fairs. **Kapalua Wine and Food Symposium** (☎ 800/527–2582): Wine and food experts and enthusiasts gather for formal tastings, panel discussions, receptions, and gourmet dinners at Kapalua Bay Resort.

July➤ **Makawao Statewide Rodeo** (☎ 808/ 572–2076): This old-time Upcountry rodeo, held at the Oskie Rice Arena in Makawao during the July 4th weekend, includes a parade and three days of festivities. **Independence Day:** The national holiday is celebrated with a tropical touch, including fairs, parades, and, of course, fireworks. Special events include the Great Kālua Pig Cook-Off in Maui, with a $1,000 cash prize for the best pig roaster in the state, a pig parade, and good eating.

July–Aug.➤ **Bon Odori Season** (☎ 808/661– 4304): Buddhist temples invite everyone to festivals that honor ancestors and feature Japanese Bon dancing.

Aug.➤ **Admission Day:** This local holiday, which is observed on the nearest Friday to the 18th to guarantee a three-day weekend, recognizes Hawai'i's statehood.

AUTUMN

SEPT.➤ **Maui Music Festival** (☎ 800/245–9229): On Labor Day weekend, well-known contemporary jazz, Hawaiian, and other musicians converge on the Ka'anapali Beach Resort for two days of nonstop music on several outdoor stages. **Taste of Lahaina** (☎ 808/667–9175): Maui's best chefs compete for top cooking honors, and samples of their entries are sold at a lively open-air party featuring live entertainment. **Maui Writers**

Conference (☎ 808/879–0061): Best-selling authors and powerhouse agents and publishers offer advice—and a few contracts—to aspiring authors and screenwriters at this Labor Day weekend gathering.

SEPT.–OCT.➤ **Aloha Week Festival:** This traditional celebration, started in 1946, preserves Hawaiian native culture. Crafts, music, dance, pageantry, street parties, and canoe races highlight the festival.

OCT.–DEC.➤ **Hawai'i Winter Baseball** (☎ 808/973–7247): Teams include promising minor leaguers from the mainland and Japan.

NOV.➤ **Hawai'i International Film Festival** (☎ 808/528–3456): The cinematic feast travels from island to island, showcasing films from the United States, Asia, and the Pacific. **Maui Invitational NCAA Basketball Tournament:** The collegiate competition brings top-ranked Mainland teams to the Lahaina Civic Center. **Kapalua International Championship Golf:** Top pro golfers meet at the Kapalua resort for the "Super Bowl" of golf with a purse of more than $600,000. **Nā Mele O Maui Festival:** Hawaiian arts, crafts, dances, music, and a lū'au are all part of this cultural event.

2 Exploring Maui

The Valley Isle, as Maui is fondly called, has made an international name for itself with its tropical allure, heady nightlife, and miles and miles of beaches. In east Maui, ferns take over forests, waterfalls cascade down crags, and moss becomes the land's lush carpeting. The rich, fertile slopes of Haleakalā, a dormant volcano in the middle of the island, yield much of Hawai'i's produce, as well as its only wine-producing grapes. In West Maui, "the Golf Coast," beaches are lined with condos, restaurants, and resorts.

THERE IS PLENTY TO SEE AND DO on the Valley Isle besides spending time on the beach. To help you organize your time, this guide divides the island into four areas to explore—West Maui, Central Maui, Haleakalā and Upcountry, and the Road to Hāna (East Maui). You can spend half a day to a full day or more in each area depending on how long you have to visit. The best way to see the whole island is by car, but there are opportunities for good walking tours.

To get yourself oriented, first look at a map of the island. You will notice two distinct circular landmasses volcanic in origin and dominated by mountains. The smaller landmass, on the western part of the island, consists of 5,788-ft Puʻu Kukui and the West Maui Mountains, some of whose reaches now grow sugarcane and pineapple. The interior of these mountains is one of the earth's wettest spots; 400 inches of rain each year have sliced the land into impassable gorges and razor-sharp ridges. Oddly enough, the area's leeward, western shore—what most people mean when they say "West Maui"—is sunny and warm year-round. Most of the island's visitor industry is centered here.

The large landmass in the eastern portion of Maui was created by Haleakalā, the cloud-wreathed volcanic peak at its center. One of the best-known mountains in the world, Haleakalā is popular with hikers and sightseers. This larger region of the island is called East Maui, with the resorts, condominiums, and beaches of Wailea, Kīhei, and Mākena flanking its leeward shore; Hāna and its wilder environs—past where the pavement stops—sit on the eastern shore.

Between the two mountain areas is Central Maui, which was once the ocean until Haleakalā spewed lava into the channel that separated East from West. Central Maui is the location of the county seat of Wailuku, from which the islands of Maui, Lānaʻi, Molokaʻi, and Kahoʻolawe are governed. It's also the base for much of the island's commerce and industry.

In the Islands, the directions *mauka* (toward the mountains) and *makai* (toward the ocean) are often used. We've included them in the text here as well.

Numbers in the text correspond to numbers in the margin and on the Maui, Lahaina, and Kahului-Wailuku maps.

Great Itineraries

Maui is designed for day trips. Many visitors never get over the spell of the sea, and never go inland to explore the island and its people. Those who do, though, launch out early from their beachside hotel or condo, loop through a district, then wind up back "home" for sunsets and mai tais. When you live on an island, you get used to going in circles. Don't be too goal-oriented as you travel around. If you rush to "get there," you might find you've missed the point of going—which is to encounter one of the most beautiful islands in the world, still mostly wilderness and largely unpopulated.

IF YOU HAVE 1 DAY

This is a tough choice. But how can you miss the opportunity to see **Haleakalā National Park** ㉝ and the volcano's enormous, other-worldly crater? Sunrise at the summit has become the thing to do. It's quite dramatic (and chilly), but there are drawbacks. Namely, you miss seeing the landscape and views on the way up in the dark; also, you have to get up early. How early? You'll need an hour and a half from the bottom of **Haleakalā Highway** (Highway 37) ㉜ to the summit. Add

to that the time of travel to the highway—at least 45 minutes from Lahaina or Kīhei. *The Maui News* posts the hour of sunrise every day.
The best experience of the crater takes all day and good legs. Hike in.
Start at the summit, hike down Sliding Sands trail, cross the crater floor,
and come back up the Halemauʻu switchbacks. (This works out best
if you leave your car at the Halemauʻu trailhead parking lot and get a
lift for the last 20-minute drive to the mountaintop.) All you need is a
packed lunch, water, and decent walking shoes. If you don't hike,
leave the mountain early enough to go explore **ʻĪao Valley State Park** ㉛
above Wailuku. This will show you the island's leafy, freshwater, jungle landscape and will compensate for the fact that you're missing the
drive to Hāna.

IF YOU HAVE 3 DAYS

Give yourself the volcano experience one day, then rest up a little with
a beach-snorkel-exploring jaunt on either East or West Maui. The East
Maui trip would have to include the **Maui Ocean Center** ⑱ (the new aquarium at Maʻalaea), a sampling of the little beaches in Wailea, then a good
dose of big golden Mākena Beach. Be sure to drive on past Mākena into
the rough lava fields, the site of Maui's last (about 200 years ago) lava
flows that formed rugged La Pérouse Bay. The ʻĀhihi-Kinaʻu Marine
Preserve has no beach, but it's a rich spot for snorkeling.

Or take the West Maui trip over the *pali* through Olowalu, **Lahaina** ④–
⑰, **Kāʻanapali** ③, and dodge off the highway to find small beaches in
Nāpili, Kahana, **Kapalua** ①, and beyond. The road gets narrow and
sensational around **Kahakuloa** ②; if you're enjoying it, keep circling
West Maui and return through the Central Valley. For your third day,
do **Hāna** ㊺. Be sure not to rush, and be sure to pull over to let residents pass. Stop in **Pāʻia** ㊴ for food, pause at **Hoʻokipa** ㊵ for the surf
action, and stop and drink in the sight of the taro fields of **Keʻanae
Arboretum** ㊻ and **Wailua Lookout** ㊽. Nearly everyone keeps going past
Hāna town to **ʻOheʻo Gulch** ㊶, the "seven pools."

IF YOU HAVE 5 DAYS

Explore Upcountry. Get to **Makawao** ㊲ and use that as your pivot point.
Head north at the town's crossroads and drive around **Haʻikū** ㊶ by
turning left at the first street (Kokomo Road), right at Haʻikū Road,
then come back uphill on any of those leafy, twisting, gulch-country
roads. After you've explored Makawao town, drive out to Kula on the
Kula Highway. This is farmland, with fields of flowers and vegetables
and small ranches with well-nourished cattle. Stop in little Kēōkea for
coffee, and keep driving on Highway 37 to the ʻUlupalakua Ranch at
the **Tedeschi Vineyards and Winery** ㉟. You can't be a Maui aficionado
unless you've spent some time Upcountry. Add some time in Central
Maui to really get to the heart of things, especially **Wailuku** ⑲–㉘ with
its old buildings and curious shops. From here you can loop out to
Pāʻia ㊴ and spend some time there enjoying beaches in the Spreckelsville
area and poking around in the boutiques and shops of this old plantation town.

When to Tour Maui

Although Maui has the usual temperate-zone shift of seasons—a bit
rainier in the winter, hotter and drier in the summer—these seasonal
changes are negligible on the leeward coasts where most visitors stay.
The only season worth mentioning is tourist season, when the roads
around Lahaina and Kīhei get crowded. Peak visitor activity occurs from
Christmas to March, then picks up again in summer. If traffic is both-
ering you, just remember that Maui is mostly unpopulated. Get out of
town and explore the countryside. During high season, the road to Hāna
tends to clog—well, not clog exactly but develop little choo-choo

trains of cars, with everyone in a line of six or a dozen driving as slowly as the first car. The solution: leave early (dawn) and return late (dusk). And if you find yourself playing the role of locomotive, pull over. Maui has a variety of community festivals, but they're spread throughout the year. Look in the local paper or ask the Maui Visitors Bureau (☞ the Gold Guide). If something's going on, check it out.

WEST MAUI

West Maui, anchored by the amusing old whaling town of Lahaina, was the focus of development when Maui set out to become a premier tourist destination. The condo-filled beach towns of Nāpili, Kahana, and Honokōwai are arrayed between the stunning resorts of Kapalua and Kāʻanapali, north of Lahaina.

A Good Drive

Begin this tour in **Kapalua** ①; even if you're not staying there, you'll want to have a look around the renowned Kapalua Bay Hotel and enjoy a meal or snack before you begin exploring. From Kapalua drive north on the Honoapiʻilani Highway (Hwy. 30). This used to be the route to Wailuku. It has been paved, but storms now and then make it partly impassable, especially on the winding, 8-mi stretch that is only one lane wide, with no shoulder and a sheer drop off into the ocean. However, you'll discover some gorgeous photo opportunities along the road, and if you go far enough, you'll come to **Kahakuloa** ②, a sleepy fishing village tucked into a cleft in the mountain. You've now come about as far as you can on this "highway." The road pushes on to Wailuku, but you may be tired of the narrow and precipitously winding course you have to take.

From Kahakuloa turn around and go back in the direction from which you came—south toward Kāʻanapali and Lahaina, past the beach towns of Nāpili, Kahana, and Honokōwai. If you wish to explore these towns, get off the Upper Honoapiʻilani Highway and drive closer to the water. If you're not staying there, you may want to visit the planned resort community of **Kāʻanapali** ③, especially the Hyatt Regency Maui and the Westin Maui. To reach them, take the third Kāʻanapali exit from Honoapiʻilani Highway (the one closest to Lahaina), then turn left on Kāʻanapali Parkway. Next, head for Lahaina. Before you start your Lahaina trek, take a short detour by turning left from Honoapiʻilani Highway onto Lahainaluna Road, and stop at the **Printing House** ④, built by Protestant missionaries in 1831. Return the way you came on Honoapiʻilani Highway, and turn left on Kēnui Street, then left on Front Street.

Lahaina is best explored on foot, so use the drive along Front Street to get oriented, then park at or near **505 Front Street** ⑤, at the south end of the town's historic and colorful commercial area. Heading back into town, turn on Prison Street and you'll come to the **Old Prison** ⑥, which was built from coral blocks. Then return to Front Street where it's a short stroll to the **Banyan Tree** ⑦, one of the town's best-known landmarks, and behind it, the old **Court House** ⑧. Next door, also in Banyan Park, stand the reconstructed remains of the waterfront **Fort** ⑨. About a half block northwest, you'll find the site of Kamehameha's **Brick Palace** ⑩. **Brig Carthaginian II** ⑪ is anchored at the dock nearby and is open to visitors. If you walk from the brig to the corner of Front and Dickenson streets, you'll find the **Baldwin Home** ⑫, restored to reflect the decor of the early 19th century. Next door is the **Master's Reading Room** ⑬, Maui's oldest building and now home to the Lahaina Restoration Foundation.

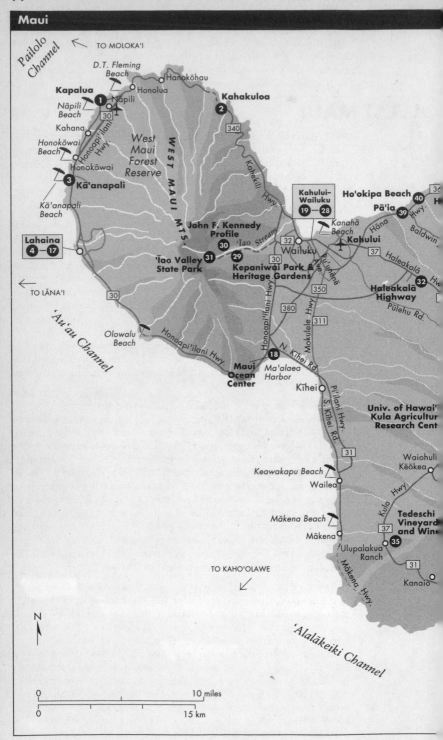

N

0   10 miles
0   15 km

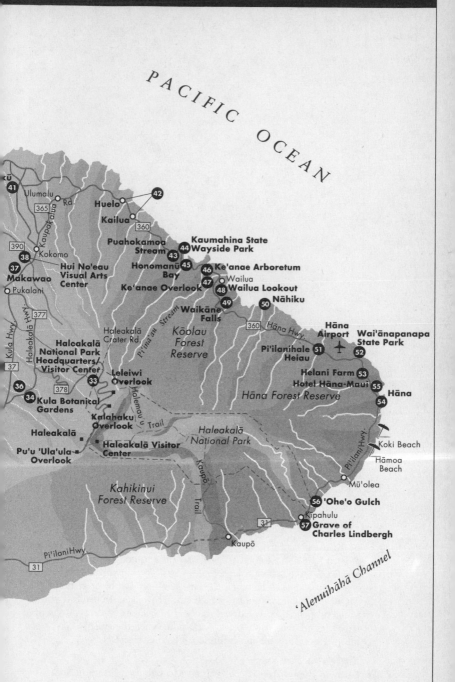

PACIFIC

OCEAN

Ulumalu

365

Kokomo

390

38

37

Makawao

Pukalani

Hui No'eau
Visual Arts
Center

Kula Hwy

377

37

Haleakalā
National Park
Headquarters/
Visitor Center

36

34

Kula Botanical
Gardens

378

33

Leleiwi
Overlook

Haleakalā
Crater Rd.

Haleakalā

Pu'u 'Ula'ula
Overlook

Kalahaku
Overlook

Haleakalā Visitor
Center

Kahikinui
Forest Reserve

Pi'ilani Hwy

31

41

Huelo

42

Kailua

360

Puahokamoa
Stream

43

Kaumahina State
Wayside Park

44

Honomanū
Bay

45

46

Ke'anae Arboretum

47

Wailua

Ke'anae Overlook

48

Wailua Lookout

49

Waikāne
Falls

50

Nāhiku

Kōolau
Forest
Reserve

360

Hāna Hwy

Hāna
Airport

Wai'ānapanapa
State Park

Pi'ilanihale
Heiau

51

52

Helani Farm

53

Hotel Hāna-Maui

55

54

Hāna

Hāna Forest Reserve

Haleakalā
National Park

Koki Beach

Hāmoa
Beach

Mū'olea

56 'Ohe'o Gulch

Kipahulu

57 Grave of
Charles Lindbergh

Kaupō

31

'Alenuihāhā Channel

TO THE BIG ISLAND OF HAWAI'I

Baldwin
Home, **12**

Banyan Tree, **7**

Brick
Palace, **10**

Brig
*Carthaginian
II*, **11**

Court House, **8**

505 Front
Street, **5**

Fort, **9**

Master's
Reading
Room, **13**

Old Prison, **6**

Printing
House, **4**

Seamen's
Hospital, **16**

Spring
House, **14**

Waiola
Church and
Cemetery, **17**

Wo Hing
Temple, **15**

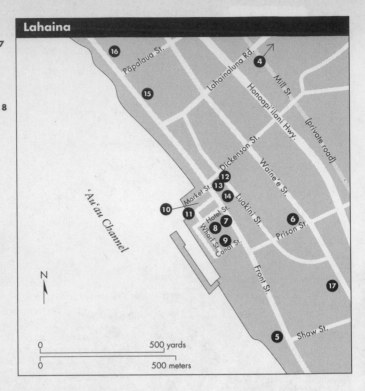

Lahaina

Wander north or south on Front Street to explore Lahaina's commercial side. At the Wharf Cinema Center, you can see the **Spring House** ⑭, built over a freshwater spring. If you continue north on Front Street, you'll come to **Wo Hing Temple** ⑮; another two blocks north and you'll find the **Seamen's Hospital** ⑯. If you're finished walking before dusk and have a hankering for just one more stop, try the **Waiola Church and Cemetery** ⑰. Walk south down Front Street, make a left onto Dickenson Street, then make a right onto Waine'e Street and walk another few blocks.

TIMING

You can walk the length of Lahaina's Front Street in fewer than 30 minutes if you don't stop along the way; just *try* not to be intrigued by the town's colorful shops and historic sites. Realistically, you'll need at least half a day—and can easily spend a full day—to check out the area's coastal beaches, towns, and resorts. The Banyan Tree in Lahaina is a terrific spot to be when the sun sets—mynah birds settle in here for a screeching symphony, which can be an event in itself. If you arrange to spend a Friday afternoon exploring Front Street, you can dine in town and hang around for Art Night, when the galleries stay open into the evening and entertainment fills the streets.

Sights to See

★ ⑫ **Baldwin Home.** An early missionary to Lahaina, Ephraim Spaulding finished building this plaster-and-whitewash coral stone home in 1835; in 1836 Dr. Dwight Baldwin—also a missionary—moved in with his family. The home is now run by the Lahaina Restoration Foundation and has been restored and furnished to reflect the period. You can view the living room with the family's grand piano, the dining room, and Dr. Baldwin's dispensary. ⊠ *696 Front St., Lahaina,* ☎ *808/661–3262.* ⊠ *$3.* ☺ *Daily 10–4.*

7 Banyan Tree. This massive tree, a popular and hard-to-miss meeting place if your party splits up for independent exploring, was planted in 1873. It is the largest of its kind in the state and provides a welcome retreat for the weary who come to sit under its awesome branches. ⊠ *Front St., between Hotel and Canal Sts., Lahaina.*

10 Brick Palace. All that's left of the palace built by King Kamehameha I around 1802 to welcome the captains of visiting ships are the excavated cornerstones and foundation in front of the Pioneer Inn. Hawai'i's first king lived only one year in the palace because his favorite wife, Ka'ahumanu, refused to stay there. It was then used as a warehouse, storeroom, and meeting house for 70 years until it collapsed. ⊠ *Makai end of Market St., Lahaina.*

★ **11 Brig *Carthaginian II.*** This vessel's sailing days are over, but it makes an interesting museum. It was built in Germany in the 1920s and is a replica of the type of ship that brought the New England missionaries around Cape Horn to Hawai'i in the early 1800s. A small museum below deck features the "World of the Whale," a colorful multimedia exhibit about whaling and local sea life. ⊠ *At dock opposite north end of Wharf St., Lahaina,* ☎ 808/661–3262. ☑ *$3.* ⊙ *Daily 10–4.*

8 Court House. This old civic building was erected in 1859, rebuilt in 1925, and restored to its 1925 condition in 1998. At one time or another it served as a customs house, a post office, a vault and collector's office, a governor's office, a police court, and a courtroom. Until restoration began, it housed the Lahaina Visitors Center and the Lahaina Art Society with its exhibits and educational programs. At the time of this writing it was not clear who would next occupy this all-purpose relic. The Visitor Center has been relocated two blocks northwest on Front Street. ⊠ *649 Wharf St., Lahaina,* ☎ 808/661–0111.

5 505 Front Street. Quaint New England–style architecture characterizes this mall, which houses small shops and restaurants connected by a wooden sidewalk. It isn't as crowded as some other areas in Lahaina, probably because between here and the nearby Banyan Tree the town turns into a sleepy residential neighborhood and some people, walking from the more bustling center of Front Street, give up before they reach the mall. Still, the casual eateries lure their share of fun-lovers. ⊠ *South end of Front St. near Shaw St., Lahaina.*

9 Fort. Used mostly as a prison, this fortress was positioned so that it could police the whaling ships that crowded the harbor. It was built after sailors, angered by a law forbidding local women from swimming out to ships, lobbed cannonballs at the town. Cannons raised from the wreck of a warship in Honolulu Harbor were brought to Lahaina and placed in front of the fort, where they still sit today. The building itself is an eloquent ruin. ⊠ *Canal and Wharf Sts., Lahaina.*

3 Kā'anapali. The theatrical look of Hawai'i tourism—planned resort communities where luxury homes mix with high-rise hotels, fantasy swimming pools, and a Disneyesque landscape—all began right here in the 1960s. Three miles of uninterrupted white beach and playground-placid water form the front yard for this artificial utopia, with its 40 tennis courts and its two championship golf courses (Kā'anapali North and South). The six major hotels are all worth visiting just for the look around, especially the Hyatt Regency Maui, with its multimillion dollar art collection. One of Maui's best attractions sits here in the Whalers Village shopping complex, the **Whale Center of the Pacific.** This small but excellent museum uses ingenious displays to teach all about the big cetaceans—and there's no charge for admission. ⊠ *2435 Kā'anapali Pkwy., Suite H16,* ☎ 808/661–5992. ☑ *Donation.* ⊙ *Daily 9:30 AM–10 PM.*

❷ Kahakuloa. This tiny fishing village seems lost in time. Untouched by progress, it's a relic of pre–jet travel Maui. Many remote villages similar to Kahakuloa used to be tucked away in the valleys of this area. This is the wild side of West Maui; true adventurers will find terrific snorkeling and swimming along this coast, as well as some good hiking trails. ⊠ *North end of Honoapi'ilani Hwy.*

❶ Kapalua. This resort, set in a beautifully secluded spot surrounded by pineapple fields, got its first big boost in 1978, when the Maui Land & Pineapple Company built the luxurious Kapalua Bay Hotel. It was joined in 1992 by a dazzling Ritz-Carlton. The hotels host dedicated golfers, celebrities who want to be left alone, and some of the world's richest folks. Kapalua's shops and restaurants are some of Maui's finest, but expect to pay big bucks for whatever you purchase. ⊠ *Bay Dr., Kapalua.*

★ Lahaina. This little whaling town has a notorious past; there are stories of lusty whalers who met head-on with missionaries bent on saving souls. Both groups journeyed to Lahaina from New England in the early 1800s. At first, Lahaina might look touristy, but there's a lot that's genuine here as well. The town has renovated most of its old buildings, which date from the time when it was Hawai'i's capital. Much of the town has been designated a National Historic Landmark, and any new buildings must conform in style to those dating before 1920. ⊠ *Honoapi'ilani Hwy., about 3 mi south of Kā'anapali.*

Ⓒ Lahaina–Kā'anapali & Pacific Railroad. Affectionately called the Sugarcane Train, this is Maui's only passenger train; it's an 1890s-vintage railway that once shuttled sugar but now moves sightseers between Kā'anapali and Lahaina. This quaint little attraction is a big deal for Hawai'i but probably not much of a thrill for those more accustomed to trains. The kids will like it. You can also get a package that combines a ride and lunch in Lahaina or a historic Lahaina tour. ⊠ *1½ blocks north of the Lahainaluna Rd. stoplight on Honoapi'ilani Hwy., Lahaina,* ☎ *808/661–0089.* ☞ *$13.50.* ☉ *Daily 9–5:30.*

⓭ Master's Reading Room. This is Maui's oldest residential building, constructed in 1834. In those days the ground floor was a mission's storeroom, and the reading room upstairs was for sailors. Now the **Lahaina Restoration Foundation** occupies the building, and its knowledgeable staff is here 8–4 to answer almost any question about historic sites in town. Ask for their walking-tour brochure. ⊠ *Front and Dickenson Sts., Lahaina,* ☎ *808/661–3262.*

❻ Old Prison. Known as Hale Pa'ahao (stuck-in-irons-house), because of its wall shackles and ball-and-chain restraints, this compound was built in the 1850s by convict laborers out of blocks of coral that had been salvaged from the demolished waterfront **Fort** (☞ *above*). Most prisoners were there for desertion, drunkenness, or reckless horse riding. Today, the building is rented for community use. ⊠ *Waine'e and Prison Sts., Lahaina.* ☉ *Daily 8–5.*

❹ Printing House. Part of Lahainaluna Seminary, founded by Protestant missionaries in 1831, the print shop turned out many of the first Hawaiian-language textbooks and other teaching aids. An exhibit features a replica of the original Rampage press and facsimiles of early printing. The oldest U.S. educational institution west of the Rockies, the seminary now serves as Lahaina's public high school. ⊠ *980 Lahainaluna Rd., Lahaina.* ☞ *Donation.* ☉ *Weekdays 10–3.*

⓰ Seamen's Hospital. Built in the 1830s to house King Kamehameha III's royal court, this property was later turned over to the U.S. government, which used it as a hospital for whalers. Next door is a typical **sugar plantation camp residence**, circa 1900. ⊠ *1024 Front St., Lahaina,* ☎ *808/661–3262.*

⑭ Spring House. Built by missionaries to shelter a freshwater spring, this historic structure is now home to a huge Fresnel lens, once used in a local lighthouse that guided ships to Lahaina. ⊠ *Wharf Cinema Center, 658 Front St., Lahaina.*

NEED A BREAK?

Has all this fresh air given you a yen for a big beefy burger? Head for **Cheeseburger in Paradise** (⊠ Front St. at Lahainaluna Rd., Lahaina, ☎ 808/661–4855). Upcountry locals, who raise their own beef, travel to Lahaina for these $5 behemoths topped with cheddar, mozzarella, or Swiss cheese.

⑰ Waiola Church and Cemetery. The Waiola Cemetery is actually older than the neighboring church, dating from the time when Kamehameha's sacred wife Queen Keōpūolani died and was buried there in 1823. The first church here was erected in 1832 by Hawaiian chiefs, and was originally named Ebenezer by the queen's second husband and widower, Governor Hoapili. It was later named Waine'e, after the district in which it is located. Aptly immortalized in James Michener's *Hawai'i* as the church that wouldn't stand, it was burned down twice and demolished in two windstorms. The present structure was put up in 1953 and named Waiola (water of life). ⊠ *535 Waine'e St., Lahaina,* ☎ *808/661–4349.*

⑮ Wo Hing Temple. Built by the Wo Hing Society in 1912 as a social center for Chinese residents, this eye-catching building now contains Chinese artifacts and a historic theater that features Thomas Edison's films of Hawai'i, circa 1898. Upstairs is the only public Taoist altar on Maui. ⊠ *858 Front St., Lahaina,* ☎ *808/661–3262.* ⊠ *Donation.* ☼ *Daily 10–4.*

CENTRAL MAUI

Kahului, an industrial and commercial town in the center of the island, is home to many of Maui's permanent residents, who find their jobs close by. The area was developed in the early '50s to meet the housing needs of workers for the large sugarcane interests here, specifically those of Alexander & Baldwin. The large company was tired of playing landlord to its many plantation workers and sold land to a developer who promised to create affordable housing. The scheme worked, and Kahului became the first planned city in Hawai'i. Ka'ahumanu Avenue (Hwy. 32), Kahului's main street, runs from the harbor to the hills. It's the logical place to begin your exploration of Central Maui.

A Good Tour

Begin at the south end of the central valley by visiting the **Maui Ocean Center** ⑱, easily spotted and accessed from the Honoapíilani Highway (Hwy. 30) at Mā'alaea. When you've had your fill of ogling sealife in this world-class aquarium and exploring Mā'alaea Boat Harbor, get back on the highway and take the second right turn, the Kūihelani Highway (Hwy. 380) to Kahului. Five miles later turn right at the traffic light, Pu'unēnē Avenue (Hwy. 350), and watch for the **Alexander & Baldwin Sugar Museum** ⑲ on the left, just before the still-operating sugar mill. The museum was opened in 1988 by "A&B," Maui's largest landowner and linchpin of its sugar industry, to detail the historic influence of sugarcane in the Islands. It's a fascinating exhibit well worth your time.

From here, explore **Kahului,** the commercial center of Maui, which looks nothing like the lush tropical paradise most people envision as Hawai'i.

HAWAIIAN MUSIC

ASK MOST VISITORS ABOUT Hawaiian music and they'll likely break into a lighthearted rendition of "Little Grass Shack." When they're done, lead them directly to a stereo.

First, play them a recording of singer Kekuhi Kanahele, whose compositions combine ancient Hawaiian chants with modern melodies. Then ask them to listen to a CD by guitarist Keola Beamer, who loosens his strings and plays slack-key tunings dating back to the 1830s.

Share a recording by falsetto virtuoso Amy Hanaiali'i Gilliom, one of the very few singers perpetuating the upper-register vocal style. Then take them to a concert by Henry Kapono, who writes and sings of the pride—and pain—of being pure Hawaiian.

These artists, like many, are proving just how multifaceted Hawaiian music has become. They're unearthing their Island roots in the form of revered songs and chants, and they're reinterpreting them for today's audiences. It's "chicken-skin" (goosebumps) stuff, to be sure, and it's made only in Hawai'i.

Granted, "Little Grass Shack" does have its place in the history books. After Hawai'i became a U.S. territory in 1900, the world discovered its music thanks to touring ensembles who turned heads with swaying hips, steel guitars, and pseudo-Hawaiian lyrics. Once radio and movies got into the act, dreams of Hawai'i came with a saccharine Hollywood sound track.

But Hawaiian music is far more complex. It harkens back to the sounds of the ancient Islanders who beat rough-hewn drums, blew haunting calls on conch shells, and intoned repetitive chants for their gods. It recalls the voices of 19th-century Christian missionaries who taught Islanders how to sing in four-part harmony, a style that's still popular today.

The music takes on international overtones thanks to gifts from foreign immigrants: the 'ukulele from Portuguese laborers, for instance, and the guitar from Mexican traders. And it's enlivened by a million renderings of "Tiny Bubbles," as mainstream entertainers like Don Ho croon Hawaiian-pop hits for Waikīkī tourists.

Island music came full circle in the late 1960s and '70s, a time termed the Hawaiian Renaissance. While the rest of the world was rocking 'n' rolling, a few dedicated artists began giving voice to a resurgence of interest in Hawaiian culture, history, and traditions.

Today's artistic trailblazers are digging deep to explore their heritage, and their music reflects that thoughtful search. They go one step further by incorporating such time-honored instruments as nose flutes and gourds, helping them keep pace with the past.

Why is Hawaiian music such a well-kept secret? Simply put, it's rarely played outside of the Islands. A handful of local performers are making their mark on the mainland and in Japan. But if you want to experience the true essence of Hawaiian music, you must come to Hawai'i. Check ads and listings in local papers for information on concerts, which take place in indoor and outdoor theaters, hotel ballrooms, and cozy nightclubs. When you hear the sound, you'll know it's Hawaiian because it'll make you feel right at home.

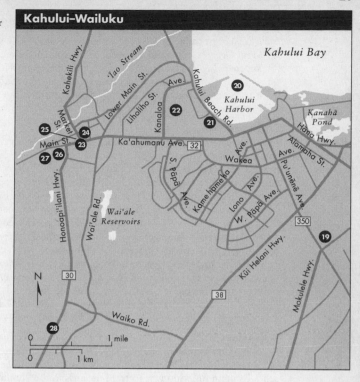

Kahului–Wailuku

Head back on Pu'unēnē Avenue all the way to its end at Ka'ahumanu Avenue, and turn left. Three blocks ahead you'll see the sputnik-looking canvas domes of Ka'ahumanu Center, Maui's largest shopping center. If you turn right at the signal just before that, you'll follow the curve of Kahului Beach Road and see any ships in port at **Kahului Harbor** ⑳. On your left are the cream-and-brown buildings of **Maui Arts & Cultural Center** ㉑; continue on the beach road until you reach Kanaloa Avenue. Make a left here and return to Ka'ahumanu Avenue passing the new **Keōpūolani Park** ㉒ and the War Memorial Stadium, site of the annual Hooters Hula Bowl. Turn right to reach Wailuku (Ka'ahumanu eventually becomes Wailuku's Main Street). To get a closer look at **Wailuku's Historic District** ㉓, turn right from Main Street onto Market Street, where you can park for free within view of the landmark **'Iao Theater** ㉔. The theater is a good place to begin your walking tour. Next door to the theater is Traders of the Lost Art, the first of many amusing shops that line **Market Street** ㉕ between Vineyard and Main streets. Then it's a short walk along Main Street to **Ka'ahumanu Church** ㉖ on High Street, just around the corner from Main and across the way from the County Court House. Retrieve your car and return to Main Street, where you'll turn right. After a few blocks, on your left, you'll see **Bailey House** ㉗. Follow Highway 30 south a couple of miles to the **Maui Tropical Plantation** ㉘.

From the plantation drive toward the mountains. Main Street turns into 'Iao Valley Road, the air cools, and the hilly terrain gets more lush. Soon you'll come to **Kepaniwai Park & Heritage Gardens** ㉙. As you drive on you'll pass a less imposing landmark called **John F. Kennedy Profile** ㉚. 'Iao Valley Road ends at **'Iao Valley State Park** ㉛, home of the erosion-formed gray and moss-green rock called 'Iao Needle. If you still have the stamina, you can end your touring with a good hike.

TIMING

The complete itinerary will take a full day. But you can explore Central Maui comfortably in little more than half a day if you whiz through the Maui Ocean Center and the Maui Tropical Plantation, or save them for another day. If you want to combine sightseeing with shopping, this is a good itinerary for it, but you'll need more time. Hikers may want to expand their outing to a full day to explore 'Iao Valley State Park, especially in spring, when any plant that can blossom does.

Sights to See

★ ⑲ **Alexander & Baldwin Sugar Museum.** "A&B," Maui's largest landowner, was one of five companies known collectively as the Big Five that spearheaded the planting, harvesting, and processing of the valuable agricultural product sugarcane. Although Hawaiian cane sugar has now been supplanted by cheaper foreign versions—as well as by sugar derived from less costly sugar beets—the crop was for many years the mainstay of the Hawaiian economy. You'll find the museum in a small, restored plantation manager's house next to the post office and the still-operating sugar refinery (black smoke billows up when cane is burning). Historic photos, artifacts, and documents explain the introduction of sugarcane to Hawai'i and how plantation managers brought in laborers from other countries, thereby changing the Islands' ethnic mix. Exhibits also describe the sugar-making process. ⊠ *3957 Hansen Rd., Pu'unēnē*, ☎ *808/871–8058.* ⊡ *$4.* ⊘ *Mon.–Sat. 9:30–4:30.*

㉗ **Bailey House.** This was the home of Edward and Caroline Bailey, two prominent missionaries who came to Wailuku to run the first Hawaiian girls' school on the island, the Wailuku Female Seminary; the school's main function was to train the girls in the "feminine arts." It once stood next door to the Baileys' home, which they called **Halehō'ike'ike** (House of Display), but locals always called it the Bailey House, and the sign painters eventually gave in.

Construction of the house, between 1833 and 1850, was supervised by Edward Bailey himself. The **Maui Historical Society** runs a museum in the plastered stone house, with a small collection of artifacts from before and after the missionaries' arrival and with Mr. Bailey's paintings of Wailuku. Some rooms have missionary-period furniture. The Hawaiian Room has exhibits on the making of tapa cloth, as well as samples of pre–Captain Cook weaponry. ⊠ *2375A Main St., Wailuku,* ☎ *808/244–3326.* ⊡ *$4.* ⊘ *Mon.–Sat. 10–4.*

㉔ **'Iao Theater.** One of Wailuku's most photographed landmarks, this charming movie house went up in Wailuku in 1927 and served as a community gathering spot. When restoration work was completed in 1996, the Maui Community Theatre returned to its Wailuku headquarters, though it still performs at Maui Arts & Cultural Center's Castle Theater, as well. The Art Deco building is now the showpiece of Wailuku's Main Street. The front of the building is now a theater-theme café offering light breakfasts, lunches, and showtime refreshments. ⊠ *68 N. Market St., Wailuku,* ☎ *808/242–6969.*

NEED A
BREAK?

Maui Bake Shop & Deli Ltd. (⊠ 2092 Vineyard St., Wailuku, ☎ 808/ 242–0064) serves salads, sandwiches, and a daily changing variety of light entrées, but what you're really going to crave here are the pastries—a feast for the eyes as well as the palate. The pastel-frosted frogs, chicks, rabbits, and mice, made of orange butter-cream cookie dough, are simply irresistible.

★ ㉛ **'Iao Valley State Park.** When Mark Twain saw this park, he dubbed it the Yosemite of the Pacific. Yosemite it's not, but it is a lovely, deep valley with the curious 'Iao Needle, a spire that rises more than 2,000 ft from the valley floor. You can take one of several easy hikes from the parking lot across 'Iao Stream and explore the junglelike area. This park offers a beautiful network of well-maintained walks, where you can stop and meditate by the edge of a stream or marvel at the native plants and flowers. Mist occasionally rises if there has been a rain, which makes being here even more magical. ⊠ *Western end of Hwy. 32.* ☜ *Free.* ◷ *Daily 7–7.*

③⓪ John F. Kennedy Profile. Hawaiians, it seems, can recognize something in almost every rock formation throughout the Islands. Still, this one does uncannily resemble the profile of the late president. ⊠ *Hwy. 32, about 1 mi east of 'Iao Valley State Park.*

②⑥ Ka'ahumanu Church. It's said that Queen Ka'ahumanu attended services on this site in 1832 and requested that a permanent structure be erected. Builders first tried adobe, which dissolved in the rain, then stone. The present wooden structure, built in 1876, is classic New England style, with white exterior walls and striking green trim. You won't be able to see the interior, however, unless you attend Sunday services. The church conducts a service entirely in the Hawaiian language each Sunday at 9:30 AM. ⊠ *Main and High Sts., Wailuku,* ☏ *808/244–5189.*

Kahului. The town of Kahului is the industrial and commercial center for Maui's year-round residents, as close to a bustling urban center as Maui gets. Most visitors arrive at the airport here and see all they will see of the town as they drive on to their hotels, unless they stop to explore Maui's largest mall, the Ka'ahumanu Center.

②⓪ Kahului Harbor. This is Maui's chief port, since it's the island's only deep-draft harbor. American-Hawai'i's 800-passenger SS *Independence* and SS *Constitution* each stop here once a week, as do cargo ships and smaller vessels, including the occasional yacht. Surfers sometimes use this spot to catch some good waves, but it's not a good swimming beach. ⊠ *Kahului Beach Rd., Kahului.*

②② Keōpūolani Park. Maui's new "Central Park" covers 101 acres and—reflecting Maui residents' traditional love of sports—it has seven playing fields. Named for the great Maui queen who was born near here and is buried in Lahaina's Waiola Church cemetery, the park is planted with native species that will take a few years to reach their potential. The park also includes a children's petting zoo, a native plant botanical garden, a picnic area, and a 3 mi walking path.⊠ *Kanaloa Ave., next to the YMCA.*

☾ ②⑨ Kepaniwai Park & Heritage Gardens. This county park is a memorial to Maui's cultural roots, with picnic facilities and ethnic displays dotting the landscape. There's an early Hawaiian shack, a New England–style saltbox, a Portuguese-style villa with gardens, and dwellings from such other cultures as China and the Philippines. Next door the **Hawai'i Nature Center** has an interactive exhibit and offers hikes that are good for children.

The peacefulness here belies the history of the area. During his quest for domination, King Kamehameha I brought his troops from the Big Island of Hawai'i to the Valley Isle in 1790 and engaged in a particularly bloody battle against the son of Maui's chief, Kahekili, near Kepaniwai Park. An earlier battle at the site had pitted Kahekili himself against an older Big Island chief, Kalani'ōpu'u. Kahekili prevailed, but the carnage was so great that the nearby stream became known as Wailuku (water of destruction) and the place where fallen warriors choked the stream's flow was called Kepaniwai (the water dam). ⊠ *Valley Rd., Wailuku.* 🎫 *Free.* ☉ *Daily 7–7.*

㉕ Market Street. An idiosyncratic assortment of shops—with proprietors to match—makes Wailuku's Market Street a delightful place for a stroll. Merchants are happy to chat with visitors, recommend a restaurant, and offer advice or directions.

㉑ Maui Arts & Cultural Center. This $32 million facility opened in 1994 after an epic fund drive led by the citizens of Maui. The top-of-the-line Castle Theater seats 1,200 people on orchestra, mezzanine, and balcony levels. Rock stars play the A& B Amphitheater. The Center (as it's called) also includes a small black box theater, an art gallery with interesting exhibits, and classrooms. The building itself is worth the visit. It incorporates work by Maui artists, and its signature lava-rock wall pays tribute to the skills of the Hawaiians. ⊠ *Just above the harbor on Kahului Beach Rd., Kahului,* ☎ *808/242–2787, box office 808/242–7469.* ☉ *Weekdays 9–5.*

⑱ Maui Ocean Center. This new aquarium that focuses on Hawaii and the Pacific will make you feel as though you're walking from the seashore down to the bottom of the reef, and then through an acrylic tunnel in the middle of the sea. Special tanks get you close up with turtles, rays, and the bizarre creatures of the tide pools. ⊠ *Enter from Honoapi'ilani Hwy. (Hwy. 30) as it curves past Mā'alaea Harbor, Mā'alaea,* ☎ *808/244–3337.* 🎫 *$17.50.* ☉ *Daily 9–5.*

㉘ Maui Tropical Plantation. This visitor attraction used to be a huge sugarcane field, but when Maui's once-paramount crop declined severely in importance, a group of visionaries decided to open an agricultural theme park. The 120-acre preserve, on Highway 30 just outside Wailuku, offers a 30-minute tram ride through its fields with an informative narration covering growing processes and plant types.

Children will also probably enjoy a historical characters exhibit, as well as fruit-testing, coconut-husking, and lei-making demonstrations and bird shows. There's a restaurant on the property and a souvenir shop that sells fruits and vegetables. On Tuesday and Thursday nights, the Maui Tropical Plantation stages a country-western show and barbecue. ⊠ *Honoapi'ilani Hwy. (Hwy. 30), Waikapu,* ☎ *808/244–7643.* 🎫 *Free; tram ride with narrated tour $8.50.* ☉ *Daily 9–5.*

㉓ Wailuku's Historic District. The National Register of Historic Places lists many of this district's old buildings, preserved with their wooden facades intact. Overall, the little town is sleepy and one would not know that it is Maui's county seat. The mayor sits at the top floor of the tallest building in town, on the corner of Main and High streets.

In ancient times Wailuku was a favored place for the inhabitants of Maui, who maintained two *heiau* (temples) on the hills above. It was easy to spot intruders from the hills, and villages grew up around the temples. The first missionaries chose this as a principal station in the 1820s. ⊠ *High, Vineyard, and Market Sts., Wailuku.*

HALEAKALĀ AND UPCOUNTRY

The fertile western slopes leading up to majestic Haleakalā are called Upcountry. This region is responsible for much of Hawai'i's produce—lettuce, tomatoes, and sweet Maui onions—but the area is also a big flower producer. As you drive along you'll notice plenty of natural vegetation, as clumps of cacti mingle with purple jacaranda, wild hibiscus, and towering eucalyptus trees.

Upcountry is also fertile ranch land, with such spreads as the 20,000-acre 'Ulupalakua Ranch, long famous for raising cattle, and the 20,000-acre Haleakalā Ranch, which throws its well-attended rodeo in Makawao each July 4th. Tedeschi Vineyards and Winery, with just a few acres of 'Ulupalakua land, is the island's only wine producer.

A Good Drive

Start in Kahului fairly early in the morning, since the clouds move over the top of the mountain as early as 11 AM. Make sure you have a full gas tank; there are no service stations on the mountain. Drive on **Haleakalā Highway** ㉜ (Hwy. 37) toward **Haleakalā National Park** ㉝ and the mountain's breathtaking summit. Try to make the drive without stopping since you'll want the best views possible.

Watch the signs: Haleakalā Highway divides. If you go straight it becomes Kula Highway, which is still Highway 37; if you veer to the left it becomes Highway 377, the road you want. After about 6 mi, make a left onto Highway 378; the switchbacks begin here. Near the top of the mountain is the Park Headquarters/Visitor Center—a good spot to stop and stretch your legs.

Continuing up the mountain, you'll come to several overlooks, including Leleiwi Overlook and Kalahaku Overlook, both with views into the crater. Not far from Kalahaku Overlook you'll find the Haleakalā Visitor Center. Eventually you'll reach the highest point on Maui, the Pu'u 'Ula'ula Overlook.

Now head back down the way you came, taking time to see and explore the lower nooks and crannies of Haleakalā. When you reach Highway 377 again, make a left. Go about 2 mi, and you'll come to **Kula Botanical Gardens** ㉞ on your left. It's worth a stop here to admire a beautiful abundance of tropical flora. Continue on Highway 377, away from Kahului, and you'll soon join Highway 37 again. Turn left and, about 8 mi farther on, you'll reach 'Ulupalakua Ranch headquarters and **Tedeschi Vineyards and Winery** ㉟, where you can sample Hawai'i's only homegrown wines.

Returning the way you came, head north toward Kahului on Highway 37. When you get to the Highway 37/377 fork, bear to the left to stay on Highway 37. This is Kula Highway; another name change will make it Haleakalā Highway again (this isn't as confusing as it sounds). About 2 mi past the fork, you'll see a turnoff to the right called Copp Road. About ½ mi later, turn left onto Mauna Place to visit the **University of Hawai'i's Kula Agricultural Research Center** ㊱ and view its extraordinary collection of protea.

Retrace your way to Kula Highway and again head toward Kahului. In about 4 mi you'll come to the bedroom community of Pukalani. If you're pressed for time you can take Highway 37 from here back to Kahului. Otherwise, head north on Highway 365 toward the *paniolo* (Hawaiian cowboy) village of **Makawao** ㊲, formerly a Portuguese settlement. **Hui No'eau Visual Arts Center** ㊳ is about mile from the Makawao crossroads as you head down Baldwin Avenue. From here it's a short drive down toward the ocean to the Hāna Highway. Make a left on the Hāna Highway to return to Kahului.

TIMING

This can be an all-day outing even without the detours to Tedeschi Vineyards and Makawao. If you start early enough to catch the sunrise from

Haleakalā's summit, you'll have plenty of time to enjoy a short hike on the mountain, have lunch in Kula, and end your day with dinner in Makawao or Ha'iku.

Sights to See

③② **Haleakalā Highway.** On this road, you'll travel from sea level to an elevation of 10,023 ft in only 38 mi—a feat you won't be able to repeat on any other car route in the world. It's not a quick drive, however; it'll take you about two hours—longer if you can't resist the temptation to stop and enjoy the spectacular views. ⊠ *Hwy. 37.*

★ **③③** **Haleakalā National Park.** A trip to Maui would not be complete without a visit here. **Haleakalā** is the centerpiece of this 27,284-acre national park, which was dedicated in 1961 to preserving the area. The 10,023-ft dormant volcano is the font from which all of East Maui flowed. It is now home to a wide variety of sights, sounds, and smells; its terrain, climate, flora, and fauna—not to mention its views—are often strange, and always memorable. The crater is actually an "erosional valley," created by centuries of wind and rain chipping away at the mountain's summit (where there may have once been a small crater), sculpting the dramatic landscape you see today. The small hills within the valley are volcanic cinder cones, each with a small crater at its top, and each the site of an eruption. The mountain has terrific camping and hiking opportunities, including a trail that loops through the crater.

Before you head up Haleakalā, call (☎ 808/871–5054) for the latest park weather conditions. Extreme gusty winds, heavy rain, and even snow in winter are not uncommon—even if it is paradise as usual down at beach level. Because of the high altitude, the mountaintop temperature is often as much as 30 degrees cooler than that at sea level. Be sure to pack an extra jacket.

You can stop and learn something of the volcano's origins and eruption history at the **Park Headquarters/Visitor Center,** at 7,000-ft elevation on Haleakalā Highway. Maps, posters, and other memorabilia are available at the gift shop here.

Leleiwi Overlook, at about an 8,800-ft elevation on Haleakalā, is one of several lookout areas in the park. If you're here in the late afternoon, it's possible you'll experience a phenomenon called the Brocken Specter. Named after a similar occurrence in East Germany's Harz Mountains, the "specter" allows you to see yourself reflected on the clouds and encircled by a rainbow. Don't wait all day for this, because it's not a daily occurrence.

The famous silversword plant grows amid the desertlike surroundings at **Kalahaku Overlook,** at the 9,000-ft level on Haleakalā. This endangered flowering plant grows only here in the crater at the summit of this mountain. The silversword looks like a member of the yucca family and produces a stalk 3 ft–8 ft tall with several hundred purple sunflowers. At this lookout the silversword is kept in an enclosure to protect it from souvenir hunters and nibbling wildlife.

Haleakalā Visitor Center, at 9,740-ft elevation on Haleakalā, has exhibits inside and a trail from here leads to White Hill, a small crater nearby. This is a short, easy walk that will give you an even better view of the valley. Hosmer Grove, just off the highway before you get to the visitor center, has camp sites and interpretive trails. Park rangers maintain a changing schedule of talks and hikes both here and at the top of the mountain; check the center's bulletin board for details.

Just before the summit, the **Crater Observatory** offers warmth and shelter, informative displays, and an eye-popping view of the cinder-cone-studded, 7-mi by 3-mi crater. The highest point on Maui is the **Pu'u 'Ula'ula Overlook,** at the 10,023-ft summit of Haleakalā. Here you'll find a glass-enclosed lookout with a 360-degree view. The building is open 24 hours a day, and this is where visitors gather for the best sunrise view. Dawn generally begins between 5:45 and 7, depending on the time of year. On a clear day, you can see the islands of Moloka'i, Lāna'i, Kaho'olawe, and Hawai'i. On a *really* clear day, you can even spot O'ahu glimmering in the distance.

On a small hill nearby, you'll see **Science City,** a research and communications center that looks like it's straight out of an espionage thriller. The University of Hawai'i and the Department of Defense don't allow visitors to enter the facility, however. The university maintains an observatory here, while the Department of Defense tracks satellites. ✉ *Haleakalā Crater Rd. (Hwy. 378), Makawao,* ☎ *808/572–9306.* ⊠ *$10 per car.* ☉ *Park headquarters and visitor center, daily 7:30–4; Haleakalā visitor center, daily sunrise–3.*

| NEED A BREAK? | **Kula Lodge** (✉ Haleakalā Hwy., Kula, ☎ 808/878–2517) serves hearty breakfasts from 6:30 to 11:15—a favorite with visitors coming down from a sunrise visit to Haleakalā's summit as well as those on their way up for a later morning tramp in the crater. Spectacular ocean views fill the windows of this mountainside lodge (☞ Chapter 4). |

㊳ Hui No'eau Visual Arts Center. This nonprofit cultural center is on the old Baldwin estate, just outside the town of Makawao. The main house, an elegant two-story Mediterranean-style villa designed in the 1920s by the defining Hawai'i architect C. W. Dickey, shines from the efforts of renovations. "The Hui," more than 60 years old, is the grand dame of Maui's well-known art scene. The acreage seems like a botanical garden, and the nonstop exhibits are always satisfying. The Hui also offers classes and maintains working artists' studios. ✉ *2841 Baldwin Ave., Makawao,* ☎ *808/572–6560.* ⊠ *Free.* ☉ *Tues.–Sun. 10–4.*

㉞ Kula Botanical Gardens. Specimens grow somewhat naturally here, and you'll see all kinds of flora that may be unfamiliar. There are *koa* trees, the wood from which is often made into finely turned bowls and hand-crafted furniture, and *kukui* trees (ancient Hawaiians used the tree's nuts, which are filled with oil, for lighting). In addition the gardens have Maui's hallmark protea, several varieties of ginger, and stands of bamboo orchid. ✉ *RR 2, Upper Kula Rd., Kula,* ☎ *808/878–1715.* ⊠ *$4.* ☉ *Daily 9–4.*

㊲ Makawao. This once-tiny town has managed to hang onto its country charm (and eccentricity) as it has grown in popularity. The district was settled originally by Portuguese and Japanese immigrants, who came to Maui to work the sugar plantations and then moved "Upcountry" to establish small farms, ranches, and stores. Descendants now work the neighboring Haleakalā and 'Ulupalakua ranches. Every Fourth of July the paniolo set comes out in force for the Makawao Rodeo. The crossroads of town, lined with places to shop, see art, and get food, reflects a growing population of people who came here just because they like it. ✉ *Hwy. 365, East Maui.*

| NEED A BREAK? | One of Makawao's most famous landmarks is **Komoda Store & Bakery** (✉ 3674 Baldwin Ave., ☎ 808/572–7261)—a classic mom-and-pop store little changed over 70-odd years—where you can get a delicious cream puff if you arrive early enough in the day. They make hundreds—but sell out each day. Cream puffs or not, Komoda's is a nifty little stop, |

HAWAI'I'S FLORA AND FAUNA

HAWAI'I HAS THE DUBIOUS distinction of claiming more extinct and endangered animal species than the rest of the North American continent. The Hawaiian crow, or 'alalā, for example, has been reduced to a population of only 15 birds, and most of these have been raised in captivity on the Big Island. The 'alalā is now facing a serious threat from another endangered bird—the 'io, or Hawaiian hawk. Still "protected" although making a comeback from its former endangered status, the nēnē goose, Hawai'i's state bird, roams freely in parts of Maui, Kaua'i, and the Big Island, where mating pairs are often spotted ambling across roads in Hawai'i Volcanoes National Park.

The mongoose is not endangered, although some residents wish it were. Alert drivers can catch a glimpse of the ferretlike mongoose darting across country roads. The mongoose was brought to Hawai'i in 1883 in an attempt to control the rat population, but the plan had only limited success since the hunter and hunted rarely met: Mongooses are active during the day, rats at night. Another creature, the rock wallaby, arrived in Honolulu in 1916 after being purchased from the Sydney Zoological Garden. Two escaped, and today about 50 of the small, reclusive marsupials live in remote areas of Kalihi Valley.

At the Kīlauea Point National Wildlife Refuge on Kauai'i, hundreds of Laysan albatross, wedge-tail shearwaters, red-footed boobies, and other marine birds glide and soar within photo-op distance of visitors to Kīlauea Lighthouse. Boobie chicks hatch in the fall and emerge from nests burrowed into cliff-side dirt banks and even under stairs—any launching pad from which the fledgling flyer can catch the nearest air current.

Hawai'i has only two native mammals. Threatened with extinction, the rare Hawaiian bat hangs out primarily at Kealakekua Bay on the Big Island. On the endangered species list, doe-eyed Hawaiian monk seals breed in northwestern Islands. With only 1,500 left in the wild, you won't catch many lounging on the beaches of Hawai'i's populated islands, but you can see rescued pups and adults along with "threatened" Hawaiian green sea turtles at Sea Life Park and the Waikīkī Aquarium on Oahu.

Tropical flowers such as plumeria, orchids, hibiscus, red ginger, heliconia, and anthuriums grow wild on all islands. Pīkake blossoms make the most fragrant leis, and fragile orange 'ilima (once reserved only for royalty), the most elegant leis. The lovely wood rose is actually the dried seed pod of a species of morning glory. Mountain apple, Hawaiian raspberry, thimbleberry, and strawberry guava provide refreshing snacks for hikers; and giant banyan trees, hundreds of years old, spread their canopies over families picnicking in parks, inviting youngsters to swing from their hanging vines.

Sprouting ruby, pompomlike lehua blossoms—thought to be the favorite flower of Pele, the volcano goddess—'ōhi'a trees bury their roots in fields of once-molten lava. Also growing on the Big Island as well as the outer slopes of Maui's Haleakalā, exotic protea flourish only at an elevation of 4,000 ft; while within Haleakalā's moonscape crater, the rare and otherworldly silversword—a 7-ft stalk with a single white spike and pale yellow flower found nowhere else on earth—blooms once and then dies.

with plenty of tasty snacks as well as all the other trappings of an old-fashioned general store.

★ ㉟ **Tedeschi Vineyards and Winery.** You can take a tour of the winery and its historic grounds, the former Rose Ranch, and sample the island's only wines: a pleasant Maui Blush, the Maui Brut-Blanc de Noirs Hawaiian Champagne, and Tedeschi's annual Maui Nouveau. The most unusual wine, Maui Blanc, is made from pineapples; you'll want to taste it before you buy—it's not appreciated by everyone. The tasting room is a cottage built in the late 1800s for the frequent visits of King Kalākaua. The cottage also contains the 'Ulupalakua Ranch History Room, which tells colorful stories of the ranch's owners, the paniolo tradition that developed here, and Maui's polo teams. The old General Store may look like a museum; in fact it's an excellent pit stop. The ranch and winery are not too out of the way when you're returning from a visit to Haleakalā, and it's definitely worth a stop. ⊠ *Kula Hwy., 'Ulupalakua Ranch,* ☎ *808/878–6058.* ☜ *Free.* ⊙ *Daily 9–5, tours daily 9–2:30.*

㊱ **University of Hawai'i's Kula Agricultural Research Center.** The first protea was planted here in the mid-'60s and since then the station has become the world's foremost protea research and development facility. Within its gates you'll see as many as 300 varieties of the exotic blooms, most with names to match: Rickrack Banksia, Veldfire Sunburst, Pink Mink, and Safari Sunset, to name just a few. You can talk to the growers to find out more about the plants, which were brought to Maui from Australia in 1965 by Dr. Philip Parvin, a University of Hawai'i horticulture professor. You must first stop at the office and sign a sheet releasing the station from any liability; they'll provide you with a map to help you find your way.

Now that you have your botanical education, proceed to one of Upcountry Maui's many commercial outlets and buy your favorite blooms. Fresh-cut or dried (protea dry beautifully), these unusual-looking blossoms make great send-home gifts, but fresh flowers leaving Hawai'i must bear an inspection stamp. Most sellers will inspect, pack, and express-ship them for you. ⊠ *Mauna Pl., Kula,* ☎ *808/878–1213.* ☜ *Free.* ⊙ *Mon.–Thurs. 7–3:30.*

THE ROAD TO HĀNA

Don't let anyone tell you the Hāna Highway is impassable, frightening, or otherwise unadvisable. Because of all the hype, you're bound to be a little nervous approaching it for the first time. But once you try it, you'll wonder if maybe there's somebody out there making it sound tough just to keep out the hordes. The 55-mi road begins in Kahului, where it is a well-paved highway. The eastern half of the road is challenging, as it is riddled with turns and bridges, and you'll want to stop often so the driver can enjoy the view, too. But it's not a grueling, all-day drive. The challenging part of the road takes only an hour and a half. By and large the road is well maintained. Still, you might check ahead when you're in Maui to find out about possible delays; the Hana police station (☎ 808/248–8311) always knows the latest.

A Good Drive

Start your trip to Hāna in the little town of **Pā'ia** ㊴, where the main street in town is Hāna Highway. You'll want to begin with a full tank of gas—there are no gas stations along the Hāna Highway, and the stations in Hāna close by 6 PM. You can also pick up a picnic lunch here and really make a delicious day of it. Lunch and snack choices along the way are limited to local fare from extremely rustic fruit stands and truck markets. Once the road gets twisty remember that many people—mostly those who live in Hāna—make this trip frequently. You'll recognize them because they're the ones who'll be zipping around every curve; they've seen this so many times before that they don't care to linger. Pull over or slow down to let them pass.

Two miles east of Pā'ia, you'll see **Ho'okipa Beach** ㊵, arguably the windsurfing capital of the world. Two mi later the bottom of Ha'ikū Road offers a right-turn side-trip to **Ha'ikū** ㊶, Maui's verdant gulch country. About 6 mi later, at the bottom of Kaupakalua Road, the roadside mileposts begin measuring the 36 mi to Hana town. The road's trademark noodling starts about 3 mi after that. All along this stretch of road, waterfalls are abundant. Turn off the radio and open the windows to enjoy the sounds and smells. There are plenty of places to pull off and park; all are ideal spots to stop and take pictures. You'll want to plan on doing this a few times, as the road's curves make driving without a break difficult. When it's raining (which is often), the drive is particularly beautiful.

As you drive on you'll pass the sleepy country villages of **Huelo** ㊷ and Kailua. At about Mile Marker 11 you can stop at the bridge over **Puahokamoa Stream** ㊸, where there are more pools and waterfalls. If you'd rather stretch your legs and use a flush toilet, continue on another mile to the **Kaumahina State Wayside Park** ㊹. Near Mile Marker 13 you can see the vast **Honomanū Bay** ㊺. Another 4 mi brings you to the **Ke'anae Arboretum** ㊻, where you can add to your botanical education or enjoy a challenging hike into a forest. Nearby you'll find the **Ke'anae Overlook** ㊼. Coming up is the halfway mark to Hāna. If you've had enough scenery, this is as good a time as any to turn around and head back to civilization.

Don't expect a booming city when you get to Hāna. It's the road that's the draw. Continue on from Mile Marker 20 for about ¾ mi to **Wailua Lookout** ㊽. After another ½ mi, you'll hit the best falls on the entire drive to Hāna, **Waikāne Falls** ㊾. At about Mile Marker 25, you'll see a road that heads down toward the ocean and the village of **Nāhiku** ㊿, once a popular native settlement. Just after Mile Marker 31, the left turn at 'Ula'ino Road doubles back for a mile, loses its pavement, and even crosses a streambed just before Kahanu Garden and **Pi'ilanihale Heiau** (51), the largest in the state. Back on the road and less than ½ mi farther is the turnoff for **Hāna Airport.** Just beyond Mile Marker 32 you'll pass **Wai'ānapanapa State Park** (52); stop here for a swim at its black-sand beach. Closer to Hāna you'll come to a private 60-acre tropical enclave, **Helani Farm** (53). **Hāna** (54) is just minutes away from here; its fabled **Hotel Hāna-Maui** (55), with its surrounding ranch, is the mainstay of Hāna's economy.

Once you've seen Hāna, you might want to drive 10 mi past the town to the pools at **'Ohe'o Gulch** (56). Now called Pi'ilani Highway, the drivable road continues, though not always gracefully, all the way around the leeward side of Haleakalā. The trip adds an hour to your return time, but you won't see this kind of huge rugged landscape anywhere else on Maui. Many people travel the mile past 'Ohe'o Gulch to see the **Grave of Charles Lindbergh** (57). The world-renowned aviator is buried next to Palapala Ho'omau Congregational Church. Past Seven Pools, past the scattered houses of Kipahulu, past tiny St. Paul's Church, on the right is the nearly hidden massive chimney of a ruined sugar mill. Just past the mill on the left side of the road is a pasture and then a galvanized-steel gate swung permanently open on a rutted track that heads toward the sea. The road goes to the Palapala Ho'omau

Congregational Church, a few hundred yards away, mostly hidden behind thick vegetation. The simple, one-room church sits on a bluff over the sea, with a small graveyard on the ocean side.

TIMING

With stops, the drive from Pā'ia to Hāna should take you between two and three hours. Lunch in Hāna, hiking, and swimming can easily turn the round-trip into a full-day outing. Since there's so much lush scenery to take in, try and plan your Road to Hāna drive for a day that promises fair, sunny weather. And be prepared for car trains that form spontaneously during the busier tourist seasons in winter and midsummer. (If you find one forming behind you, pull over). If you make this trip in winter, when the north shore waves are the highest, you may have the chance to watch astonishing windsurfing feats at Ho'okipa Beach, but sometimes the winter conditions are too dangerous even for daredevils.

Sights to See

⑤⑦ Grave of Charles Lindbergh. The world-renowned aviator chose to be buried here because he and his wife, writer Anne Morrow Lindbergh, spent a lot of time living in the area in a home they built. He was buried here in 1974, next to Palapala Ho'omau Congregational Church. Remember, this is a churchyard, so be considerate and leave everything exactly as you found it. ⊠ *Palapala Ho'omau Congregational Church, Kīpahulu.*

OFF THE BEATEN PATH **KAUPŌ ROAD –** This stretch of road beyond Kīpahulu has rough stretches, most notably a 4-mi unpaved portion in Kaupo; bad storms will occasionally cause temporary washouts and closures. It's a beautiful drive, however, and people travel it every day in two-wheel-drive cars. The pay-off is the chance to see the leeward "back side" of I luleukalā—rugged, grand, and unpopulated. In pre-discovery days, this whole part of the island was heavily populated. You can still see the old rock walls and house platforms that were abandoned 150 years ago. Along the way, the little Kaupō Store, about 15 mi past Hāna, sells a variety of essential items, such as groceries, fishing tackle, and hardware; it's also a good place to stop for a cold drink. You'll also pass the renovated Hui Aloha Church, a tiny, wood-frame structure surrounded by an old Hawaiian graveyard. In Kanaio, you'll pass through the zone of Haleakalā's last eruption, 200 years ago. You'll eventually wind up at 'Ulupalakua.

④① Ha'ikū. At one time, this town vibrated around a couple of enormous pineapple canneries; now the place is reawakening to itself as a self-reliant community. At the town center, the old cannery has turned into a rustic mall; nearby warehouses are following suit. Continue 2 mi up Kokomo Road to see a large *pu'u* (cinder cone) capped with a grove of columnar pines, and the 4th Marine Division Memorial Park. During World War II American GIs trained here for battles on Iwo Jima and Saipan. Locals have nicknamed the cinder cone "Giggle Hill," because it was a popular place for Maui girls to entertain their favorite servicemen. You might want to return to Hāna Highway by following Ha'ikū Road east. This is one of Maui's prettiest drives, and it passes West Kuiaha Road, where a left turn will bring you to a second renovated cannery. ⊠ *Intersection of Ha'ikū and Kokomo Rds.*

★ ⑤④ **Hāna.** For many years, the fabled Hotel Hāna-Maui was the only attraction for diners and shoppers determined to spend some time and money in Hāna after their long drive. The **Hāna Cultural Center Museum** (☎ 808/248–8622), on Ukea Street, helps to meet that need. Besides operating a well-stocked gift shop, it displays artifacts, quilts, a replica of an authentic *kauhale* (an ancient Hawaiian living complex, with thatched huts and food gardens, and other Hawaiiana). The knowledgeable staff can explain it all to you.

As you wander around Hāna, keep in mind that this is a company town. Although sugar was once the mainstay of Hāna's economy, the last plantation shut down in the '40s. In 1946 rancher Paul Fagan built the Hotel Hāna-Maui and stocked the surrounding pastureland with cattle. Suddenly, it was the ranch and its hotel that were putting food on most tables.

The cross you'll see on the hill above the hotel was put there in memory of Fagan. After his death in the mid-'60s, ownership of the ranch and town passed to 37 shareholders, most of whom didn't care about their property. Then the Rosewood Corporation purchased most of Hāna's valuable land and put megamillions into restoring the Hotel Hāna-Maui. In 1989 Rosewood sold its Hāna holdings to a Japanese company, which appointed Sheraton as manager. Sheraton renovated the old hotel and added the plantation-look Sea Ranch health spa across the road, and the isolated resort became a favorite hideaway for health-conscious celebrities. The property was sold again in 1995 to the New York–based Manolis Company, which promptly announced plans to build a golf course on part of the land; many local residents just as promptly announced their opposition to the proposal. The golf-course permit lapses in fall 1998; at press time the property was up for sale.

Because the town is so small, most of the people you'll see are the hands-on suppliers of the services and amenities that make hotel guests happy. Moreover, many locals have worked at the hotel for years; a fascinating family tree that hangs near the lobby shows the relationships among all the employees. If you're at all curious, be sure to talk to some of the townspeople. They're candid, friendly, and mostly native Hawaiian— or at least born and raised in Hāna. ⊠ *Hāna Hwy., Mile Marker 35.*

Hāna Airport. Think of Amelia Earhart. Think of Waldo Pepper. If these picket-fence runways don't turn your thoughts to the derring-do of barnstorming pilots, you haven't seen enough old movies. Only the smallest planes can land and depart here, and when none of them happen to be around, the lonely wind sock is the only evidence that this is a working airfield. ⊠ *Hāna Hwy., past Mile Marker 30,* ☎ *808/ 248–8208.*

53 **Helani Farm.** Known as the birthplace of tropical flowers on Maui, this 60-acre enclave with its signature tree house used to be open to the public on a drop-in basis. Now, 20-minute guided tours are by appointment only and reserved for truly serious horticulture enthusiasts. The place is still worth an unscheduled stop, though, because the flower shop at the entrance sells bouquets of 10 tropicals for only $2 and also has gift boxes. ⊠ *Helani Farm, Hāna,* ☎ *808/248–8274 or 800/385–5241.* 🎫 *$10.*

45 **Honomanū Bay.** At Mile Marker 14 the Hāna Highway drops into and out of this enormous valley, with its rocky black-sand beach. The Honomanū Valley was carved by erosion during Haleakalā's first dormant period. At the canyon's head, there are 3,000-ft cliffs and a 1,000-ft waterfall, but don't try to reach them. There's not much of a trail, and what does exist is practically impassable. ⊠ *Hāna Hwy. before Ke'anae.*

★ **40** **Ho'okipa Beach.** There is no better place on this or any other island to watch the world's best windsurfers in action. The surfers know five different surf breaks here by name. Unless it's a rare day without wind or waves, you're sure to get a show here. It's not safe to park on the shoulder; use the ample parking lot at the county park entrance. ⊠ *2 mi past Pā'ia on Hwy. 36.*

⑤⑤ Hotel Hāna-Maui. This fabled hotel, a favorite of privacy-seeking celebrities, is one of the best in the state. The newer Sea Ranch cottages across the road are also part of the Hāna-Maui; the cottages were built to look like authentic plantation housing, but only from the outside. ⊠ *Hāna Hwy., Hāna,* ☎ *808/248-8211.*

㊷ Huelo. This sleepy little farm town has two quaint and lovely churches but little else of interest to tourists. Yet it's a good place to meet local residents and learn about a rural lifestyle you might not have expected to find in the Islands. The same could be said, minus the churches, for nearby **Kailua** (Mile Marker 6), home to Alexander & Baldwin's irrigation employees. ⊠ *Hāna Hwy., near Mile Marker 5.*

㊹ Kaumahina State Wayside Park. The park has a picnic area, rest rooms, and a lovely overlook to the Ke'anae Peninsula. Hardier souls can camp here—with a permit (☎ 808/984-8109 weekdays 8–4). ⊠ *Hāna Hwy., Mile Marker 12, Kailua.* 🔲 *Free.*

㊻ Ke'anae Arboretum. Here's a place to learn the names of the many plants and trees now considered native to Hawai'i. The meandering Pi'ina'au Stream adds a graceful touch to the arboretum and provides a swimming pond besides. You can take a fairly rigorous hike from the arboretum, if you can find the trail at one side of the large taro patch. Be careful not to lose the trail once you're on it. A lovely forest waits at the end of the hike. ⊠ *Hāna Hwy., Mile Marker 17, Ke'anae.* 🔲 *Free.*

㊼ Ke'anae Overlook. From this observation point, you'll notice the patchwork-quilt effect the taro farms create below. The ocean provides a dramatic backdrop for the farms; in the other direction there are awesome views of Haleakalā through the foliage. This is a great spot for photos. ⊠ *Hāna Hwy. near Mile Marker 17, Ke'anae.*

NEED A BREAK?

Just past Ke'anae on Hāna Highway pull over at **Uncle Harry's** (☎ 808/248-7019), a refreshment stand run by the family of fondly remembered Harry Mitchell, a Hawaiian elder and social activist who held no official title. A little shop has souvenirs and Hawaiian crafts for sale, and the family has restored a grass house to demonstrate how their ancestors lived. The Mitchells have some Hawaiian food available, as well as fruit, home-baked breads, and beverages. Just don't expect the stainless steel and Formica slickness of, say, Denny's.

㊿ Nāhiku. This was a popular settlement in ancient times, with hundreds of residents. Now only about 80 people live in Nāhiku, mostly native Hawaiians and some back-to-the-land types. A rubber grower planted trees here in the early 1900s. The experiment didn't work out, so Nāhiku was essentially abandoned. The road ends at the sea in a pretty landing. This is the rainiest, densest part of the East Maui rain forest. ⊠ *Makai side of Hāna Hwy., Mile Marker 25.*

⑤⑥ 'Ohe'o Gulch. Meg Ryan's rhapsody in the 1994 film *I.Q.*, about Maui's "seven sacred pools," may have ruined this spot forever, filling visitors with wrong-headed expectations. Here's the straight scoop: Maui residents call this place 'Ohe'o Gulch; there are many waterfalls well over 100 ft high, but there is no 100-ft-high waterfall that anyone could safely slide down; there are more than seven pools (the actual number depends on rainfall and what you consider a "pool"); and sunbathing and hiking are both popular activities, but swimming here can be hazardous, and there are no lifeguards. From the paved parking lot, you can walk a short way to the first of the pools. Rocks are available for sunbathing, and caves may be explored. In spring and summer it can get quite crowded here, and it doesn't even thin out when it rains. The best way to escape the crowd is to hike upstream. The 2-mi trail to dynamic **Waimoku Falls** passes two thrilling footbridges and a boardwalk through a bamboo forest. ⊠ *Pi'ilani Hwy., 10 mi south of Hāna.*

★ ❸❾ **Pā'ia.** This little town on Maui's north shore was once a sugarcane enclave, with a mill and plantation camps. Shrewd immigrants quickly opened shops to serve the workers, who probably found it easier to buy supplies near home. The town boomed during World War II when the Marines set up camp in nearby Ha'ikū. After the war, however, sugar producer Alexander & Baldwin closed its Pā'ia operation, many workers moved on, and the town's population began to dwindle.

In the '70s Pā'ia became a hippie town as dropouts headed for Maui to open boutiques, galleries, and unusual eateries. In the '80s windsurfers discovered nearby Ho'okipa Beach, and brought an international flavor to Pā'ia. You can see this in the youth of the town and in the budget inns that have cropped up to offer accommodations to those who windsurf for a living. Pā'ia is certainly a fun place.

Apart from windsurfing, what keeps Pā'ia in business these days is feeding Hāna-bound visitors. If you are setting out on the road to Hāna and *not* hankering to sample the local fare at the extremely rustic fruit stands and truck markets that will be your only choices along the Hāna Highway, you might also want to purchase a picnic lunch in Pā'ia. Nearly any restaurant in town will pack up whatever you need. **Picnics** (⊠ 30 Baldwin Ave., ☎ 808/579–8021) specializes in food for the road.

If you want to do some shopping as well, Pā'ia is a friendly little town. You can find clothing and handcrafted keepsakes or snacks and sweets in abundance. Pā'ia is also home to Lama Tenzin, a Tibetan monk who lives and teaches at a small open temple called **Karma Rimay O Sal Ling**, on Baldwin Avenue half a mile from the traffic light. ⊠ *Hwys. 390 and 36, north shore.*

❺❶ **Pi'ilanihale Heiau.** The largest prehistoric monument in Hawai'i, this temple platform was built for a great 16th-century Maui king named Pi'ilani. This king also supervised the construction of a 10-ft wide road that completely encircled the island. (That's why his name is part of most of Maui's difficult-to-pronounce highway titles.) Hawaiian families continue to maintain and protect the sacred site as they have for centuries, and they have not been eager to turn it into a tourist attraction. In 1998, however, two-hour appointment-only guided tours became available. Tours include 122-acre **Kahanu Garden**, a federally funded research center focusing on the ethnobotany of the Pacific. ⊠ *Left on 'Ula'ino Rd. at Mile Marker 31,* ☎ *808/248–8912.* ⌨ *Donation.* ☉ *By appointment.*

❹❸ **Puahokamoa Stream.** The bridge over Puahokamoa Stream is the first of many you'll cross en route from Pā'ia to Hāna. It spans pools and waterfalls. Picnic tables are available, so many people favor this as a stopping point, but there are no rest rooms. ⊠ *Hāna Hwy. near Mile Marker 11.*

❺❷ **Wai'ānapanapa State Park.** With a permit you can stay in state-run cabins here for less than $30 a night—the price varies depending on the number of people—but reserve early; they often book up a year in advance. The park is right on the ocean, and it's a lovely spot to picnic, hike, or swim. An ancient burial site is nearby, as well as a heiau. Wai'ānapanapa also has one of Maui's only black-sand beaches and some freshwater caves for adventurous swimmers to explore. ⊠ *Hāna Hwy. near Mile Marker 32, Hāna,* ☏ *808/248–8061.* 📠 *Free.*

49 Waikāne Falls. Though not necessarily bigger or taller than the other falls, these are the most dramatic—some say the best—falls you'll find on the Road to Hāna. That's partly because the water is not diverted for sugar irrigation; the taro farmers in Wailua need all the runoff. This is another good spot for photos. ⊠ *Hāna Hwy. past Mile Marker 21, Wailua.*

48 Wailua Lookout. From the parking lot, you can see Wailua Canyon, but you'll have to walk up steps to get a view of Wailua Village. The landmark in Wailua Village is a church made of coral, built in 1860. Once called St. Gabriel's Catholic Church, the current Our Lady of Fatima Shrine has an interesting legend surrounding it; as the story goes, a storm washed just enough coral up onto the shore to build the church, but then took any extra coral back to sea. ⊠ *Hāna Hwy. near Mile Marker 21, Wailua.*

3 Dining

In many of Maui's eateries, Continental classics such as chateaubriand and veal scallopine have given way to dishes such as coconut-chili beef and yellowfin tuna–breadfruit cakes. Although most of the island's food was once shipped in frozen, it is now passé to order goods from the mainland. The island's abundance of ingredients, from some 20 types of wild banana to fresh fish caught off the island's shores, together with Asian and Western techniques has spawned a new style of cooking— contemporary Hawaiian cuisine. The result: exciting and glorious fare.

SOME, BUT NOT ALL, of the island's best restaurants are in hotels—not surprising, considering that tourism is the island's number-one industry. In the resorts you'll find some of Maui's finest Continental restaurants and some good coffee shops as well. In addition, because many of the upscale hotels sit right on the beach, you'll often have the benefit of an oceanfront ambience.

Except as noted, reservations are not required at Maui restaurants, but it's never a bad idea to phone ahead to book a table. Restaurants are open daily unless otherwise noted.

Few restaurants on Maui require jackets. An aloha shirt and pants for men and a simple dress or pants for women are acceptable in all but the fanciest establishments. For price category explanations, *see* On the Road with Fodor's at the beginning of the book.

West Maui

American

$$–$$$ ✕ **Longhi's.** This Lahaina establishment has been around since 1976,
★ serving great Italian pasta as well as sandwiches, seafood, beef, and chicken dishes. All the pasta is homemade and the in-house bakery is constantly busy preparing breakfast pastries, desserts, and hot-out-of-the-oven bread. Longhi's is the only restaurant on Maui to win *Wine Spectator*'s prestigious Best Award of Excellence. Even on a warm day, you won't need air-conditioning here with two spacious, breezy, open-air levels to choose from. The black-and-white tile floors are a nice touch. ✉ *888 Front St., Lahaina,* ☎ *808/667–2288. AE, D, DC, MC, V.*

$–$$ ✕ **Lahaina Coolers.** This breezy little café with a surfboard hanging
★ from its ceiling serves up such tantalizing fare as shrimp pesto linguine with prawns, basil, garlic, and cream; and Evil Jungle Pasta (grilled chicken in spicy Thai peanut sauce), as well as pizzas, steaks, burgers, and such desserts as a chocolate taco filled with tropical fruit and berry salsa. Pastas are made fresh in-house. Don't be surprised to see a local fisherman walk through the dining area with a freshly caught snapper, or a harbor captain reeling in a hearty breakfast. ✉ *180 Dickenson St., Lahaina,* ☎ *808/661–7082. AE, MC, V.*

Continental

$$$–$$$$ ✕ **Swan Court.** You enter this elegant eatery via a grand staircase and
★ what seems like a tropical, cathedral-ceiling ballroom, where black and white swans glide across a waterfall-fed lagoon. The menu applies European and Pacific Rim flavors to fresh, locally grown vegetables, seafood, and meats. Try the crispy scallop dim sum (a type of wonton) in plum sauce; creamy lobster coconut bisque brimming with chunks of fish, lobster, shrimp, and button mushrooms; or charbroiled lamb chops in macadamia satay sauce. Arrive early and ask for a table on the left side, where the swans linger in the evening. The restaurant is also open for a breakfast buffet. ✉ *Hyatt Regency Maui, Kā'anapali Beach Resort, 200 Nohea Kai Dr., Lahaina,* ☎ *808/661–1234. AE, D, DC, MC, V.*

$$–$$$$ ✕ **Bay Club.** A candle-lit dinner at this lovely spot on a rocky promon-
★ tory overlooking the ocean is a romantic way to cap off a fun-filled day in the sun, especially if you've been swimming at crescent-shape Kapalua beach just a few yards from the door. However, you won't want to bring sandy feet into the richly paneled, casually elegant interior. Anything on the menu is recommended, especially the fresh catch of the day. For a truly relaxing evening with a view, lean back, sip a

38

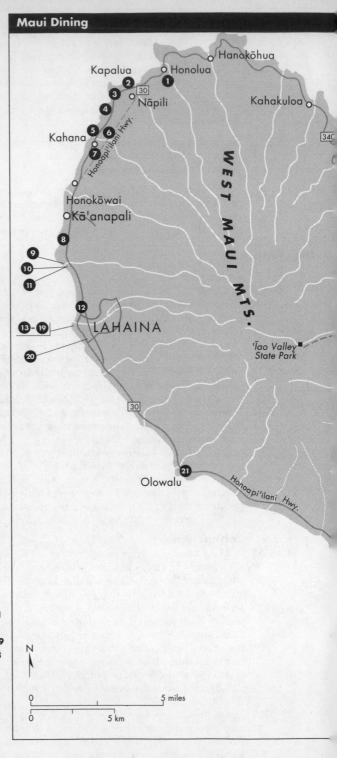

Maui Dining

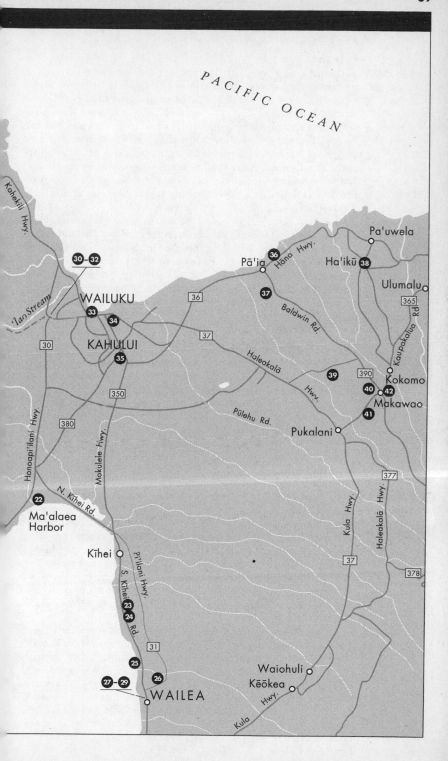

PACIFIC OCEAN

Pa'uwela

Pā'ia 36 Hāna Hwy. Ha'ikū 38

Kahekili Hwy.

30–32

WAILUKU 36 37

Ulumalu

365

33 34 Baldwin Rd.

'Īao Stream

KAHULUI 37

30

35 Haleakalā

39 390 Kokomo

Hwy. 40 42

Makawao

41

350 Pūlehu Rd.

380 Pukalani

Honoapi'ilani Hwy. Mokulele Hwy.

377

22

Ma'alaea N. Kīhei Rd.
Harbor

Kula Hwy.

Haleakalā Hwy.

Kīhei

Pi'ilani Hwy.

S. Kīhei Rd.

37

378

23

24

31

25

Waiohuli

27–29 26

Kēōkea

WAILEA

Kula Hwy.

Kula

glass of cabernet or Riesling from the excellent wine list, and watch the sun slip gloriously past the Maui horizon. ⊠ *Kapalua Bay Hotel, 1 Bay Dr., Kapalua,* ☏ *808/669–5656. AE, D, DC, MC, V.*

French

$$$–$$$$ ✕ **Gerard's.** The French are famous for their exquisite food prepara-
★ tion and savory sauces. This charming establishment has honored that tradition since it opened in 1982. Owner and celebrated chef Gerard Reversade started cooking at the age of 10, and at 12 was baking croissants from scratch. Now he prepares rack of lamb with poached garlic; medallions of venison with pepper sauce, and fish so fresh it's almost wriggling. The menu changes once a year, but many favorites—such as the sinfully good crème brûlée—remain. If you should see Michael Jordan or Robert Redford dining at a nearby table, pretend not to notice. ⊠ *Plantation Inn, 174 Lahainaluna Rd., Lahaina,* ☏ *808/661–8939. AE, D, DC, MC, V.* ☺ *No lunch.*

$$–$$$$ ✕ **Chez Paul.** Since 1975 this tiny roadside restaurant between Lahaina
★ and Ma'alaea in Olowalu has been serving excellent classical French cuisine, such as fresh island fish poached in white wine with shallots, cream, and capers, to a packed house of repeat customers. The nondescript building belies the fine art, 14 linen-draped tables, the 22-seat private dinng room, the wine cellar, and charming atmosphere inside. Don't blink or you'll miss this small group of buildings huddled in the middle of nowhere. ⊠ *Hwy. 30, 4 mi south of Lahaina,* ☏ *808/661–3843. Reservations essential. AE, D, MC, V.* ☺ *No lunch.*

Hawai'i Regional/Pacific Rim

$$$–$$$$ ✕ **'Ānuenue Room.** In Hawaiian, ānuenue means "rainbow." It's an apt name for the Ritz-Carlton's signature restaurant where you may be lucky enough to catch a rainbow arcing over the ocean. In the meantime, you can enjoy a rainbow of such menu choices as caramelized salmon in orange shoyu glaze, seared veal filet mignon with black truffle risotto, or Dungeness crab cakes. Service is excellent, as you might expect at the Ritz. ⊠ *Ritz-Carlton, Kapalua, 1 Ritz-Carlton Dr., Kapalua,* ☏ *808/669–1665. AE, D, DC, MC, V.*

$$–$$$$ ✕ **David Paul's Lahaina Grill.** When Crazy Shirts magnate Rick Ralston was looking for a chef to open a new restaurant in Lahaina in 1990, David Paul wasn't interested—until he saw the location in the romantic, Victorian-era Lahaina Hotel, which Ralston had restored. Since then, the popular restaurant has expanded twice, and offers a well stocked wine cellar, in-house bakery, wine and cheese tastings on weekdays from 5 to 6, piano stylings on a baby grand in the lounge, and free "Fear of Cooking" classes. The award-winning menu is revised seasonally, but you can count on finding the signature tequila shrimp and firecracker rice along with such scrumptious desserts as triple-berry pie. ⊠ *127 Lahainaluna Rd., Lahaina,* ☏ *808/667–5117. AE, DC, MC, V.*

$$–$$$ ✕ **Avalon Restaurant and Bar.** Ferns and fronds form the tropical
★ decor and lend a relaxing ambiance to California chef Mark Ellman's home-grown eatery, tucked away in a quiet courtyard off bustling Front Street. Signature items at this trendy locale include shrimp with shiitake mushrooms and sundried tomatoes; and whole 'ōpakapaka (snapper) in garlic and black bean sauce. Don't miss the "new wave" sushi bar, featuring such innovations as the lollipop: A carved cucumber stuffed with raw fish. A combination of fresh fruits in caramel sauce paired with macadamia nut ice cream is the only dessert. ⊠ *844 Front St., Lahaina,* ☏ *808/667–5559. AE, D, DC, MC, V.*

$$–$$$ ✕ **Hula Grill.** This family-oriented, bustling, 300-seat restaurant set in a re-created 1930's Hawaiian beach house is the informal counterpart to genial chef-restaurateur Peter Merriman's first popular eatery on the

Big Island, and the food is every bit as good. South Pacific snapper, baked with tomato, chili, and cumin aioli, is served with black bean, Maui onion, and avocado relish. Or try a slab of spare ribs, steamed imu-style in banana leaves, then kiawe wood-grilled with mango barbecue sauce. Every table has an ocean-beach view, or you can actually dine on the beach, toes in the sand, at the Barefoot Bar where Hawaiian entertainment is presented every evening. ⊠ *Whalers Village, 2435 Kāʻanapali Pkwy., Kāʻanapali,* ☎ *808/667–6636. AE, DC, MC, V.*

$$–$$$ ✕ **Plantation House Restaurant.** It's hard to decide which is best here, the food or the view. Rolling hills, grassy volcanic ridges lined with pine trees, and fairways that appear to drop off into the ocean provide an idyllic setting for such entrées as duck breast "under the influence" of cabernet-port reduction sauce, roasted Molokaʻi pork chops with mushroom-mashed potatoes and caramelized Maui onion sauce, and fresh fish charbroiled on soba noodles and vegetable stir-fry with ginger-sesame broth. This high up in the West Maui mountains, the breeze through the restaurant's large shuttered windows can be cool, so you may want to bring a sweater, or sit by the fireplace. ⊠ *Plantation Course Clubhouse, 2000 Plantation Club Dr., past Kapalua,* ☎ *808/669–6299. AE, MC, V.*

$$–$$$ ✕ **Roy's Kahana Bar & Grill.** Anyone who's ever eaten at one of Roy Yamaguchi's restaurants knows how good the cuisine is, and this Roy's is no exception. Such Asian-Pacific specialties as shrimp with sweet, spicy chili sauce keep regulars returning for more. Locals say this is a great place to get together with friends for fun and good food. ⊠ *Kahana Gateway Shopping Center, 4405 Honoapiʻilani Hwy., Kahana,* ☎ *808/669–6999. AE, D, DC, MC, V.*

$$ ✕ **Roy Yamaguchi's Nicolina.** Instead of adding on to his established restaurant next door, innovative chef Roy Yamaguchi just started a whole new restaurant that caters to the spice-loving crowd. Indulge on grilled southwestern-style chicken with chili hash and smoked tomato sauce, or smoked and peppered duck with ginger sweet potatoes and Szechuan-Mandarin sauce. You may even find some zippy salsas and a jalapeño pepper or two. ⊠ *Kahana Gateway Shopping Center, 4405 Honoapiʻilani Hwy., Kahana,* ☎ *808/669–5000. AE, D, DC, MC, V.*

Italian

$–$$ ✕ **Scaroles Ristorante.** A longtime favorite of visitors and locals, this place doesn't look like much from the outside, but inside, the friendly atmosphere and authentic northern Italian cooking make up for any lack of chic and draw plenty of loyal fans. In fact, some customers have complained that the bustling place is too small and that squeezing in like a sardine, Italian-style, is no fun. The pasta, chicken, veal, and seafood dishes are all worthy choices, as is the ricotta cheesecake for dessert. They'll even allow you to bring your own libations. ⊠ *930 Waineʻe St., Lahaina,* ☎ *808/661–4466. Reservations essential. D, DC, MC, V.*

Japanese

$–$$ ✕ **Nikko.** Fourteen table-top grills are the performing stages for knife-wielding chefs demonstrating the ancient art of Teppanyaki cooking. Meat and seafood are their tasty targets, and outstanding fare is your reward for watching the show at this oceanview restaurant. "Samurai Sunset" early dinner specials are served from 6 to 6:30. ⊠ *Maui Marriott Hotel, Kāʻanapali Beach Resort, 100 Nohea Kai Dr., Kāʻanapali,* ☎ *808/667–1200. AE, D, DC, MC, V.*

Mexican-American

$–$$ ✕ **Aloha Cantina.** Masses of Mexican-theme posters and artifacts hang on the walls while simulated palm tree trunks hold up a fake leafy ceiling sparkling with hot-pepper-shape tree lights. On your first breakfast visit try a stack of macadamia nut pancakes covered with coconut syrup. For lunch, order the grilled snapper paired with white wine sauce and coleslaw and wrapped in a flour tortilla—in other words, a fish taco. It's a hit. Also on the varied Maui Mex-American menu you'll find a Mexican pizza, a jalapeño garden burger, a chicken Caesar taco, Thai Cobb salad, and tortilla soup. Worth several visits. ⊠ *839 Front St., Lahaina,* ☎ *808/661–8788. AE, MC, V.*

Seafood

$$–$$$ ✕ **Erik's Seafood Grotto.** This seafood diner is so proud of its large se-lection of fresh fish, it displays the whole offering nightly as a photo opportunity. Additional house specialties include bouillabaisse chock full of clams, scallops, lobster, shrimp, and fish and served with toasted garlic bread; and *cioppino,* a seafood stew served over homemade fet-tuccine. A stop at the oyster bar is a worthwhile detour: Try half-shells topped with horseradish mayonnaise and baked with Gruyère cheese. Come to this nautical spot between 5 and 6 and catch the $12.95–$13.95 early-bird specials. ⊠ *Kahana Villas, 4242 Lower Honoapi'ilani Hwy., Kahana,* ☎ *808/669–4806. AE, D, DC, MC, V.*

$$–$$$ ✕ **Pacific'O.** You can sit outdoors at umbrella-shaded tables a few feet from the water's edge, or find a spot inside Pacific'O's light and breezy interior. With protective reefs to keep the swelling seas nearby at bay, it's easy to see why this spot was chosen by King Kamehameha the Great as his personal playground. He would have enjoyed the cuisine, too, which includes the Asian, Polynesian, and European flavors of such delectables as shrimp and basil wonton, banana imu-style fish with vanilla bean sauce, 'ahi parfait with passion fruit dressing, and marinated scal-lops and shrimps seared with red Thai curry and coconut milk sauce. Live jazz is also on the menu Thursday through Saturday nights from 9 to midnight. ⊠ *505 Front St., Lahaina,* ☎ *808/667–4341. AE, D, DC, MC, V.*

$$ ✕ **Lokelani.** Here you'll find elegant dining with attentive service in a
★ relaxed garden-style atmosphere. The chefs do a standout job meld-ing traditional preparations with Asian and Polynesian flavors. The re-sult includes such appetizers as Asian shrimp stuffed with spicy crab meat in sweet Thai sauce and banana salsa; 'ahi tempura with ginger shiitake mushrooms; and grilled Muscovy duck summer rolls filled with papaya, basil, and kaiware sprouts in sweet Thai chili sauce. The menu suggests the perfect wine for each dish, including such desserts as chocolate macadamia nut–cream cheese pie and coffee crème brûlée. ⊠ *Maui Marriott, 100 Nohea Kai Dr., Kā'anapali,* ☎ *808/667–1200, ext. 51. AE, D, DC, MC, V.*

$–$$ ✕ **Kimo's.** Outstanding seafood is just one of the options here. Also good are Hawaiian-style chicken and pork dishes, burgers, sandwiches, vegetarian pasta, and sashimi. The smoked marlin appetizer is espe-cially tasty. On a warm Lahaina summer day, it's a treat to relax at an umbrella-shaded table on the open-air lānai, sip a pineapple-passion-guava fruit drink, and watch sailboats and parasailers glide in and out of the harbor. Try the signature dessert, Hula Pie: vanilla macadamia nut ice cream topped with chocolate fudge and whipped cream in an Oreo-cookie crust. ⊠ *845 Front St., Lahaina,* ☎ *808/661–4811. AE, DC, MC, V.*

Thai

$–$$ ✕ **Orient Express.** Have your Thai food and enjoy it too—hot, medium, or mild—at this decidedly Asian locale with red lacquer and yellow flowers evident everywhere. Eating Thai is always an adventure with such menu choices as beef strips marinated in coconut milk and spices, skewered on bamboo sticks and grilled, or shrimp cooked with bamboo shoots, water chestnuts, and dried chilies. ⊠ *Nāpili Shores Resort, 5316 Lower Honoapi'ilani Hwy., Nāpili,* ☎ *808/669–8077.* ⊘ *No lunch. AE, MC, V.*

Central Maui

Italian

$$ ✕ **Marco's Grill & Deli.** This convenient eatery outside the Kahului airport is home to some of the best-priced and best-tasting Italian fare on Maui. Fettuccine alfredo, linguine with sausage, and vodka rigatoni are all on the extensive menu, along with an unforgettably good Reuben sandwich and the best Greek salad you'll ever find. The local business crowd fills the place for breakfast, lunch, and dinner; it's become so popular that a second Marco's will open in Kīhei by press time. Look for the green awning. ⊠ *444 Hāna Hwy., Kahului,* ☎ *808/877–4446. AE, D, DC, MC, V.*

Japanese

$ ✕ **Restaurant Matsu.** The Maui Mall can appear pretty deserted with so many folks opting for the multilevel Ka'ahumanu Shopping Center a few blocks away, but that doesn't mean there aren't some gems here. This tiny, nondescript kitchen and lunchroom is one of them. Its authentic Japanese fare is well-known to local residents who come for the sushi, noodles, soup, tempura vegetables, and fish entrées served over the counter daily. ⊠ *Maui Mall, Ka'ahumanu Ave., Kahului,* ☎ *808/871–0822. No credit cards.*

Steak

$$–$$$ ✕ **Chart House.** Of the three Chart House locations, this one gets the best reviews from locals. Overlooking Kahului Harbor and decorated with the model ships, boat hulls, and surf prints expected of a harborside steak house, this branch offers big lunch portions and hearty fish, steaks, and prime rib dinners—along with their famous mud pie dessert. ⊠ *500 N. Pu'unēnē Ave., Kahului,* ☎ *808/877–2476. AE, D, MC, V.*

Thai

$–$$ ✕ **Saeng's Thai Cuisine.** Making a choice from the six-page menu here requires determination, but the food is worth the effort, and most dishes can be tailored to your taste buds: hot, medium, or mild. Begin with spring rolls and a dipping sauce; move on to such entrées as Evil Prince Chicken (cooked in coconut sauce with Thai herbs) or red curry shrimp, and finish up with tea and tapioca pudding. The dining room is decorated with Asian artifacts, flowers, and a waterfall, and tables on a veranda will satisfy outdoor lovers. ⊠ *2119 Vineyard, Wailuku,* ☎ *808/244–1567. AE, MC, V.*

$–$$ ✕ **Siam Thai.** Behind a somewhat weathered storefront you'll find some of the best Thai food on Maui. This local favorite serves traditional chicken-coconut soup, beef and chicken sautéed with ginger and bamboo shoots, curries, and vegetarian dishes—about 60 selections in all. The food tends to be spicy, the portions small, and huge crowds arrive at lunchtime. Some patrons opt for takeout because there's not much in the way of decor. ⊠ *123 Market St., Wailuku,* ☎ *808/244–3817. AE, D, DC, MC, V.*

Vietnamese

$–$$ ✕ **A Saigon Café.** The only storefront sign announcing this small, delightful hideaway is one reading OPEN. Once you find it, treat yourself to *banh hoi chao tom,* more commonly called shrimp pops burritos (ground marinated shrimp, steamed and grilled on a stick of sugarcane). It's fun and messy. You might also be in the mood for vegetarian fare. They have that, too. The interior is decorated in white with Vietnamese carvings and other interesting artwork. ⊠ *1792 Main St., Wailuku,* ☎ *808/243–9560. D, MC, V.*

East Maui

American
$$–$$$ ✕ **Joe's Bar & Grill.** With friendly service, a great view of Lāna'i and such dishes as New York steak with caramelized onions, wild mushrooms, and Gorgonzola cheese crumble, there are lots of reasons to stop in at this spacious, breezy spot. Owners Joe and Bev Gannon, who run the immensely popular Hāli'imaile General Store, have brought their flair for food home to roost in this treetop-level restaurant at the Wailea Tennis Club, where you can dine in comfort while watching exciting court action from a front-row balcony seat. ⊠ *131 Wailea Ike Pl., Wailea,* ☎ *808/875–7767. AE, MC, V.*

$–$$ ✕ **Hapa's Brewhaus & Restaurant.** Maui's newest microbrewery has such lagers as Maui Moonset, Paradise Pale, and Black Lava on tap; a comprehensive selection of wines; and an assortment of great eats that includes pizza, calzones, pastas, chicken-teriyaki burgers, vegetarian stir-fry, sashimi, and lobster bisque. The roomy facility also has a game room with one pool table and some dart boards, and live entertainment from 9:30 to 1 Monday through Saturday. ⊠ *Lipoa Center, 41 E. Lipoa St., Kīhei,* ☎ *808/879–9001. D, DC, MC, V.*

$–$$ ✕ **Sandcastle at Wailea.** Tucked away in the middle of the Wailea Shopping Village, this convenient eatery serves tasty burgers and fries, creative salads, and hefty sandwiches in an indoor garden-style setting that is surprisingly secluded considering the bustling shopping activity outside. ⊠ *3750 Wailea Alanui, Wailea,* ☎ *808/879–0606. D, MC, V.*

Continental/Tropical
$$$$ ✕ **Seasons.** Acclaimed executive chef George Mavrothalassitis prepares standout dishes that marry fresh Island ingredients with flavors from Provence (Chef Mavro's homeland), China, Japan, Thailand, and the Pacific islands. Sensational ocean vistas add to the delicious ambience. ⊠ *Four Seasons Resort Maui, 3900 Wailea Alanui, Wailea,* ☎ *808/ 874–8000. AE, D, DC, MC, V.* ☉ *No lunch.*

Hawai'i Regional/Pacific Rim
$$–$$$ ✕ **Hāli'imaile General Store.** What do you do with a lofty wooden building that used to be a camp store in the 1920s and is surrounded by a tiny town in the middle of sugarcane and pineapple fields? If you're Bev Gannon, you turn it into a legendary Island fine-dining tradition. The Szechuan barbecued salmon and rack of lamb Hunan-style are classics. For a filling and innovative appetizer, try a sashimi napoleon, a tower of crispy wonton layered with smoked salmon. The outstanding house salad is topped with Maui onions, mandarin oranges, walnuts, and crumbled blue cheese on request. ⊠ *900 Hāli'imaile Rd., left at the exit off Hwy. 37, 5 mi from the Hānā Hwy., Hali'imaile,* ☎ *808/ 572–2666. MC, V.*

$$–$$$ ✕ **Hula Moons.** This delightful oceanside spot is full of memorabilia chronicling the Island life of Don Blanding, a writer, artist, and poet who became Hawai'i's unofficial ambassador of aloha. The outstanding menu blends fresh, locally grown produce with Pacific Rim and European preparations. Try the scallops with Chinese black bean sauce, charbroiled T-bone steak with pineapple compote and Moloka'i sweet potatoes, or a just-off-the-boat fresh catch of the day. You can dine inside, poolside, or outside on the terrace while you choose your vintage from an extensive wine list. ⊠ *Aston Wailea Resort, 3700 Wailea Alanui, Wailea,* ☎ *808/879–1922. AE, D, DC, MC, V.*

$$–$$$ ✕ **A Pacific Cafe.** Hawai'i Regional cuisine, the culinary edge in the
★ Islands these days, began with a few innovative Island chefs, such as
Jean-Marie Josselin, whose creations are now served by four establishments. Such flavor combinations as pan-seared mahimahi with
garlic, a sesame crust, and lime-ginger sauce; roasted duck with gar-
lic-mashed potatoes and sundried-cherry and star anise sauce; and
seared scallops in crisp polenta crust with caramel sauce and seared
corn and avocado salsa are just some of the mouthwatering choices.
The restaurant's tropical, whimsical decor has been described as "the
Flintstones meet the Jetsons." ✉ *Azeka Place II Shopping Center,
1279 S. Kīhei Rd., Kīhei,* ☏ *808/879–0069. AE, D, DC, MC, V.* ☺
No lunch.

Italian

$$$–$$$$ ✕ **Carelli's.** Dine beachside with the sound of gentle waves washing
the shore, while sampling steamed clams in white wine, butter, and gar-
lic; pasta stuffed with lobster in lemon-basil cream sauce; or chicken
breast stuffed with ricotta cheese and organic spinach. Carelli's is a
gourmet's delight, but if you'd like to know how good the cuisine here
really is, just ask some of the customers: Jack Nicholson, Goldie Hawn,
and Joe Montana, to name a few. ✉ *2980 S. Kīhei Rd., Keawakapu,*
☏ *808/875–0001. Reservations essential. AE, MC, V.*

$$–$$$ ✕ **Casanova Italian Restaurant & Deli.** In true Italian style, congenial
co-owner Steven Burgelin is on hand most evenings to greet and chat
up guests at this neighborhood spot on the slopes of Haleakalā. If you're
pining for pasta, imagine chicken and porcini mushrooms stuffed into
bite-size ravioli and topped with a sage butter sauce, or ricotta and
spinach dumplings languishing in a creamy Gorgonzola sauce. Another
savory flavor here is pizza cooked in a brick, wood-burning oven im-
ported from Italy. Don't even try to resist such desserts as flourless choco-
late mousse cake with raspberry sauce. Casanova is also known for
it's extra-large dance floor and entertainment by well-known Island
and mainland musicians (☞ Chapter 5). ✉ *1188 Makawao Ave.,
Makawao,* ☏ *808/572–0220. D, DC, MC, V.*

$$–$$$ ✕ **Trattoria Ha'ikū.** The rural hills of Tuscany and the leafy gulches of
Ha'ikū not only look alike but, with the opening of this classy little
country dinner house, they now taste alike, too. The understated the-
ater of this jungle discovery—with its white linens, splashing fountains,
and graceful tuxedo-shirted waiters—does a wonderful job of inter-
preting the classic Italian *trattoria,* or family-operated inn. Ingredients
are regional (vegetables from local contract gardens, fresh-catch Maui
fish, herbs from the restaurant's own garden). The preparation is sim-
ple and delicious (as odd as it sounds, the spaghetti-and-meatballs is
unforgettable). And the portions are generous (their special cut for steak
Florentine would please two lumberjacks). House wines, a good Chi-
anti and Pinot Grigio, are served the Italian way—in 5-ounce juice glasses.
The house itself is actually a renovated mess hall, built in the 1920s,
for workers at the adjacent pineapple cannery. ✉ *Olde Ha'ikū Can-
nery, corner of Ha'ikū and Kokomo Rds.,* ☏ *808/575–2820. MC, V.*

Mexican

$–$$ ✕ **Polli's.** This Mexican restaurant in the paniolo town of Makawao
★ not only has a wide selection of such delicious taste treats as seafood
enchiladas, chimichangas, quesadillas, and fajitas, but also offers to
prepare any item on the menu with seasoned tofu or vegetarian taco
mix instead of meat—and the meatless dishes are just as good. A special treat are the *bunuelos*—light pastries topped with cinnamon,
maple syrup, and a scoop of ice cream. The intimate interior plastered
with colorful sombreros and other knickknacks will make you think

you've wandered into a south-of-the-border cantina. ⊠ *1202 Makawao Ave., Makawao,* ☎ *808/572–7808. AE, D, DC, MC, V.*

Seafood

$$–$$$$ ✕ **Ma'alaea Waterfront Restaurant.** At this harborside establishment
★ fresh fish is prepared in a host of sumptuous ways: Baked in buttered parchment paper; imprisoned in ribbons of angel hair potato; or topped with tomato salsa, smoked chili pepper, and avocado. Tourists come early to dine at sunset on the outdoor patio. The varied menu also offers outstanding rack of lamb and veal scallopini. Pass the Maui Ocean Center and veer left into Ma'alaea Village, then follow the blue WA-TERFRONT RESTAURANT signs to the third condominium. ⊠ *50 Hau'oli St., Ma'alaea,* ☎ *808/244–9028. AE, D, DC, MC, V.*

$$–$$$ ✕ **Mama's Fish House.** As you enjoy the landscaped grounds and
★ ocean views at this cliff-top restaurant, check out the stone path engraved with whimsical Hawaiian geckos. But the real treat here is the fish, prepared in seven mouthwatering ways—baked in a creamy herb sauce, sautéed with macadamia nuts, or grilled with spicy wasabi butter, for example. That's why this thatched-hut restaurant with a Hawaiian nautical theme is packed every evening. The chicken, steak, and kālua pig dishes are worth trying, as well. About 1½ mi east of Pa'ia on the Hāna Highway, look for Mama's classic '40s-era Ford trucks parked on grassy knolls at both entrances; self parking and valet. ⊠ *799 Poho Pl., Kū'au,* ☎ *808/579–8488. Reservations essential. AE, D, DC, MC, V.*

Steak

$$ ✕ **Makawao Steak House.** Where better to go for great steaks than ranch country. This paniolo restaurant, nestled in a restored house that was built in 1927 on the slopes of Haleakalā, serves downright good prime rib, rack of lamb, and fresh fish with consistency you can count on and friendly service. Three fireplaces and an intimate lounge create a cozy, welcoming atmosphere. ⊠ *3612 Baldwin Ave., Makawao,* ☎ *808/572–8711. D, DC, MC, V.* ۞ *No lunch.*

Picnics

On Maui you'll find plenty of secluded spots for a laptop lunch for two. Also, if you're on your way to Haleakalā or Hāna, you might want to take a picnic along. Many hotels will prepare the essentials for you, or try one of these Maui delis:

Casanova Italian Restaurant & Deli (⊠ 1188 Makawao Ave., Makawao, ☎ 808/572–0220) packs Italian specialties for the road, for the beach, or for back at the condo, from 8:30 AM to 6:30 PM.

Picnics (⊠ 30 Baldwin Ave., Pā'ia, ☎ 808/579–8021) has experience and style when preparing lunch for the road. Their carry-out meals start at $8 per person. A $50 extravaganza for two–four people comes in a basket with cooler, tablecloth, and a "Road to Hāna" cassette.

4 Lodging

Maui has it all—from beachside villas to cozy B&Bs. Most of the island's big resorts and hotels are in the west, while lodges and inns are in the east. It takes time to find the perfect home away from home, so be sure to plan ahead.

MAUI HAS THE HIGHEST PERCENTAGE of upscale hotel rooms in the state, and the island has the highest average accommodation cost of any Hawaiian island—the average lodging rate on Maui can run as much as $70 more per night than on the other Islands. Maui also has the state's highest concentration of condominium units. Many are oceanfront and offer the ambience of a hotel suite without the cost. Most lodgings have outdoor swimming pools.

The county hasn't officially sanctioned B&Bs, not wanting to siphon business from the hotels. However, they exist, and they exist now in such numbers that county officials have begun to struggle, a bit too late, to define, organize, and regulate them. Many have their units in separate guest houses, which allow privacy while still giving you a chance to get to know your hosts, and many offer a secluded retreat on the cool, Upcountry slopes of Haleakalā. Rates for most B&Bs range from $35 a night to as much as $150.

What you'll pay depends in part on where you want to stay. West Maui is the center of tourism, with more rooms available here than elsewhere on the island; most are high-quality and expensive. Two major resort areas anchor West Maui: the Kā'anapali Beach Resort, with its six hotels and seven condominiums, and the Kapalua Bay Resort, with two hotels and several condo complexes.

East Maui is a mixed bag when it comes to accommodations. You can find just about any rate and just about any degree of comfort. That's partly because the area is so huge, encompassing the Wailea and Mākena resorts along the southwestern shore; Kīhei, a hodgepodge strip running north from Wailea (Kīhei is especially popular with families vacationing from other islands, it's easy for children to find playmates by the pool); Upcountry Maui, the area that rises into the clouds of Haleakalā; and Hāna, secluded in the easternmost part of Maui. For price category explanations, *see* On the Road with Fodor's at the beginning of the book.

West Maui

$$$$ 🏨 **Embassy Vacation Resort.** This all-suite hotel with spacious one- and
★   two-bedroom suites may be Maui's best-kept secret. Rooms are decorated in olive and tan. Inviting touches include an oversize bathroom with large soaking tub and glass-enclosed shower, a minikitchen, an entertainment center, and wicker chaise longues. Guest privileges to a nearby 18-hole golf course and tennis courts are also included, and the hotel has a rooftop 18-hole miniature golf course. ⊠ *104 Kā'anapali Shores Pl., Lahaina 96761,* ☎ *808/661–2000 or 800/462–6284,* 𝔽𝔸𝕏 *808/667–5821. 413 suites. 3 restaurants, fans, in-room modem lines, in-room VCRs, pool, hot tub, exercise room, beach, shops, video games, children's program (ages 4–10), coin laundry, airport shuttle (West Maui airport only). AE, D, DC, MC, V.*

$$$$ 🏨 **Hyatt Regency Maui.** A recent $16 million face-lift upgraded public spaces and guest rooms, improved access for people with disabilities, and added some new facilities—an outdoor Jacuzzi, a wedding gazebo, and a beachfront bar—to this renowned Maui fantasyland filled with art, waterfalls, and a collection of exotic animals, including penguins. ⊠ *Kā'anapali Beach Resort, 200 Nohea Kai Dr., Lahaina 96761,* ☎ *808/661–1234 or 800/233–1234,* 𝔽𝔸𝕏 *808/667–4499. 815 rooms.*

In case you want to be welcomed there.

We're here to see that you're always welcomed at establishments everywhere. That's why millions of people carry the American Express® Card – for peace of mind, confidence, and security, around the world or just around the corner.

do more

Cards

And just in case.

We're here with American Express® Travelers Cheques and Cheques *for Two*.® They're the safest way to carry money on your vacation and the surest way to get a refund, practically anywhere, anytime.

Another way we help you...

do more.®

Travelers
Cheques

4 restaurants, 6 bars, in-room safes, 12 no-smoking floors, pool, 2 golf courses, 6 tennis courts, health club, beach, shops, library, children's program (ages 3–12), chapel. AE, D, DC, MC, V.

$$$$ ☒ **Kā'anapali Ali'i.** Yes, this is a condominium, but you'd never know it; the four 11-story buildings are put together so well you still have the feeling of seclusion. Instead of tiny rooms, you can choose between one- and two-bedroom apartments. Each features lovely amenities: a chaise in an alcove, a bidet, a sunken living room, a whirlpool, oak kitchen cabinets, and a separate dining room. Run by a company called Classic Resorts, the Kā'anapali Ali'i is maintained like a hotel—with daily maid service, an activities desk, and a 24-hour front desk. ☒ *50 Nohea Kai Dr., Lahaina 96761,* ☎ *808/667–1400 or 800/642–6284,* ℻ *808/661–1025. 264 units. 2 pools, sauna, 18-hole golf course, 6 tennis courts, beach. AE, D, DC, MC, V.*

$$$$ ☒ **Kapalua Bay Hotel.** Built in 1978 fronting what was once voted America's best beach, at lovely Kapalua Bay, this hotel has a real Maui feel to it: The exterior is understated white and natural wood. The open lobby, filled with flowering vanda and dendrobium orchids, has a view of the ocean. The plantation-style rooms are decorated in earth tones with green accents, and all have views of Lāna'i and Moloka'i. A shopping plaza outside the main hotel entrance has some fine restaurants and boutiques. Guests receive preferred rates and tee times at three 18-hole golf courses in Kapalua. ☒ *1 Bay Dr., Kapalua 96761,* ☎ *808/ 669–5656 or 800/367–8000,* ℻ *808/669–4694. 209 rooms. 3 restaurants, 2 pools, 6 tennis courts, beach. AE, DC, MC, V.*

$$$$ ☒ **Kapalua Bay Villas.** Privately owned and individually decorated one- and two-bedroom units may be rented through the Kapalua Bay Hotel. Condos are assigned to one of five luxury categories and regularly inspected to ensure that standards are maintained. Renters enjoy a free shuttle to the hotel and guest rates for golf, tennis, and other hotel amenities. ☒ *1 Bay Dr., Kapalua 96761,* ☎ *808/669–5656 or 800/367–8000,* ℻ *808/669–4694. 125 units. AE, D, DC, MC, V.*

$$$$ ☒ **Maui Marriott.** Rooms here are large and tastefully done in pastel tones and bamboo furnishings, and nearly 90% have ocean views. Besides enjoying access to a beachside massage tent and privileges at two 18-hole golf courses in Kā'anapali, guests can join classes featuring aerobics; hula; Hawaiian arts, crafts, and language; food preparation; and a number of sports. The best thing here, however, is the service: The staff is genuinely friendly and helpful. ☒ *100 Nohea Kai Dr., Lahaina 96761,* ☎ *808/667–1200 or 800/228–9290,* ℻ *808/667–8300. 720 rooms. 4 restaurants, 2 lobby lounges, 2 pools, 2 hot tubs, 5 tennis courts, health club, beach, bicycles, shops, children's program (ages 5–12). AE, D, DC, MC, V.*

$$$$ ☒ **Nāpili Kai Beach Club.** These lodgings on 10 beautiful beachfront acres appeal to a loyal following. Hawaiian-style rooms are done in seafoam green, mauve, and rattan; shoji doors open onto your lānai, with the beach and ocean right outside. Packages that include a car, breakfast, and other extras are available to guests who stay five nights or longer. ☒ *5900 Lower Honoapi'ilani Rd., Nāpili Bay 96761,* ☎ *808/669–6271 or 800/367–5030,* ℻ *808/669–5740. 162 rooms. Kitchenettes, 4 pools, hot tub, 2 putting greens, beach. AE, MC, V.*

$$$$ ☒ **Ritz-Carlton, Kapalua.** This beachfront hotel features spacious, com-
★ fortable rooms with oversize marble bathrooms, lānai overlooking the three-level pool, and all the grace, elegance, and service that this classy hotel chain is known for. Most rooms have ocean views. Guests on the Club floors have a private lounge with complimentary snack and beverage service all day long. All guests have golf privileges at three 18-hole courses in Kapalua. ☒ *1 Ritz-Carlton Dr., Kapalua 96761,* ☎ *808/669–6200 or 800/262–8440,* ℻ *808/665–0026. 548 rooms. 4*

50

Maui Lodging

Aloha Cottages, **31**

Aston Wailea
Resort, **22**

Embassy Vacation
Resort, **6**

Four Seasons
Resort, **23**

Grand Wailea, **24**

Heavenly Hāna
Inn, **30**

Hotel Hāna-Maui, **32**

Hyatt Regency
Maui, **13**

Kā'anapali Ali'i, **11**

Kā'anapali Beach
Hotel, **9**

Kama'ole Sands, **18**

Kapalua Bay Hotel, **2**

Kapalua Bay Villas, **3**

Kea Lani Hotel Suites
& Villas, **25**

Kula Lodge, **29**

Lahaina Hotel, **14**

Mana Kai Maui, **19**

Maui Lu Resort, **17**

Maui Marriott, **12**

Maui Prince, **26**

Nāpili Kai Beach
Club, **4**

Olinda Country
Cottage & Inn, **28**

Papakea Beach
Resort, **5**

Pheasant Run, **27**

Pioneer Inn, **16**

Plantation Inn, **15**

Renaissance Wailea
Beach Resort, **20**

Ritz-Carlton,
Kapalua, **1**

Royal Lahaina
Resort, **7**

Sheraton Maui, **8**

Wailea Villas, **21**

Westin Maui, **10**

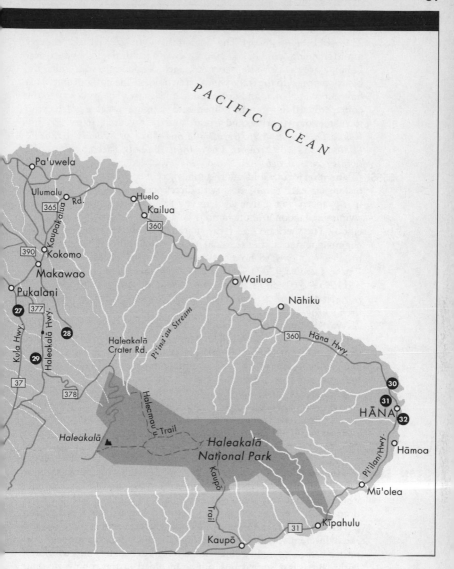

restaurants, 5 lobby lounges, pool, beauty salon, 10 tennis courts, health club, beach, shops, children's programs. AE, D, DC, MC, V.

$$$$ 🏨 **Royal Lahaina Resort.** The lānai at this Outrigger Hotels property afford stunning ocean or golf-course views. What distinguishes the Royal Lahaina are the two-story cottages, each divided into four units; the bedrooms open to the trade winds on two sides. The upstairs units each have a private lānai, and downstairs units share. The walkway to the courtyard wedding gazebo is lined with stepping stones engraved with the names of past brides and grooms and their wedding dates. ✉ 2780 Keka'a Dr., Lahaina 96761, ☎ 808/661–3611 or 800/447–6925, FAX 808/661–3538. 592 rooms. 3 restaurants, 3 pools, 18-hole golf course, tennis courts, beach. AE, D, DC, MC, V.

$$$$ 🏨 **Sheraton Maui.** Gold and rust tones accent custom-made wicker furnishings in each room, most with direct ocean views, at this spectacular property. In the lush gardens you'll find an enormous freshwater swimming lagoon and the famous Pu'u Keka'a sunset cliff-diving ceremony. The Sheraton's 53-ft catamaran takes off regularly for snorkel, champagne sunset, and seasonal whale-watch sailings; there are guest privileges at two 18-hole golf courses nearby. ✉ 2605 Kā'anapali Pkwy., Lahaina 97671, ☎ 808/661–0031 or 800/782–9488, FAX 808/661–0458. 510 rooms. 3 restaurants, 3 lobby lounges, in-room safes, refrigerator, pool, 3 tennis courts, fitness center, beach, summer children's programs. AE, D, DC, MC, V.

$$$$ 🏨 **Westin Maui.** This is a hotel for active people who like to be out and about and won't spend all their time in their rooms, which are rather small for the price. But compensations are provided—an "aquatic playground" with five heated swimming pools, privileges at two 18-hole golf courses in Kā'anapali, and the centralmost position on Kā'anapali Beach. The landscaping is lush; there are abundant waterfalls—15 at last count—and lagoons. A valuable Asian and Pacific art collection is displayed throughout the property. ✉ 2365 Kā'anapali Pkwy., Lahaina 96761, ☎ 808/667–2525 or 800/228–3000, FAX 808/661–5831. 761 rooms. 3 restaurants, 4 lobby lounges, 5 pools, beauty salon, hot tub, health club, beach, children's programs. AE, D, DC, MC, V.

$$$–$$$$ 🏨 **Plantation Inn.** Charm and luxury set apart this inn reminiscent of
★ a Southern plantation home. Filled with Victorian and Far East furnishings, it's set on a quiet street in the heart of Lahaina. Secluded lānai draped with hanging plants face a central courtyard, pool, and garden pavilion perfect for morning coffee. Each guest room or suite is decorated differently, with hardwood floors, French doors, antiques, four-poster beds, and ceiling fans. Some have kitchenettes and whirlpool baths. Breakfast served poolside is included in the room rate, and downstairs one of Hawai'i's best French restaurants, Gerard's, adds to the allure. ✉ 174 Lahainaluna Rd., Lahaina 96761, ☎ 808/667–9225 or 800/433–6815, FAX 808/667–9293. 18 rooms. Restaurant, refrigerators, pool, hot tub, free parking. AE, MC, V.

$$$ 🏨 **Kā'anapali Beach Hotel.** This property is right in the middle of all the Kā'anapali action and has much more reasonable rates than its neighbors. Instead of glitz and flash, you'll find a comfortable hotel with a friendly Hawaiian staff. There are complimentary classes in hula, lei making, and 'ukulele playing, and guests have privileges at the two 18-hole Kā'anapali golf courses. ✉ 2525 Kā'anapali Pkwy., Lahaina 96761, ☎ 808/661–0011 or 800/262–8450, FAX 808/667–5978. 430 rooms. 2 restaurants, lobby lounge, pool, beach. AE, D, DC, MC, V.

$$$ 🏨 **Papakea Beach Resort.** This resort is an active place to stay if you consider all the classes held here, such as swimming, snorkeling, and pineapple cutting. In Honokōwai, Papakea has built-in privacy because its units are spread out among 11 low-rise buildings on some 13 acres of land. You aren't really aware that you're sharing the property with

363 other units. Bamboo-lined walkways between buildings and fish-stocked ponds create a serene mood. There's a two-day minimum stay. Despite its name, there is no beach on the premises, although there are several nearby. ✉ *3543 Honoapi'ilani Hwy., Lahaina 96761,* ☎ *808/669–9680 or 800/367–5637,* ℻ *808/669–0751. 36 studios; 224 1-bedroom and 224 2-bedroom units. 2 pools, hot tub, saunas, putting green, 4 tennis courts. AE, MC, V.*

$$$ 🏨 **Pioneer Inn.** Known officially as the Best Western Pioneer Inn–Maui, this historic building has occupied its ringside seat on Lahaina's action since 1901. Its dockside ambience capitalizes on Lahaina's 19th-century whaling days. All rooms are air-conditioned, and New England–style mahogany furnishings recapture Lahaina's missionary era. It's often possible to stay in one of the small rooms for under $100 a night. You might not want to spend your entire vacation here, as the area can be a bit noisy in the evenings, but for a night or two of bargain-price historic atmosphere, the place can't be beat. ✉ *658 Wharf St., Lahaina 96761,* ☎ *808/661–3636 or 800/457–5457,* ℻ *808/667–5708. 34 rooms. 3 restaurants. AE, D, DC, MC, V.*

$$ 🏨 **Lahaina Hotel.** Honolulu businessman Rick Ralston, also responsible for the rebirth of the Mānoa Valley Inn on O'ahu, has stocked this 12-room Maui property with antique beds, wardrobes, and chests, as well as delightful country-print curtains and spreads. Downstairs, the trendy David Paul's Lahaina Grill, near the lively corner of Front Street and Lahainaluna Road, attracts diners. ✉ *127 Lahainaluna Rd., Lahaina 96761,* ☎ *808/661–0577 or 800/669–3444,* ℻ *808/667–9480. 12 rooms. Restaurant. AE, D, MC, V.*

East Maui

$$$$ 🏨 **Aston Wailea Resort.** The tropical lobby and interior spaces showcase a remarkable collection of Hawaiian and Pacific Rim artifacts. All the spacious rooms have private lānai and are styled with a tropical theme in wicker and beige. The grounds are beautiful, with walks along paths accented with palm, banana, and torch ginger. There are golf privileges at three nearby courses, as well as tennis privileges at the Wailea Tennis Club. ✉ *3700 Wailea Alanui Dr., Wailea 96753,* ☎ *808/879–1922 or 800/922–7866,* ℻ *808/874–8331. 516 rooms. 2 restaurants, 3 pools, hot tub, beach. AE, D, DC, MC, V.*

$$$$ 🏨 **Four Seasons Resort.** This is a Maui favorite, partially because of
★ its location, on one of the Valley Isle's finest beaches with all the amenities of the well-groomed Wailea Resort, including access to three 18-hole golf courses and a "Wimbledon West," with 11 championship tennis courts. The property itself has great appeal, with terraces, courtyards, gardens, waterfalls, and fountains. Nearly all the rooms have an ocean view and combine traditional style with tropical touches. You'll find terry-cloth robes and whole-bean coffee grinders in each room. ✉ *3900 Wailea Alanui, Wailea 96753,* ☎ *808/874–8000 or 800/334–6284,* ℻ *808/874–6449. 380 rooms. 3 restaurants, 2 bars, pool, health club, 2 tennis courts, beach. AE, D, DC, MC, V.*

$$$$ 🏨 **Grand Wailea.** Sunny opulence is everywhere at this 42-acre resort.
★ Elaborate water features include a 2,000-ft multilevel "canyon river-pool" with slides and grottoes. The Spa Grande cossets guests with rejuvenating offerings, from aerobics classes to exotic water-and-massage therapies. Luxury pervades the spacious ocean-view rooms, beautifully outfitted with such amenities as an overstuffed chaise longue, a comfortable writing desk, and an oversize tub and separate shower. Guests have access to three 18-hole golf courses, and tennis privileges are available. ✉ *3850 Wailea Alanui Dr., Wailea 96753,* ☎ *808/875–1234 or 800/888–6100,* ℻ *808/874–2442. 761 rooms. 5 restau-*

rants, 6 bars, 3 pools, health club, beach, children's programs, chapel. AE, D, DC, MC, V.

$$$$ ⚇ **Hotel Hāna-Maui.** One of the best places to stay in Hawai'i is this
★ small, secluded hotel in Hāna surrounded by a 7,000-acre ranch. The original hotel buildings have white plaster walls and trellised verandas, while inside, the spacious rooms have bleached wood floors, furniture upholstered in natural fabrics, and such decorator touches as fine art and orchids. The newer Sea Ranch Cottages across the road surround a state-of-the-art fitness center. A shuttle carries guests to a secluded beach nearby. ⊠ Box 9, Hāna 96713, ☎ 808/248–8211 or 800/321–4262, FAX 808/248–7264. 96 units. Restaurant, bar, 2 pools, massage, tennis courts, exercise room, horseback riding, jogging, beach, library. AE, D, DC, MC, V.

$$$$ ⚇ **Kama'ole Sands.** This is a huge property for Kīhei—11 four-story buildings wrap around a grassy slope on which are clustered swimming and wading pools, a small waterfall, whirlpool baths, and barbecues. All units have kitchens, laundry facilities, and private lānai. Managed by Castle Resorts & Hotels, this condominium property has a 24-hour front desk and an activities desk and is across the road from Kīhei Beach. ⊠ 2695 S. Kīhei Rd., Kīhei 96753, ☎ 808/874–8700 or 800/367–5004, FAX 808/879–3273. 11 studios; 211 1-bedroom, 83 2-bedroom, and 4 3-bedroom condo units. Restaurant, pool, wading pool, 4 tennis courts. AE, D, DC, MC, V.

$$$$ ⚇ **Kea Lani Hotel Suites & Villas.** This Moorish-domed, all-suite resort offers seclusion and privacy at oceanside two- and three-bedroom villas, each with its own small pool and within easy reach of attractions in Wailea and West Maui. Accommodations in the main hotel are spacious one-bedroom suites with dining lānai and marble bathrooms. Guests have access to three 18-hole golf courses, and tennis privileges are available. ⊠ 4100 Wailea Alanui, Wailea 96753, ☎ 808/875–4100 or 800/882–4100, FAX 808/875–1200. 413 suites, 37 villas. 3 restaurants, 2 lobby lounges, deli, in-room VCRs, refrigerators, 3 pools, beauty salon, 2 hot tubs, health club, beach, shops, children's programs. AE, D, DC, MC, V.

$$$$ ⚇ **Maui Prince.** The attention to service, style, and presentation are apparent from the minute you walk into the delightful open-air lobby of the hotel. Rooms on three levels surround the courtyard, which is home to a Japanese garden with a bubbling stream. Each evening a small ensemble performs chamber music in the courtyard. Room decoration is understated, in tones of mauve and beige. Unfortunately, there's an earth berm between the hotel and the beach—part of the agreement the hotel had to make with the zoning commission and local residents—so an ocean view isn't possible from the first floor. ⊠ 5400 Mākena Alanui Rd., Mākena 96753, ☎ 808/874–1111 or 800/321–6284, FAX 808/879–8763. 290 rooms. 4 restaurants, pool, 2 18-hole golf courses, 6 tennis courts, beach. AE, DC, MC, V.

$$$–$$$$ ⚇ **Renaissance Wailea Beach Resort.** On fantastic Mōkapu Beach, most of the hotel's rooms are contained in a seven-story, T-shape building. Tapestries and gorgeous carpets enhance the public areas; outside, you'll find exotic gardens, waterfalls, and reflecting ponds. The VIP Mōkapu Beach Club building houses 26 luxury accommodations and has its own concierge, pool, and beach cabanas. Guest rooms are decorated in shades of cream and each has a lānai. Guests have access to the nearby golf and tennis facilities. ⊠ 3550 Wailea Alanui Dr., Wailea 96753, ☎ 808/879–4900 or 800/992–4532, FAX 808/874–6128. 345 rooms. 4 restaurants, lobby lounge, refrigerators, 2 pools, hot tub, basketball, health club, Ping-Pong, shuffleboard, beach, children's programs. AE, D, DC, MC, V.

$$$–$$$$ ⊞ **Wailea Villas.** The Wailea Resort opened with three fine condominiums, calling them, appropriately, Wailea 'Ekahi, Wailea 'Elua, and Wailea 'Ekolu (Wailea One, Two, and Three). Since then, Wailea has added the Grand Champions Villas, and the adjoining Mākena Resort has built Mākena Surf and Polo Beach Club. All have beautifully landscaped grounds, large units with exceptional views, and access to five of the island's best beaches. Wailea 'Elua Village, Polo Beach Club, and Mākena Surf are the more luxurious properties, with rates to match. The three original villas are an expansive property, with all the amenities of the fine Wailea Resort, including daily maid service and a concierge. ⊠ *3750 Wailea Alanui Dr., Wailea 96753,* ☎ *808/879–1595 or 800/367–5246,* ℻ *808/874–3554. 9 studios; 94 1-bedroom, 157 2-bedroom, and 10 3-bedroom apartments. 6 pools. AE, MC, V.*

$$–$$$ ⊞ **Kula Lodge.** This venue isn't typically Hawaiian: The lodge resembles a chalet in the Swiss Alps, and two of its five units have a gas fireplace. Charming and cozy, in spite of the nontropical ambience, this is a perfect spot for a romantic interlude. Units are in two wooden cabins; four have lofts in addition to the ample bed space downstairs. On 3 wooded acres, the lodge has views of the valley and ocean enhanced by the surrounding forest and tropical gardens. The property has a restaurant and lounge, as well as a gift shop and a protea store that will pack flowers for you to take home; units do not have phones or TVs. ⊠ *RR 1, Box 475, Kula 96790,* ☎ *808/878–2517 or 800/233–1535,* ℻ *808/878–2518. 5 units. Restaurant. MC, V.*

$$–$$$ ⊞ **Mana Kai Maui.** This lodging is a real find in Kīhei, partly because
★ of the property itself and partly because it sits on the end of one of the nicest beaches in the state, just down the strip from the Renaissance Wailea. Here you can get a studio without a kitchen, or a one- or two-bedroom unit with a kitchen. The decor is modest—what people in the Islands might call typical tropical—but recently renovated, and the view of the ocean right beyond the lānai steals your attention anyway. The Mana Kai has a very good beachfront restaurant, open for all meals. There's daily maid service and no minumum-stay requirement. ⊠ *2960 S. Kīhei Rd., Kīhei 96753,* ☎ *808/879–1561; for reservations and information, contact Condominium Rentals Hawai'i:* ⊠ *362 Huku Li'i Pl., Suite 204, Kihei 96753,* ☎ *808/879–2778 or 800/367–5242,* ℻ *808/879–7825. 98 units. Restaurant, lobby lounge, air-conditioning, refrigerators, pool, beach, shops, beauty salon. AE, MC, V.*

$$–$$$ ⊞ **Olinda Country Cottage & Inn** The restored Tudor home and adjacent cottage are so far up Olinda Road above Makawao you'll keep thinking you must have passed it, but keep driving to reach the inn, which sits amid a 8.6-acre protea farm surrounded by forest and some wonderful hiking trails. There are three delightful accommodations in the Inn: two upstairs bedrooms with private baths, and the downstairs Pineapple Sweet with its French doors; but best of all is the ultraromantic cottage, which looks like a dollhouse from the outside. It would be easy to settle in for a long winter here, but bring slippers and warm clothes—the mountain air can be chilly. ⊠ *536 Olinda Rd., Makawao 96768,* ☎ ℻ *808/572–1453 or* ☎ *800/932–3435. 2 rooms with bath, 1 room shares bath, 2 cottages. Hiking, laundry. CP. No credit cards.*

$$ ⊞ **Aloha Cottages.** If you want to meet the people in little Hāna town, check into one of these cottages, run by Fusae Nakamura. Tourism is Mrs. Nakamura's way of earning extra money for her family now that she's retired, and she takes her vocation seriously. The one three-bedroom and three two-bedroom units and one studio all have kitchens or kitchenettes. The rooms are sparsely furnished but clean and adequate. The carefully tended fruit trees on the neighboring property provide a special touch—Mrs. Nakamura often supplies her guests with the harvest, which includes papaya, bananas, and avocados. ⊠ *Hāna 96713,* ☎ *808/248–8420. 5 cottages. No credit cards.*

$$ ⊡ **Heavenly Hāna Inn.** An impressive Japanese gate marks the entrance at this upscale inn. The three suites, one a two-bedroom unit, all have TVs. Decor is spare, with Japanese overtones; the furniture was built by Hāna residents. ⊠ *Box 790, Hāna 96713,* ☎ *808/248–8442. 3 suites. No credit cards.*

$$ ⊡ **Maui Lu Resort.** The first hotel in Kīhei and now operated by Aston Resorts, this place is reminiscent of a rustic lodge. The main lobby was the summer home of the original owner—a Canadian logger—and over the years, the Maui Lu has added numerous wooden buildings and cottages to its 28 acres. Of the 120 rooms, 50 are right on the beach, and some have their own private coves. The rest are across Kīhei Road, on the main property. The decor isn't fancy, but it isn't motel-tacky either. ⊠ *575 S. Kīhei Rd., Kīhei 96753,* ☎ *808/879–5881 or 800/922–7866,* ⅏X *808/879–4627. 120 rooms. Restaurant, lounge, refrigerators, in-room safes, pool, 2 tennis courts, beach. AE, D, DC, MC, V.*

$ ⊡ **Pheasant Run.** For that warm-sky Upcountry ranch feeling, head for Pheasant Run, in pasture with a magnetic panorama of the entire island. The owner is a master builder, and this sprawling house has obviously been his labor of love. There are bonuses for animal-lovers— the company of a Dr. Dolittle–inspired assortment of animals, including Ollie, a surfing dog. The beautifully designed rental, one bedroom and two stories, is separated from the main house by a breezeway. ⊠ *692 Naele Rd., Kula 96790,* ☎ *808/878–6739,* ⅏X *808/572–2265. 1 room. Laundry. No credit cards.*

5 Nightlife and the Arts

Watching a sunset from a tropical perch, taking a moonlight stroll along a near-perfect crescent beach, or dining in a meadow are among the best nightlife options on Maui.

NIGHTLIFE ON MAUI CAN BE of the make-your-own-fun variety. As on all the Neighbor Islands, the pace is a bit slower than what you'll find in Waikīkī. Dancing, lūʻau shows, dinner cruises, and so on are found mainly in the resort areas. Kāʻanapali in particular can really get hopping, with myriad activities for visitors of all ages. The old whaling port of Lahaina also parties with the best of them—its Halloween observances are legendary—and attracts a younger, often towheaded crowd who all seem to be visiting from towns on the West Coast.

Most of Maui's cultural activities are community efforts, with theater, film, and symphony productions held in the island's central towns of Kahului and Wailuku. Since it opened in 1994, the **Maui Arts & Cultural Center** (⊠ Maui Central Park, Kahului, ☎ 808/242–2787) has become the venue for more and more of the island's best live entertainment. The complex includes the 1,200-seat Castle Theater, which hosts classical, country, and world-beat concerts by touring musicians; a 4,000-seat amphitheater for large outdoor concerts; and the 350-seat McCoy Theater for plays and recitals. Art, crafts, and hula lessons are offered regularly in the center's workshops and studios. For information on current programs, check the Events Box Office (☎ 808/242–7469) or the daily newspaper, *The Maui News*. Most major credit cards are accepted at the venues listed below.

For nightlife of a different sort, children and astronomy buffs will enjoy stargazing at **Tour of the Stars,** a unique nightly one-hour program on the roof of the Hyatt Regency Maui in Kāʻanapali. You can look through giant binoculars and a deep-space telescope. The program is run by a real astronomer. ⊠ *Hyatt Regency Maui's Lahaina Tower, 200 Nohea Kai Dr., Kāʻanapali,* ☎ *808/661–1234, ext. 4727.* ➳ *$12.* ☉ *Nightly at 8, 9, and 10; meet in hotel lobby.*

Bars and Clubs

Contemporary Music

Makai Bar (⊠ Maui Marriott, Kāʻanapali Beach Resort, ☎ 808/667–1200). Live Hawaiian and contemporary music nightly, awesome sunset views, and the best pūpū on Maui according to a *Maui News* readers' poll, are at this comfortable spot on the Kāʻanapali coast.

Molokini Lounge (⊠ Maui Prince Hotel, Mākena Resort, ☎ 808/874–1111). This is a pleasant bar with an ocean view, and you can even see Molokini Island before the sun goes down. Live music is presented, often Hawaiian in theme. There's a dance floor for late-night revelry.

Country and Western

Lone Star Cookhouse (⊠ 1234 Lower Main St., Wailuku, ☎ 808/242–6616; ⊠ 1913 S. Kīhei Rd., Kīhei, ☎ 808/975–2838). When you find yourself hankerin' for strummin' and twang, move 'em out to this country-western hangout and two-step to the latest tunes. Tables are moved to make way for a dance floor when a live band takes the stage. The cookhouse serves burgers and fries as well as authentic Texas barbecue, smoked brisket, and ribs; there's an all-you-can-eat soup and salad bar. Reggae, rock-and-roll, and alternative sounds might find their way into the audio mix here, too.

Maui Paniolo Posse (☎ 808/669–4946). Appreciated by those who are hooked on country-western dancing but aren't fond of smoky bars, Ron, Micki, and their friends teach fun and fast-paced line dancing at various venues around Maui: Lahaina Civic Center, Pukalani Civic Center, and Kīhei Civic Center. Call for a current schedule. They usually have snacks to share, but everyone adds to the pot.

Jazz

Pacific'O (✉ 505 Front St., Lahaina, ☎ 808/667–4341). There's only one place to hear live jazz on the beach. It's a mellow, pacific sort of jazz—naturally—and it plays from 9 till midnight on Thursday through Saturday nights. A little something to accompany the cocktails and jazz? The shrimp wontons with Hawaiian salsa is a winner.

Rock Music

Casanova (✉ 1188 Makawao Ave., Makawao, ☎ 808/572–0220), voted "Best Late Night on Maui" in a *Maui News* reader survey, claims to be the best place for singles to meet and the largest dance floor on Maui. When a DJ is not spinning hits, contemporary musicians rock on with blues, country-western, rock-and-roll, and reggae. Past favorites have included Kool and the Gang, Los Lobos, and Taj Mahal. Expect a cover charge on nights featuring entertainment.

Cheeseburger in Paradise (✉ 811 Front St., Lahaina, ☎ 808/661–4855) is known for, what else, big beefy cheeseburgers. Locals also know it as a great place to tune in to live bands playing rock-and-roll, Top 40, and oldies sounds from 4:30 PM to closing. There's no dance floor, but the second-floor balcony is a good place to watch Lahaina's Front Street action.

Hapa's Brewhaus & Restaurant (✉ Lipoa Center, 41 E. Lipoa St., Kīhei, ☎ 808/879–9001 or, for the entertainment hot line, 808/875–1990). Good food and some fine homemade brews are on the menu here along with sports TV, rock and funk bands, disco, hula shows, comedy, and a game room. These folks have gone all out to create a first-rate club with a large stage, roomy dance floor, state-of-the-art lighting and sound systems, and tier seating so that everyone gets a good view. Even non-smokers will find the club comfortable: The air-conditioning system removes secondhand smoke.

Hard Rock Cafe (✉ Lahaina Center, 900 Front St., Lahaina, ☎ 808/ 667–7400). Maui's version of the Hard Rock is popular with young locals as well as visitors who like their music *loud*.

Luigi's Pasta & Pizzeria (✉ Maui Mall, 70 E. Ka'ahumanu Ave., Kahului, ☎ 808/877–3761). Nightlife is limited in Kahului, but this inviting little Italian restaurant provides a fun evening out. The after-9 PM action alternates between karaoke and dancing to Top 40 recorded hits.

Moose McGillycuddy's (✉ 844 Front St., Lahaina, ☎ 808/667–7758). The Moose offers no cover live music on Tuesday and Thursday; otherwise, it's recorded music, but it's played so loud you'd swear it's live. This entertaining place tends to draw a young crowd, who come for the burgers and beer, to dance, and to meet one another. Specials include all-you-can-eat king crab and, on other nights, a 22-ounce porterhouse.

Planet Hollywood (✉ 744 Front St., Lahaina, ☎ 808/667–7877). There's no live music, but making the scene here is popular entertainment. Movie and television memorabilia, a celebrity handprint wall, and movie preview trailers make this place more than just another place to eat. The Maui edition of this chain adds island touches to its basic pasta, burgers, and rock-music fare—such local specialties as Maui potato chips and Hawaiian pizza. (Pineapple is a better pizza topping than you might imagine.)

Radio Cairo Maui (✉ 2439 S. Kīhei Rd., Kīhei, ☎ 808/879–4404) is proof that the late-night music and dance action in the condo town of Kīhei is in full swing. Sunday and Monday nights, jazz is on the agenda. The rest of the week, take your pick of oldies, Top 40, or well-known contemporary Hawaiian artists. Also on view is a unique collection of African art.

Tsunami (⊠ Grand Wailea, 3850 Wailea Alanui Dr., Wailea, ☎ 808/875–1234). You can dance to recorded Top 40 hits in this sophisticated, high-tech disco where laser beams zigzag high above a futuristic dance floor. The music plays from 9 PM to 3 AM. Thursday is Ladies' Night, Friday is "Flashback Fever," and Saturday focuses on contemporary dance. On other nights, the room is used for private parties. Expect a $5 cover charge (this is a bar), except on Ladies' Night, when it's free. Don't wear beach clothes.

World Cafe (⊠ 900 Front St., Lahaina, ☎ 808/661–1515). Combine a variety of tasty food, a video game room, lots of pool tables, televised sports, two dance floors on two levels, and a mix of recorded and live music that includes contemporary Hawaiian, old-time rock-and-roll, and reggae, and you have the hottest 15,000 square ft of night-club space in West Maui. Just to make sure the action never stops, the management has added country-western dance lessons, a grass-roots comedy club, and a female impersonation show, all of which necessitate a cover charge. This is a great place for people-watching.

Dinner and Sunset Cruises

America II Sunset Sail. The star of this two-hour cruise is the craft itself—a 1987 America's Cup 12-m class contender that is exceptionally smooth and steady, thanks to its renowned winged-keel design. ⊠ *Lahaina Harbor, Slip 5, Lahaina,* ☎ *808/667–2195.* 🖃 *$25.*

Kaulana Cocktail Cruise. This two-hour sunset cruise (with a bit of whale-watching thrown in, in season) features a *pūpū* menu (hot and cold hors d'oeuvres), open bar, and live music. ⊠ *Lahaina Harbor, Lahaina,* ☎ *808/871–1144.* 🖃 *$39.*

Pride Charters. A 65-ft catamaran built specifically for Maui's waters, the *Pride of Maui* features a large cabin, a large upper sundeck for unobstructed viewing, and a stable, comfortable ride. Morning and afternoon cruises; breakfast, lunch, and beverages are provided. ⊠ *Ma'alaea Harbor, Ma'alaea,* ☎ *808/242–0955.* 🖃 *$30.*

Scotch Mist Charters. A two-hour champagne sunset sail is offered on the 25-passenger Santa Cruz 50 sloop *Scotch Mist II.* ☎ *808/661–0386.* 🖃 *$35.*

Windjammer Cruises. This cruise includes a prime rib and Alaskan salmon dinner, and live entertainment on the 70-ft, 93-passenger *Spirit of Windjammer,* a three-mast schooner. ⊠ *283 Wili Ko Pl., Suite 1, Lahaina,* ☎ *808/661–8600.* 🖃 *$69.*

Film

Hawai'i International Film Festival. This acclaimed salute to celluloid used to be restricted to Honolulu, but now festival films are also presented on the Neighbor Islands, including Maui. Each November, the festival brings together filmmakers from Asia, the Pacific Rim, and North America to view feature films, documentaries, and shorts. The films are shown at the Holiday Theaters in the Ka'ahumanu Center and at selected resort hotels, where related activities also take place. To find out about specific films and dates, phone the International Film Festival Office (☎ 808/528–3456) in Honolulu.

Lū'au and Revues

Drums of the Pacific. The Hyatt presents a fine Polynesian revue on the hotel's Sunset Terrace. The all-you-can-eat-and-drink buffet dinner includes such fare as fresh fish, kālua pig, chicken, coconut beef, and other Polynesian treats. Afterward, the show features an exciting Samoan fire dance as well as other traditional dances and chants from such island locales as Hawai'i, Tahiti, and New Zealand. ⊠ *Hyatt Regency Maui, Kā'anapali,* ☎ *808/661–1234, ext. 4420.* 💲 *$62 .* ☉ *Dinner nightly at 4:45, show at 7.*

Marriott Lū'au. Learn to make Hawaiian crafts and play authentic early Hawaiian games before you sit down to one of the best lū'au in the Islands. This traditional presentation, which includes an imu ceremony, fire dancing, nonstop mai tais, and a delicious buffet dinner, has been featured on NBC's "Today Show." ⊠ *Maui Marriott, Kā'anapali,* ☎ *808/667–1200, ext. 380.* 💲 *$60.* ☉ *Nightly at 5.*

Nāpili Kai Beach Club Keiki Hula Show. Expect to be charmed as well as entertained when 30 children ages 7–16 take you on a dance tour of Hawai'i, New Zealand, Tahiti, Samoa, and other Polynesian islands. The talented youngsters make their own ti-leaf skirts and fresh flower leis that they give to the audience at the end of the show. This is a nonprofessional but delightfully engaging review, and the 80-seat, oceanfront room is usually sold out. ⊠ *Nāpili Kai Beach Club, 5900 Honoapi'ilani Hwy., Nāpili,* ☎ *808/669–6271.* 💲 *$35.* ☉ *Dinner Fri. at 6, show at 7:30.*

Old Lahaina Lū'au. Some consider this the best lū'au you'll find on Maui—it's small, personal, and authentic. Its new home is an outdoor theater designed specifically for traditional Hawaiian entertainment; it feels like an old seaside village. In addition to fresh fish and grilled steak and chicken, you'll get all-you-can-eat traditional lū'au fare: kālua pig, chicken long rice, *lomilomi* salmon (massaged until tender and served with minced onions and tomatoes), *haupia* (coconut pudding), and other treats. You'll also get all you can drink. Guests sit either on tatami mats or at tables. Then there's the entertainment, featuring a musical journey from Old Hawai'i to the present with hula, chanting, and singing. ⊠ *1287 Front St., Lahaina (makai of the Lahaina Cannery Mall),* ☎ *808/667–1998.* 💲 *$62.* ☉ *Nightly 5:30–8:30.*

Wailea's Finest Lū'au. The Aston Wailea Resort's oceanfront lawn is certainly a beautiful spot to hold a lū'au. The traditional feast begins with a lei greeting and imu ceremony, and the evening includes a world champion fire-knife dancer and colorful Hawaiian hula show. ⊠ *Aston Wailea Resort, Wailea,* ☎ *808/879–1922.* 💲 *$52.* ☉ *Tues., Thurs., and Fri. at 5.*

Wailea Sunset Lū'au. The Renaissance Wailea Beach Resort puts on its excellent Hawaiian lū'au three times a week. It features an open bar, an imu ceremony, a lū'au buffet, music by a Hawaiian band, and a Polynesian show with dancers performing pieces from around the Pacific—including one wielding a fire knife. ⊠ *Renaissance Wailea Beach Resort, 3550 Wailea Alanui Dr.,* ☎ *808/879–4900. Reservations essential.* 💲 *$57.* ☉ *Tues., Thurs., and Sat. 5:30–8:30.*

Music

Maui Philharmonic Society. The Society has presented such prestigious performers as Ballet Hispanico, the Shostakovich String Quartet, and the New Age pianist-composer Philip Glass. Performances take place

HULA, THE DANCE OF HAWAI'I

LEGENDS IMMORTALIZE LAKA as the goddess of hula, a gentle deity who journeyed from island to island, sharing the dance with all who were willing to learn. Laka's graceful movements, spiritual and layered with meaning, brought to life the history, the traditions, and the genealogy of the islanders. Ultimately taught by parents to children and by *kumu* (teachers) to students, the hula preserved without a written language the culture of these ancient peoples.

Some legends trace the origins of hula to Moloka'i, where a family named La'ila'i was said to have established the dance at Ka'ana. Eventually the youngest sister of the fifth generation of La'ila'i was given the name Laka, and she carried the dance to all the islands in the Hawaiian chain.

Another legend credits Hi'iaka, the volcano goddess Pele's youngest sister, as having danced the first hula in the hala groves of Puna on the Big Island. Hi'iaka and possibly even Pele were thought to have learned the dance from Hōpoe, a mortal and a poet also credited as the originator of the dance.

In any case, hula thrived until the arrival of puritanical New England missionaries, who with the support of Queen Ka'ahumanu, an early Christian convert, attempted to ban the dance as an immoral activity throughout the 19th century.

Though hula may not have been publicly performed, it remained a spiritual and poetic art form, as well as a lively celebration of life presented during special celebrations in many Hawaiian homes. David Kalakaua, the popular "Merrie Monarch" who was king from 1874 to 1891, revived the hula. Dancers were called to perform at official functions. In 1906, Nathaniel Emerson wrote, "Its (hula's) view of life was idyllic, and it gave itself to the celebration of those mythical times when gods and goddesses moved on earth as men and women, and when men and women were as gods."

Gradually, ancient hula, called *kahiko,* was replaced with a lively, updated form of dance called *'auana.* Modern costumes of fresh ti-leaf or raffia skirts replaced the voluminous *pa'u* skirts made of *kapa* (cloth made of beaten bark), and the music became more melodic, as opposed to earlier chanted routines accompanied by *pahu* (drums), *'ili 'ili* (rocks used as castanets), and other percussion instruments. Such tunes as "Lovely Hula Hands," "Little Grass Shack," and the "Hawaiian Wedding Song" are considered hula *'auana.* Dancers might wear graceful *holomu'u* with short trains, or ti leaf skirts with coconut bra tops.

In 1963, the Merrie Monarch festival was established in Hilo on the Big Island, and has since become the most prestigious hula competition in the state. Staged annually the weekend after Easter, contestants of various *halau* (hula schools) from Hawai'i and the mainland compete in the categories of Miss Aloha Hula, hula kahiko, and hula 'auana (modern). For more information, contact the **Merrie Monarch Hula Festival** (✉ Hawai'i Naniloa Hotel, 93 Banyan Dr., Hilo, HI 96720, ☎ 808/935–9168).

Moloka'i stages its own Ka Hula Piko festival to celebrate the birth of hula every May. Singers, musicians, and dancers perform in a shaded glen at Papohaku Beach State Park and nearby, Islanders sell food and Hawaiian crafts. During the week preceding the festival, John Kaimikaua, the founder, and his halau present hula demonstrations, lectures, and storytelling at various Moloka'i sites. For more information, contact the **Moloka'i Visitors Association** (✉ Box 960, Kaunakakai, HI 96748, ☎ 808/553–3876 or 800/800–6367).

in various spots around the island. ⊠ *J. Walter Cameron Center, 95 Mahalani St., Wailuku 96793,* ☎ *808/244–3771.*

Maui Symphony Orchestra (☎ 808/244–5439). The symphony orchestra usually performs at the **Maui Arts & Cultural Center** (⊠ Maui Central Park, Kahului, ☎ 808/242–2787, box office 808/242–7469), offering five season concerts and a few special musical sensations as well. The regular season includes a Christmas concert, an opera gala, a classical concert, and two pops concerts outdoors.

Theater

Baldwin Theatre Guild. Dramas, comedies, and musicals are presented by this group about eight times a year. The guild has staged such favorites as *The Glass Menagerie, Brigadoon,* and *The Miser.* Musicals are held in the Community Auditorium, which seats 1,200; all other plays are presented in the Baldwin High School Mini Theatre. ⊠ *1650 Ka'ahumanu Ave., Kahului,* ☎ *808/984–5673.* ▩ *$8.*

Maui Academy of Performing Arts. For a quarter-century this group has offered fine performances as well as dance and drama classes for children and adults. It has presented such plays as *Peter Pan, Jesus Christ Superstar,* and *The Nutcracker.* At this writing, MAPA had just secured a new home in Wailuku at the old National Dollar Store building and had begun to renovate it into a small theater and two dance studios. ⊠ *Main and Market Sts., Wailuku,* ☎ *808/244–8760.* ▩ *$10–$12.*

Maui Community Theatre. Now staging about six plays a year, this is the oldest dramatic group on the island, started in the early 1900s. Each July, the group also holds a fund-raising variety show, which can be a hoot. ⊠ *'Iao Theatre, 68 N. Market St., Wailuku,* ☎ *808/242–6969.* ▩ *Musicals $10–$15, nonmusicals $8–$13.*

Seabury Hall Performance Studio. This college-preparatory school above Makawao town offers a season of often supercharged shows in its satisfying small theater and two dance studios. The school's formula is to mix talented kids with seasoned adults and innovative, even off-beat, concepts. Dance concerts are always a hit. ⊠ *480 Olinda Rd., 1 mi north of Makawao crossroads,* ☎ *808/573–1257.* ▩ *$7–$12.*

6 Outdoor Activities, Beaches, and Sports

Visiting Maui's miles and miles of beaches is not the only activity on the island. You might hang glide, fish, sail, snorkel, surf, or waterski. And though it surprises visitors to this tropical paradise, the paniolo *(cowboy) culture of Upcountry makes horseback riding only natural here.*

Beaches

Maui has about 120 mi of coastline. Not all of this is beach, of course, but Maui's striking white crescents do seem to be around every bend. All of Hawai'i's beaches are free and open to the public—even those that grace the front yards of fancy hotels—so you can feel free to make yourself at home on any one of them. Blue beach-access signs indicate right-of-ways through condominium and resort properties.

Although they don't appear often, be sure to pay attention to any signs or warning flags on the beaches. Warnings of high surf or rough currents should be taken seriously. Before you seek shade under a swaying palm tree, watch for careening coconuts; though the trade winds seem gentle, they are strong enough to knock the fruit off the trees and onto your head. Also be sure to apply that sunscreen diligently. Maui is closer to the equator than the beaches to which you're probably accustomed, so although you may think you're safe, take it from those who've gotten a beet-red burn in 30 minutes or less—you're not. Drinking alcoholic beverages on beaches in Hawai'i isn't allowed.

West Maui offers quite a few beach choices. If you start at the northern end of West Maui and work your way down the coast, you'll find the beaches described below.

D. T. Fleming Beach is one of West Maui's most popular beaches. This charming, mile-long sandy cove is better for sunbathing than for swimming, because the current can be quite strong. There are rest room facilities, including showers, picnic tables and grills, and paved parking. ✉ *Hwy. 30 about 1 mi north of Kapalua Resort.*

On the northern side of Nāpili Bay is the smaller and even more pristine **Kapalua Beach.** You may have to share sand space with a number of other beachgoers, however, because the area is quite popular for lazing, swimming, and snorkeling. There are showers, rest rooms, and a paved parking lot. ✉ *Past Bay Club restaurant off Lower Honoapi'ilani Hwy., before Kapalua Bay Hotel.*

The lovely **Nāpili Beach** is right outside the Nāpili Kai Beach Club, a popular little resort for honeymooners. This sparkling white crescent makes a perfect cove for strolling and sunbathing. Despite condominiums and other development around the bay, the only facilities available here are showers at the far right end of the beach, and a low tap by the beach-access entrance where you can wash the sand off your feet, but you're only a few miles south of Kapalua. ✉ *5900 Lower Honoapi'ilani Hwy., from upper highway follow cutoff road closest to Kapalua Resort and look for Nāpili Pl. or Hui Dr.*

Honokōwai Beach is a bust if you're looking for that classic Hawaiian stretch of sand. Still, children will enjoy the lawn area and rocks that have formed a pool. This beach, in the midst of condominium row, does have rest rooms, showers, picnic tables, and paved parking. ✉ *3636 Lower Honoapi'ilani Rd., across from Honokōwai Superette.*

Fronting the big hotels at Kā'anapali is one of Maui's best people-watching spots, **Kā'anapali Beach.** This is not the beach if you're looking for peace and quiet, but if you want lots of action, lay out your towel here. Cruises, windsurfers, and parasailers head out from this beach while the beautiful people take in the scenery. Although no facilities are available, the nearby hotels have rest rooms and some, like the Marriott, have outdoor showers. You're also close to plenty of shops and concessions. ✉ *Follow any of 3 Kā'anapali exits from Honoapi'ilani Hwy., and park at any of the hotels.*

Cheap Snorkeling

South of Lahaina at Mile Marker 14 are the narrow stretches of white sand known as **Olowalu Beaches,** a swimming and snorkeling haven. There's no parking here—people just pull off the road—and there are no facilities except a small general store nearby where you can get a soda, but it's one of Maui's best sandy spots. With mask and fins, you'll see yellow tangs, parrot fish, and sometimes the state fish, the *humuhumunukunukuāpua'a.* You can call it a humu, if you like. ⊠ *Hwy. 30, Mile Marker 14, south of Lahaina.*

Farther south of Olowalu, you'll find **Wailea's five crescent beaches,** which stretch for nearly 2 mi with relatively little interruption by civilization. Several hotels call Wailea home, and more condominiums are under construction. So far, the buildings haven't infringed on the beaches in a noticeable way. With any luck, the population boom won't affect this area either. Swimming is good here; the crescents protect the shoreline from rough surf. Few people populate these beaches—mostly hotel guests who have briefly forsaken the pools of the nearby lodgings—which makes Wailea a peaceful haven. Rest rooms and showers are available. ⊠ *Drive south of Kilei, along western shore of East Maui.*

Just south of Wailea is the town of **Mākena,** with two good beaches. **Big Beach** is 3,000 ft long and 100 ft wide. The water off Big Beach is fine for swimming and snorkeling, and you'll find showers, rest rooms, and paved parking here. If you walk over the cinder cone at Big Beach, you'll reach **Little Beach,** which is used for nude sunbathing. Officially, nude sunbathing is illegal in Hawai'i, but several bathers who've pushed their arrests through the courts have found their cases dismissed. Understand, though, that you take your chances if you decide to indulge in this favorite local practice at Little Mākena.

If you're staying in the Central Maui area, try **Kanahā Beach** in Kahului. A long, golden strip of sand bordered by a wide grassy area, this is a popular spot for windsurfers, joggers, and picnicking Maui families. Kanahā Beach has toilets, showers, picnic tables, and grills. ⊠ *Drive through the airport and back out to the car-rental road (Koeheke), turn right, and keep going.*

If you want to see some of the world's finest windsurfers, stop at **Ho'okipa Beach** on the Hāna Highway. The sport has become an art—and a career, to some—and its popularity was largely developed right at Ho'okipa. This is also one of Maui's hottest surfing spots. Waves get as high as 15 ft. This is not a good swimming beach, nor the place to learn windsurfing yourself, but plenty of picnic tables and barbecue grills are available for hanging out. ⊠ *Hwy. 36, 1 mi past Pā'ia.*

In Hāna, **Kōkī Beach** offers unusually good bodysurfing because the sandy bottom stays shallow for a long way out. There are no facilities here, but the spot is rich in Hawaiian lore. It sits beneath a prominent cinder cone called Ka Iwi O Pele ("Pele's Bone"), and the small island off shore, 'Ālau Island, is the place where the demigod Maui fished the Hawaiian islands out of the sea. Watch conditions; the riptide here can be mean. Just down the road is the beach James Michener called the best in the Pacific—crescent-shape **Hāmoa Beach.** Park on the roadside and walk down either one of the steep paths. Hotel Hāna-Maui keeps facilities here for its guests but has politely included a shower and rest room for the public. ⊠ *Haneo'o Loop Rd., 2 mi east of Hāna town.*

Participant Sports

Biking

Maui County has designated hundreds of miles of bikeways on Maui's roads, making biking safer and more convenient than in the past.

Painted bike lanes make it possible for a rider to travel all the way from Mākena to Kapalua, and you'll see dozens of these hardy souls pedaling under the hot Maui sun. Some visitors rent a bike just to ride around the resort where they're staying. Whatever your preference, you have several rental choices, including **A & B Rental** (⊠ 3481 Lower Honoapi'ilani Hwy., Lahaina, ☎ 808/669–0027), **West Maui Cycles** (⊠ 4310 Lower Honoapi'ilani Hwy., Lahaina, ☎ 808/669–1169), **Hawai'i Sail and Sport**(⊠ 101 N. Kīhei Rd., Kīhei, ☎ 808/879–0178), and **Maui Sports and Cycle** (⊠ Long's Center, Kīhei, ☎ 808/875–8448, and ⊠ Dolphin Plaza, ☎ 808/875–2882). Bikes rent for $10–$20 a day.

Camping and Hiking

Like the other Hawaiian islands, Maui is riddled with ancient paths. These were the roads the Polynesians used to cross from one side of the island to another. Most of these paths are now too difficult to find. But if you happen to stumble upon something that looks like it might have been a trail, chances are good it was used by the ancients. In fact, most trails on Maui are not well marked. Only three areas have clearly marked trailheads. Luckily, these are some of the best hikes on the island. There's also a nature center, which has walks suited for children.

In Maui's center, **Haleakalā Crater** in Haleakalā National Park is an obvious hiking haven, with several trails. As you drive to the top of the 10,023-ft dormant volcano on the Haleakalā Highway, you'll first come to **Hosmer Grove,** less than a mile after you enter the park. This is a lovely forested area, with an hour-long nature trail. You can pick up a map at the trailhead, and park rangers offer guided hikes on a changing schedule. There are six campsites (no permit needed), pit toilets, drinking water, and cooking shelters. There's also **Halemau'u Trail,** near the 8,000-ft elevation. The walk to the crater rim is a relative stroll, then it's a switchback trail nearly 2 mi to the crater floor. Nearly 4 mi from the trailhead, you'll find **Hōlua Cabin,** which you can reserve—at least three months in advance—through the National Park Service (⊠ Box 369, Makawao 96768, ☎ 808/572–9306). You can pitch a tent, but you'll need a permit that's issued on a first-come, first-serve basis at Haleakalā National Park Headquarters/Visitors Center (⊠ Haleakalā Crater Rd.,☎ 808/572–9306) at the 7,000-ft elevation point on Haleakalā; they're open daily 7:30–4.

If you opt to drive all the way to the top of Haleakalā, you'll find a trail called **Sliding Sands,** which starts at about the 10,000-ft elevation, descending to the crater floor 4 mi away. The scenery is spectacular; it's colorful and somewhat like the moon. You can reach the above-mentioned Hōlua Cabin in about 7 mi if you veer off to the left and head out of the crater on the Halemau'u Trail. If you continue on the Sliding Sands Trail, however, you'll come to **Kapalaoa Cabin** within about 6 mi, and at about 10 mi you'll hit **Palikū Cabin,** both also available from the park service with at least three months' notice. All three cabins have bunks, firewood, water, and a stove, and are limited to 12 people. They can be reached in less than a day's walk. Palikū Cabin has tent camping nearby with toilets and drinking water. Tent permits, again, are issued at park headquarters on the day you want to use them.

On the southern slope of Haleakalā is **Polipoli Forest,** which will remind you of a Walt Disney movie. It was once heavily forested, until cattle and goats chewed away most of the natural vegetation. Starting in about 1930, the government began a program to reforest the area, and soon cedar, pine, cypress, and even redwoods took hold. Because of the elevation, it's a bit cooler here and sometimes wet and misty.

To reach the forest, drive on Highway 377 past Haleakalā Road to Waipoli Road. Go up the hill until you reach the park. Next to the lot, you'll see a small campground and a cabin you can rent from the Division of State Parks. Write far in advance for the cabin (✉ Box 1049, Wailuku 96793, ☎ 808/244–4354); for the campground, you can wait until you arrive in Wailuku, then visit the State Parks office (✉ 54 High St.). Once you're at Polipoli, there are three trails from which to choose.

'Ohe'o Gulch in East Maui is part of Haleakalā National Park, but it's very different from the crater. That's because it's over on the Hāna side of the park—which actually extends far beyond the mountain you see in the clouds. This is a lush, rainy, tropical area. You can reach 'Ohe'o Gulch by continuing on the Hāna Highway about 10 mi past Hāna. 'Ohe'o Gulch includes the fabled pools, where the two major trails begin. The first trail is **Makahiku Falls,** a ½-mi jaunt from the parking lot to an overlook. You can go around the barrier and get closer to the falls if you want. From here, you can continue on the second trail for another 1½ mi to encounter 400-ft **Waimoku Falls.** The trail spans a sensational gorge and leads through a clonking, mystifying forest of giant bamboo. There's camping down at the grassy seacliffs, with no permit required, although you can stay only three nights. Toilets, grills, and tables are available here, but no water.

In 'Iao Valley, the **Hawai'i Nature Center** (✉ 875 'Iao Valley Rd., Wailuku 96793, ☎ 808/244–6500) leads interpretive hikes for children and their families.

Fitness Centers

Most fitness centers on Maui are in hotels. If your hotel does not have a facility, ask if privileges are available at other hotels. Outside the resorts, the most convenient and best-equipped are **Gold's Gym** (✉ 840 Waine'e St., Lahaina, ☎ 808/667–7474; ✉ Lipoa Ctr., 41 E. Lipoa St., Kīhei, ☎ 808/874–2844; ✉ 850 Kolu St., Wailuku, ☎ 808/242–6851), and **World Gym** (✉ 300 Ohukai Rd., G-112, Kīhei Commercial Ctr., Kīhei, ☎ 808/879–1326), which all have complete fitness facilities.

Golf

How do you keep your mind on the game in a place like Maui? It's very hard, because you can't ignore the view, but Maui has become one of the world's premier golf-vacation destinations. The island's major resorts all have golf courses, each of them stunning. They're all open to the public, and most lower their greens fees after 2:30 on weekday afternoons.

Kapalua Golf Club has three 18-holers—the Village Course and the Bay Course, designed by Arnold Palmer, and the Plantation Course, designed by Ben Crenshaw. Kapalua is well known among television-sports watchers. ✉ *300 Kapalua Dr., Kapalua,* ☎ *808/669–8044.* 🏌 *Greens fee $95–$100 guests, $140–$150 nonguests, including cart; club rental $30–$40.*

The lovely **Mākena Golf Course** has two 18-hole courses, North and South, designed by Robert Trent Jones, Jr. Of all the resort courses, this one is the most remote. At one point, golfers must cross a main road, but there are so few cars that this poses no problem. ✉ *5415 Mākena Alanui Rd., Kīhei,* ☎ *808/879–3344.* 🏌 *Greens fee $80 guests, $140 nonguests; rates include cart.*

Kā'anapali Golf Courses are two of Maui's most famous. The layout consists of two 18-hole courses: The North Course was designed by Robert Trent Jones, Sr., and the South Course architect was Arthur Jack

Snyder. ⊠ *Kā'anapali Beach Resort, Kā'anapali,* ☎ *808/661–3691.* 🖾 *Greens fee $100 guests, $120 nonguests, including cart.*

Silversword Golf Course is just up the hill from Kīhei. ⊠ *1345 Pi'ilani Hwy., Kīhei,* ☎ *808/874–0777.* 🖾 *Greens fee $70, including cart.*

The **Wailea Golf Club** also has three courses: the Gold and the Blue, which were designed by Arthur Jack Snyder, and the newer Emerald, designed by Robert Trent Jones, Jr. In his design, Snyder incorporated ancient lava-rock walls to create an even more unusual golfing experience. ⊠ *100 Wailea Golf Club Dr., Wailea,* ☎ *808/875–5111.* 🖾 *Greens fee $110 Wailea guests, $140 nonguests, including cart.*

Maui has municipal courses as well, where the fees are lower. Be forewarned, however, that the weather can be cooler and wetter, and the locations may not be convenient. The **Waiehu Municipal Golf Course** is on the northeast coast of Maui a few miles past Wailuku. ⊠ *Off Hwy. 340 in West Maui,* ☎ *808/244–5934.* 🖾 *Greens fee $25 weekdays, $30 weekends; cart $15.*

Hang Gliding

Through a headset, USHGA instructor Armin Engert of **Hang Gliding Maui** (☎ 808/878–3806) will teach you the basics of weight-shift control while you cruise for 45 minutes on the wind currents over Maui in a motorized open-cockpit Ultralight. There's a weight limit of 200 pounds for this trip, which costs $150 plus $30 for each additional 15 minutes. For a tandem glide from the summit of Haleakalā to the beach below is a 35-minute descent, the weight limit is 185 pounds, and the price of $250 includes membership in the U.S. Hang Gliding Association and 24 snapshots of your adventure taken by a wing-mounted camera.

Parasailing

If you have a yen to be floating in the sky like a bird but lack the derring-do of a barnstormer, parasailing is the perfect alternative to skydiving (you gently rise several hundred feet up from the ground instead of leaping out of an aircraft at 10,000 ft) or hang gliding (the safety rope holds you in your flight pattern). This is an easy and fun way to earn your wings: Just strap on a harness attached to a parachute, and a power boat pulls you up and over the ocean from a launching dock or from a boat's platform.

Several companies on Maui will take you for a ride that usually lasts about 10 minutes, and costs $30–$50. For safety reasons, **West Maui Parasailing** (☎ 808/661–4060) requires that passengers weigh more than 100 pounds, or two must be strapped together in tandem. **Lahaina Para-Sail** (☎ 808/661–4887) lays claim to the only parasail vessel on Maui that is Coast Guard certified for 25 passengers and has bathroom facilities on board. They'll be glad to let you experience a "toe dip" or "freefall" if you request it, and their minimum weight to fly alone is 75 pounds.

Tennis

The state's finest tennis facilities are at the **Wailea Tennis Club** (⊠ 131 Wailea Ike Pl., Kīhei, ☎ 808/879–1958 or 800/332–1614), often called "Wimbledon West" because of its two grass courts; there are also 11 Plexipave courts and a pro shop. You'll pay $25 an hour per person for the hard courts. The grass courts are by well-in-advance reservation only. Weekday mornings there are clinics to help you improve your ground strokes, serve, volley, or doubles strategy.

At the Mākena Resort, just south of Wailea, the **Mākena Tennis Club** (⊠ 5400 Mākena Alanui Rd., Kīhei, ☎ 808/879–8777) has six courts. Rates are $16 per court hour for guests, $18 for nonguests. After an hour, if there's space available, there's no charge.

Over on West Maui, the **Royal Lahaina Tennis Ranch** (✉ 2780 Keka'a Dr., ☎ 808/661–3611, ext. 2296), in the Kā'anapali Beach Resort, offers 11 recently resurfaced courts and a pro shop. Rates are a flat $10 per person per day whether you are a guest or not.

The **Hyatt Regency Maui** (✉ 200 Nohea Kai Dr., Kā'anapali, ☎ 808/661–1234, ext. 3174) has six courts, with rentals and instruction. All day passes cost $15 for guests, $20 for nonguests.

Kapalua Tennis Garden (✉ 100 Kapalua Dr., Kapalua, ☎ 808/669–5677) serves the Kapalua Resort with 10 courts and a pro shop. You'll pay $10 an hour if you're a guest, $12 if you're not, and you're welcome to stay longer for free if there is no one waiting.

Maui Beach & Tennis Club (✉ 100 Nohea Kai Dr., Kā'anapali, ☎ 808/667–1200, ext. 66689) at the Maui Marriott has five Plexipave courts, with three lit for night play, and a pro shop. Daily rates are $10 for guests and $12 for nonguests.

There are other facilities around the island, usually one or two courts in smaller hotels or condos. Most of them, however, are open only to their guests. The best free courts are the five at the **Lahaina Civic Center** (✉ 1840 Honoapi'ilani Hwy., Lahaina, ☎ 808/661–4685), near Wahikuli State Park; they're available on a first-come, first-serve basis.

Water Sports

Note that, to reduce interference with whales, no "thrill craft"—specifically parasails and Jet Skis—are allowed in Maui waters from December 15 to April 15.

DEEP-SEA FISHING

If fishing is your sport, Maui is the place for it. You'll be able to throw in hook and bait for fish like 'ahi, *aku* (a skipjack tuna), barracuda, bonefish, *kawakawa* (bonito), mahimahi, Pacific blue marlin, *ono* (wahoo), and *ulua* (jack crevalle). On Maui you can fish throughout the year, and you don't need a license.

Plenty of fishing boats run out of Lahaina and Mā'alaea harbors. If you charter a boat by yourself, expect to spend in the neighborhood of $600 a day. But you can share the boat with others who are interested in fishing the same day for about $100. Although there are at least 10 companies running boats on a regular basis, these are the most reliable: **Finest Kind Inc.** (✉ Slip 7, Box 10481, Lahaina 96767, ☎ 808/661–0338), **Hinatea Sportfishing** (✉ Slip 27/Lahaina Harbor, Lahaina 96761, ☎ 808/667–7548), and **Lucky Strike Charters** (✉ Box 1502, Lahaina 96767, ☎ 808/661–4606). **Ocean Activities Center** (✉ 1847 S. Kīhei Rd., Suite 203A, Kīhei 96753, ☎ 808/879–4485 or 800/798–0652) can arrange fishing charters as well. You're responsible for finding your own transportation to the harbor.

KAYAKING

A sport that's been gaining in popularity recently, kayaking off the coast of Maui can be a leisurely paddle or more of a challenge, depending on weather conditions and location. If this is your first time in one of these banana-shape boats, it's best to go with a guide until you're comfortable with the equipment, have learned a few techniques for coping with ocean swells and waves, and know which parts of Maui's coastline are best suited to your skill level. A guided trip costs $20–$30 per hour, and the longer ones usually include lunch. Kayak rentals run about $25–$35 a day. Wear a sun visor, and count on getting wet.

Leroy, at the Beach Activities Center of the **Maui Marriott** (✉ 100 Nohea Kai Dr., Kā'anapali, ☎ 808/667–1200, ext. 374) makes you feel at home on the ocean with a short trip to Kā'anapali's Black Rock for possible turtle sightings. The Marriott's kayaks, with back rests and foot-pedal rudder control, will spoil you for lesser equipment, and if your arms get tired, Leroy will tow you and your craft back to port. Two other outfitters that can help you get started are **South Pacific Kayak** (✉ 2439 S. Kīhei Rd., Kīhei, ☎ 808/875–4848), and **Kelii's Kayak Tours** (☎ 808/879–3957 or 888/874–7652).

SAILING

Because of its proximity to the smaller islands of Moloka'i, Lāna'i, Kaho'olawe, and Molokini, Maui can provide one of Hawai'i's best sailing experiences. Most sailing operations like to combine their tours with a meal, some throw in snorkeling or whale-watching, while others offer a sunset cruise.

One of the best and longest-running operations is **Trilogy Excursions** (✉ 180 Lahainaluna Rd., Lahaina 96761, ☎ 808/661–4743 or 800/874–2666). Their full-day, multihull-catamaran cruise to Lāna'i includes a guided van tour of the island, a barbecue lunch, beach volleyball, and a "Snorkeling 101" class, where you can test your skills in the waters of Hulopo'e Marine Preserve (Trilogy has exclusive commercial access). Snorkeling gear is supplied. They also offer a Molokini snorkel cruise.

Other companies offering cruises include **Maui–Moloka'i Sea Cruises** (✉ 831 Eha St., Suite 101, Wailuku 96793, ☎ 808/242–8777), **Sail Hawai'i** (☎ 808/879–2201), **Scotch Mist Charters** (☎ 808/661–0386), the Hyatt Regency Maui's **Kiele V** (✉ 200 Nohea Kai Dr., Lahaina, ☎ 808/661–1234), and **Pride Charters** (✉ 208 Kenolio Rd., Kīhei 96753, ☎ 808/875–0955), which has a glass-bottom catamaran, hot-water showers, and live entertainment.

SCUBA DIVING

Believe it or not, Maui is just as scenic underwater as it is above. In fact, some of the finest diving spots in Hawai'i lie along the Valley Isle's western and southwestern shores. If you're a certified diver, you can rent gear at any Maui dive shop simply by showing your PADI or NAUI card. Unless you're familiar with the area, however, it's probably best to hook up with a dive shop for an underwater tour. Additionally, the only really decent shore dive is at Honolua Bay, a marine reserve above Kapalua Resort. The water is usually rough during the winter, but there's always a chance you will spot some of Maui's winter visitors—humpback whales (☞ Whale-Watching Tours box, *below*).

Maui has no lodging facilities tailored to divers, but there are many dive shops that sell and rent equipment and give lessons and certification. Before signing on with any of these outfitters, however, it's a good idea to ask a few pointed questions.

Some popular stores include **Capt. Nemo's Ocean Emporium** (✉ 150 Dickenson St., Lahaina, ☎ 808/661–5555), **Dive Shop** (✉ Kīhei boat ramp, S. Kīhei Rd., ☎ 808/879–2201), **Ed Robinson's Diving Adventures** (☎ 808/879–3584 or 800/635–1273), **Happy Maui Diving and Tours** (✉ 840 Waine'e St., Suite 106, Lahaina, ☎ 808/669–0123), **Lahaina Divers** (✉ 143 Dickenson St., Lahaina, ☎ 808/667–7496), and **Maui Dive Shop** (✉ Lahaina Cannery Mall, ☎ 808/661–5388). All provide equipment with proof of certification, as well as introductory dives for those who aren't certified. Introductory boat dives generally run about $80.

Area dive sites include:

Honolua Bay, in West Maui, is a marine preserve with many varieties of coral and tame tropical fish, including large ulua, *kāhala,* barracuda, and manta rays. With depths of 20 ft–50 ft, this is a popular spot for introductory dives. Dives are generally given only during the summer months.

Molokini Crater, at 'Alalākeiki Channel, is a crescent-shape islet formed by the top of a volcano. This marine preserve's depth range (10 ft–80 ft), combined with the attraction of the numerous tame fish dwelling here that can be fed by hand, make it a popular introductory dive site.

SNORKELING

If you want a personal introduction to Maui's undersea universe, the undisputable authority is marine biologist **Ann Fielding's Snorkel Maui.** She's the Carl Sagan of Hawai'i's reef cosmos—formerly with University of Hawai'i, Waikīkī Aquarium, and the Bishop Museum and the author of several guides to island sealife. She'll not only show you fish; she'll introduce you to *individual* fish. This is a good first experience for dry-behind-the-ears types. ⊠ *Box 1107, Makawao 96768,*☎ *808/572-8437.*

Of course, the same dive companies that take scuba aficionados on tours will take snorkelers as well. One of Maui's most popular snorkeling spots can be reached only by boat: Molokini Crater, that little bowl of land off the coast of the Mākena Resort. For about $55, you can spend half a day at Molokini, with meals provided.

Ocean Activities Center (⊠ 1847 S. Kīhei Rd., Suite 203A, Kīhei, ☎ 808/879–4485) does a great job, although other companies also offer a Molokini snorkel tour.

You can find some good snorkeling spots on your own. If you need gear, **Snorkel Bob's** (⊠ Nāpili Village Hotel, 5425 Lower Honoapi'ilani Rd., Nāpili, ☎ 808/669–9603; ⊠ 34 Keala Pl., Kīhei Town Center, ☎ 808/879–7449; ⊠ 161 Lahainaluna Rd., Lahaina, ☎ 808/661–4421) will rent you a mask, fins, and snorkel, and throw in a carrying bag, map, and snorkel tips for as little as $5 per day.

Secluded **Windmill Beach** (⊠ take Hwy. 30 3½ mi north of Kapalua, then turn onto the dirt road to the left) has a superb reef for snorkeling. A little more than 2 mi south, another dirt road leads to **Honolua Bay;** the coral formations on the right side of the bay are particularly dramatic. You'll find **Nāpili Bay,** one beach south of the Kapalua Resort, also quite good for snorkeling.

Almost the entire coastline from Kā'anapali south to Olowalu offers fine snorkeling. Favorite sites include the area just out from the cemetery north of Wahikuli State Park, near the lava cone called **Black Rock,** on which Kā'anapali's Sheraton Maui Hotel is built (tame fish will take bread from your hand there), and the shallow coral reef south of **Olowalu** General Store.

The coastline from Wailea to Mākena is also generally good for snorkeling. The best is found near the rocky fringes of Wailea's **Mōkapu, Ulua, Wailea,** and **Polo** beaches.

Between Polo Beach and Mākena Beach (turn right on Mākena Road just past Mākena Surf Condo) lies **Five Caves,** where you'll find a maze of underwater grottoes below offshore rocks. This spot is recommended for experienced snorkelers only, since the tides can get rough. At Mākena, the waters around the **Pu'uōla'i** cinder cone provide great snorkeling.

SURFING

Although on land it may not look as if there are seasons on Maui, the tides tell another story. In winter the surf is up on the northern shores of the Hawaiian Islands, while summer brings big swells to the southern side. Near-perfect winter waves on Maui can be found at **Honolua Bay,** on the northern tip of West Maui. To get there, continue 2 mi north of D. T. Fleming Park on Highway 30 and take a left onto the dirt road next to a pineapple field; a path takes you down the cliff to the beach.

Next best for surfing is **Hoʻokipa Beach Park** (off Hwy. 36, a short distance east of Pāʻia), where the modern-day sport began on Maui. This is the easiest place to watch surfing, because there are paved parking areas and picnic pavilions in the park. A word of warning: the surfers who come here are pros, and if you're not, they may not take kindly to your getting in their way.

Pushing the envelope of big wave surfing has reached a new level here in the channel waters off Maui, where surfers get pulled out to sea and then whipped into the big waves. At Hoʻokipa Beach Park, viewers with a good pair of binoculars might be able to see out past the windsurfers to view an example of tow-in surfing: Jet Ski pilots pull state-of-the-art big wave surfers out to the 1-mi marker, where the waves can average 30 ft–40 ft during winter swells. Amazing grace!

You can rent surfboards and boogie boards at many surf shops, such as **Second Wind** (⊠ 111 Hāna Hwy., Kahului, ☎ 808/877–7467), **Lightning Bolt Maui** (⊠ 55 Kaʻahumanu Ave., Kahului, ☎ 808/877–3484), and **Ole Surfboards** (⊠ 277 Wili Ko Pl., Lahaina, ☎ 808/661–3459).

Maui Surfing School (☎ 808/875–0625) guarantees one two-hour lesson is all it takes to have "anyone who can walk" standing on a surfboard and riding the gentle waves of Lahaina Harbor. Costs are $60 per person (maximum class size of eight), including equipment rental; group discounts are available.

WINDSURFING

It's been more than 15 years since Hoʻokipa Bay was discovered by boardsailors, but in those years since 1980, the windy beach 10 mi east of Kahului has become the windsurfing capital of the world. The spot is blessed with optimal wave-sailing wind and sea conditions and, for experienced windsurfers, can offer the ultimate experience. Other locations around Maui are good for windsurfing as well—Honolua Bay, for example—but Hoʻokipa is absolutely unrivaled.

Even if you're a windsurfing aficionado, chances are good you didn't bring your equipment. You can rent it—or get lessons—from these shops: **Maui Ocean Activities** (⊠ Lahaina, ☎ 808/667–1964), **Maui Windsurfing Company and Cort Larned Windsurfing School** (⊠ 520 Keolani Pl., Kahului, ☎ 808/877–4816), **Ocean Activities Center** (⊠ 1847 S. Kīhei Rd., Kīhei, ☎ 808/879–4485), and **Maui Windsurfari** (⊠ 425 Koloa St., Kahului, ☎ 808/871–7766). Lessons range from $30 to $60 and can last anywhere from one to three hours. Equipment rental also varies—from no charge with lessons to $20 an hour. For the latest prices and special deals, it's best to call around once you've arrived.

Spectator Sports

Baseball

From mid-October to mid-December the four teams of **Hawaiʻi Winter Baseball** compete. The teams consist mostly of local players, plus a few promising minor leaguers from the mainland. The **Maui Stingrays**

WHALE-WATCHING

APPEALING TO BOTH children and adults, whale-watching is one of the most exciting activities in the United States. During the right time of year on Maui—between November and April—you can see whales breaching and blowing just offshore. The humpback whales' attraction to Maui is legendary. More than half the North Pacific's humpback population winters in Hawai'i, as they've been doing for years. At one time there were thousands of the huge mammals, but the world population has dwindled to about 1,500. In 1966 they were put on the endangered species list, which restricts boats and airplanes from getting too close.

Experts believe the humpbacks keep returning to Hawaiian waters because of the warmth. Winter is calving time for the behemoths, and the young whales, born with little blubber, probably couldn't survive in the frigid Alaskan waters. No one has ever seen a whale give birth, but the experts studying whales off Maui know that calving is their main winter activity, since the 1- and 2-ton youngsters suddenly appear while the whales are in residence.

Quite a few operations run whale-watching excursions off the coast of Maui, with many boats departing from the wharves at Lahaina and Ma'alaea each day. **Pacific Whale Foundation** (⊠ Kealia Beach Plaza, 101 N. Kīhei Rd., Kīhei 96753, ☎ 808/879–8811) pioneered whale-watching back in 1979 and now runs four boats, plus sea kayaks and special trips to encounter turtles and dolphins. During humpback season (Dec. 15–May 1) PWF has a marine naturalist stationed at McGregor Point Lookout (on the *pali* or cliffs heading into Lahaina) and also weekdays at 12:15 on the observation deck of their Kīhei office.

Also offering whale-watching in season are **Ocean Activities Center** (⊠ 1847 S. Kīhei Rd., Suite 203, Kīhei 96753, ☎ 808/879–4485); **Island Marine** (⊠ 113 Prison St., Lahaina 96761, ☎ 808/661–8397); and **Pride Charters** (⊠ 208 Kenolio Rd., Kīhei, ☎ 808/874–8835), whose two-hour whale-watch cruise is narrated by a naturalist from Whales Alive and Keiko (Free Willie) Foundation. Ticket prices average $22–$35.

(☎ 808/242–2950) play their home games at War Memorial Stadium in Wailuku. Reserved seats cost $6, general admission is $5.

Golf

Maui has a number of golf tournaments, most of which are of professional caliber and worth watching. Many are also televised nationally. One of those attention-getters is the **Mercedes Championships** (☎ 808/669–2440), formerly called the Lincoln-Mercury Kapalua International, held now in January. This is the first official PGA tour event, held on Kapalua's Plantation Course. The Aloha Section of the Professional Golfers Association of America hosts the **GTE Hawaiian Tel Hall of Fame** (☎ 808/669–8877) championship at the Plantation Course in May, and a clambake feast on the beach tops off the **Kapalua Clambake Pro-Am** (☎ 808/669–8812) in July.

At Kā'anapali, the **EMC Maui Kā'anapali Classic SENIOR PGA Golf Tournament** pits veteran professionals in a battle for a $1 million purse each October.

Over in Wailea, on June's longest day of the year, self-proclaimed "lunatic" golfers start out at first light to play 100 holes of golf in the annual **Ka Lima O Maui,** a fund-raiser for local charities.

Outrigger-Canoe Races

Polynesians first traveled to Hawai'i by outrigger canoe, and racing the traditional craft has always been a favorite pastime in the Islands. Canoes were revered in Old Hawai'i, and no voyage could begin without a blessing, ceremonial chanting, and a hula performance to ensure a safe journey. At Whaler's Village in May, the two-day launch festivities for the **Ho'omana'o Challenge Outrigger Sailing Canoe World Championship** (☎ 808/661–3271) also include a torchlighting ceremony, arts and crafts demonstrations, and a chance to observe how the vessels are rigged—as well as the start of the race.

Polo

Polo is popular with Mauians. From April to June, Haleakalā Ranch, on Highway 377, 1 mi past the summit turnoff (Hwy. 378), hosts the "indoor" contests, which are played outdoors in a field flanked by sideboards. During the outdoor polo season from September through November, matches are held at Olinda Field, 1 mi above the paniolo town of Makawao on Olinda Road. There is a $3 admission charge for most games, which start at 2 PM on Sunday. Two special events to catch if you're in town include Memorial Day's **Champagne Brunch** match and the **High Goal Benefit** game, which is held on the first Sunday in November and features teams from such countries as Argentina, England, and Australia. For information, contact Moani (☎ 808/877–5544).

Rodeos

With dozens of working cattle ranches throughout the Islands, many youngsters learn to ride a horse before they can drive a car. Mauians love their rodeos and put on several for students at local high schools throughout the year. Paniolos get in on the act, too, at three major annual events: the **Oskie Rice Memorial Rodeo,** usually staged the weekend after Labor Day; the **Cancer Benefit Rodeo** in April, held at an arena 3 mi east of Pā'ia; and Maui's biggest event, drawing competitors from all islands as well as the U.S. mainland, the **4th of July Rodeo,** which comes with a full-on parade and other festivities that last for days. Spectator admission fees to the competitions vary from free to $7. Cowboys are a tough bunch to tie down to a phone, but you can try calling the **Maui Roping Club** (☎ 808/572–2076) for information.

Surfing and Windsurfing

Not many places can lay claim to as many windsurfing tournaments as Maui. The Valley Isle is generally thought to be the world's preeminent windsurfing location, and draws boardsailing experts from around the globe who want to compete on its waves. In March the **Hawaiian Pro Am Windsurfing** competition gets under way. In April the **Da Kine Hawaiian Pro Am** lures top windsurfers, and the **Aloha Classic World Wave Sailing Championships** takes place in October. All are held at Ho'okipa Bay, right outside the town of Pā'ia, near Kahului. For competitions featuring amateurs as well as professionals, check out the **Maui Race Series** (☎ 808/877–2111), six events held at Kanahā beach in Kahului in summer when winds are the strongest and lack of big waves makes conditions excellent for the slalom (speed racing) course. Competitors maneuver their boards close to shore, and the huge beach provides plenty of seating and viewing space. Ho'okipa Bay's large waves are also prime territory for surfers. The **Local Motion Surfing** competition heats up the action in May, and in January the **Maui Rusty Pro,** held jointly at Honolua Bay, invites professionals to compete for a $40,000 purse.

Tennis

At the **Kapalua Jr. Vet/Sr. Tennis Championships** in May, where the minimum age is 30, players have been competing in singles and doubles events since 1979. On Labor Day, the **Wilson Kapalua Open Tennis Tournament,** Maui's grand prix of tennis, calls Hawai'i's hottest hitters to volley for a $12,000 purse at Kapalua's Tennis Garden and Village Tennis Center. Also at the Tennis Center, Women's International Tennis Association professionals rally with avid amateurs in a week of pro-am and pro-doubles competition during the **Kapalua Betsy Nagelsen Tennis Invitational** in December. All events are put on by the **Kapalua Tennis Club** (☎ 808/669–5677).

In East Maui, 1999 marks the 15th year for the **Wailea Open Tennis Championship,** held in July on the Plexipave courts at the **Wailea Tennis Club** (☎ 808/879–1958).

7 Shopping

*You'll enjoy browsing in the shops
that line Front Street in Lahaina
or the boutiques that are packed into
the major resorts. Kahului and Lahaina
also have some good-size shopping
malls.*

WHETHER YOU HEAD FOR one of the malls (☞ *below*) or opt for the boutiques hidden around the Valley Isle, one thing you should have no problem finding is clothing made in Hawai'i. The Hawaiian garment industry is now the state's third-largest economic sector, after tourism and agriculture.

Maui has an abundance of locally made art and crafts in a range of prices. In fact, a group that calls itself Made on Maui exists solely to promote the products of its members—items that range from pottery and paintings to Hawaiian teas and macadamia caramel corn. You can identify the group by its distinctive Haleakalā logo.

Business hours for individual shops on the island are usually 9–5, seven days a week. Shopping centers tend to stay open later (until 9 or 10 at least one night of the week).

Art

Maui has more art per square mile than any other Hawaiian island—maybe more than any other U.S. county. There are artists' guilds and co-ops, as well as galleries galore, all over the island. Art shows are held throughout the year at the Maui Arts & Cultural Center. Marine sculptors and painters showcase their work during **Celebration of Whales** at the Four Seasons Resort Wailea in January. The Lahaina Arts Society presents **Art in the Park** under the town's historic banyan tree every Friday and Saturday from 9–5. Moreover, the town of Lahaina hosts **Art Night** every Friday from 7–10; galleries open their doors (some serve refreshments), and musicians stroll the streets.

Hui No'eau Visual Arts Center (⊠ 2841 Baldwin Ave., Makawao, ☎ 808/572–6560) presents juried and nonjuried exhibits by local artists.

Lahaina Galleries has two locations in West Maui (⊠ 728 Front St., Lahaina, ☎ 808/667–2152 and ⊠ Kapalua Resort, ☎ 808/669–0202).

Martin Lawrence Galleries (⊠ Lahaina Market Place, Front St. and Lahainaluna Rd., Lahaina, ☎ 808/661–1788) represents noted mainland artists, including Andy Warhol and Keith Haring, in a bright and friendly gallery opened in 1991.

One of the most interesting galleries on Maui is the **Maui Crafts Guild** (⊠ 43 Hāna Hwy., Pā'ia, ☎ 808/579–9697). Set in a two-story wooden building alongside the highway, the Guild is crammed with work by local artists; the best pieces are the pottery and sculpture. Upstairs, antique kimonos, hand-painted silks, and batik fabric are on display.

Maui Hands (⊠ 3620 Baldwin Ave., Makawao, ☎ 808/572–5194; ⊠ Ka'ahumanu Center, Kahului, ☎ 808/877–0368) has work by dozens of local artists, including paniolo-theme lithographs by Sharon Shigekawa, who knows whereof she paints: She rides each year in the Kaupō Roundup. The shop is in the town's old theater.

Viewpoints (⊠ 3620 Baldwin Ave., Makawao, ☎ 808/572–5979) calls itself Maui's only fine-arts collective; it is a cooperative venture of about two dozen Maui painters and sculptors, representing a wide variety of styles.

Village Gallery has two locations—one in Lahaina (⊠ 120 Dickenson St., ☎ 808/661–4402) and one in the Ritz-Carlton, Kapalua (⊠ 1 Ritz-Carlton Dr., ☎ 808/669–1800)—featuring such popular local artists as Betty Hay Freeland, Wailehua Gray, Margaret Bedell, George Allen, Joyce Clark, Pamela Andelin, Stephen Burr, and Macario Pascual.

Wyland Galleries (⊠ 697 Front St., Lahaina, ☎ 808/661–7099; ⊠ 711 Front St., Lahaina, ☎ 808/667–2285; ⊠ 136 Dickenson St., Lahaina, ☎ 808/661–0590) is the only Maui shop to sell the work of Wyland, the marine artist whose giant airbrushed whales adorn the exterior walls of buildings across the United States. The gallery also sells paintings and sculptures by other marine artists.

Clothing

Island Wear

Hilo Hattie (⊠ Lahaina Center, Lahaina, ☎ 808/661–8457), Hawai'i's largest manufacturer of aloha shirts and mu'umu'u, also carries brightly colored blouses, skirts, and children's clothing.

Liberty House has the kind of Island wear—colorful shirts and mu'umu'u, as well as other graceful styles—worn by people who live year-round on Maui. The store has several branches on the island, including shops in the Westin Maui, Hyatt Regency, Four Seasons Wailea, and Embassy Vacation Resort; and in Azeka Place Shopping Center in Kīhei, Lahaina Center, and Ka'ahumanu Center in Kahului. The largest Liberty House store is the one at Ka'ahumanu Center (☎ 808/877–3361).

Panama Jack's (⊠ Lahaina Cannery Mall, Lahaina, ☎ 808/661–3344) carries everything a man needs for a complete Hawaiian wardrobe: aloha shirts, beachwear, swimsuits, sunglasses, sandals, and accessories.

Pineapple Bay Clothing (⊠ Lahaina Cannery Mall, Lahaina, ☎ 808/ 667–0402) has Hawaiian prints, cool and comfortable linens and cottons, and the ever versatile sarong.

Reyn's (⊠ Kapalua Bay Hotel, Kapalua, ☎ 808/669–5260; ⊠ Lahaina Cannery Mall, Lahaina, ☎ 808/661–5356; ⊠ Hyatt Regency Maui, Kā'anapali, ☎ 808/661–0215; ⊠ Whalers Village, Kā'anapali, ☎ 808/ 661–9032) has high-quality aloha shirts in the subtler shadings local men favor for business attire.

Ukulele Clothing Co. (⊠ Ka'ahumanu Center, Kahului, ☎ 808/871– 7290; ⊠ 834 Front St., Lahaina, ☎ 808/667–2521) has terrific casual wear in subtle prints and solids.

Resort Wear

Not all Maui's casual clothing is floral. You can find island-worthy sportswear in shops all over the Valley Isle, including most of the stores that sell Island wear, as well as these:

Honolua Surf Company (⊠ 845 Front St., Lahaina, ☎ 808/661–8848; ⊠ Whalers Village, Kā'anapali, ☎ 808/661–5455; ⊠ Lahaina Cannery Mall, Lahaina, ☎ 808/661–5777) sells casual clothing and sportswear for young women.

Kramer's Men's Wear (⊠ Lahaina Cannery Mall, Lahaina, ☎ 808/661– 5377) has a good selection of men's clothing in large sizes.

Paradise Clothing (⊠ Whalers Village, Kā'anapali, ☎ 808/661–4638) carries Speedo brand swimwear for men, women, and children.

SGT Leisure (⊠ 701 Front St., Lahaina, ☎ 808/667–0661; ⊠ Whalers Village, Kā'anapali, ☎ 808/667–9433) has resortwear by Tori Richards and other designers. **SGT Leisure Cabana** (⊠ Wailea Shopping Center, Wailea, ☎ 808/874–5647) is the company's first men's store on Maui, but ladies, too, shop here for the '40s and '50s vintage silk shirts by Avanti. Also at the Wailea Shopping Center, another SGT Leisure

(☎ 808/879–5186), referred to as the logo shop, sells silk-screened and embroidered apparel designed by the company's owners. The stores also carry bags, hats, and other accessories.

At **Tropical Tantrum Outlet Store** (⊠ 395 Dairy Rd., Kahului, ☎ 808/871–9558) you'll find a wide selection of stylish resort wear, as well as aloha shirts and mu'umu'u, for 50% less than the company's retail store prices. This well-known outfitter has four retail stores on Maui (⊠ Azeka Place Shopping Center, Kīhei, ☎ 808/874–3835; ⊠ Ka'ahumanu Center, Kahului, ☎ 808/871–8088; ⊠ Kama'ole Shopping Center, Kīhei, ☎ 808/875–4433; and ⊠ 275 Ka'ahumanu Ave., Kahului, ☎ 808/877–0441).

Flea Market

The **Maui Swap Meet** flea market is the biggest bargain on Maui, with crafts, gifts, souvenirs, fruit, flowers, jewelry, antiques, art, shells, and lots more. ⊠ *Kahului Fairgrounds, Hwy. 350, off S. Pu'unēnē Ave., Kahului.* ☜ *50¢.* ⊙ *Sat. 5:30–noon.*

Food

Many visitors to Hawai'i opt to take home some of the local produce: pineapples, papayas, coconut, or Maui onions. You can find jams and jellies—some of them "Made on Maui" products—in a wide variety of tropical flavors. Cook Kwee's Maui Cookies have gained quite a following, as have Maui Potato Chips. Both are available in most Valley Isle grocery stores. Coffee sellers now have Maui-grown and -roasted beans alongside the better-known Kona varieties.

Remember that fresh fruit must be inspected by the U.S. Department of Agriculture before it can leave the state, so it's safer to buy a box that has already passed muster.

Airport Flower & Fruit Co. (☎ 808/243–9367 or 800/922–9352) sells ready-to-ship pineapples, Maui onions, papayas, and fresh coconuts.

Take Home Maui (⊠ 121 Dickenson St., Lahaina, ☎ 808/661–8067 or 800/545–6284) will supply, pack, and deliver produce free to the airport or your hotel.

Gifts

Dan's Green House (⊠ 133 Prison St., Lahaina, ☎ 808/661–8412) has some truly unusual offerings—adorable baby animals: pigs, goats, birds, and cotton-eared marmoset or golden-handed tamarin monkeys that go for $2,000 a pair.

Lahaina Printsellers Ltd. has Hawai'i's largest selection of original antique maps and prints pertaining to Hawai'i and the Pacific. They also sell museum-quality reproductions and original oil paintings from the Pacific Artists Guild.

Maui's Best (⊠ Ka'ahumanu Center, Kahului, ☎ 808/877–7959; ⊠ Wailea Shopping Village, Wailea, ☎ 808/879–4734; ⊠ Azeka Place Shopping Center, ☎ 808/874–9216) has a wide selection of gifts from Maui and around the world.

Ola's Makawao (⊠ 1156 Makawao Ave., Makawao, ☎ 808/573–1334) contains a delightful assortment of whimsical gifts and affordable, contemporary, functional art made by artists from Hawai'i and the U.S. mainland. They are also the exclusive western-U.S. distributors for chocolates by JoMart Candies.

BONUS MILES MAKE GREAT SOUVENIRS.

Earn Miles With Your MCI Card.

Take the MCI Card along on this trip and start earning miles for the next one. You'll earn frequent flyer miles on all your calls and save with the low rates you've come to expect from MCI. Before you know it, you'll be on your way to some other international destination.

Sign up for MCI by calling 1-800-FLY-FREE

Is this a great time, or what? :-)

Earn Frequent Flyer Miles.

AmericanAirlines
A'Advantage

Continental Airlines
OnePass

▲ Delta Air Lines
SkyMiles

HAWAIIAN AIRLINES

MIDWEST EXPRESS AIRLINES

NORTHWEST AIRLINES
WORLDPERKS

Rapid Rewards
SOUTHWEST AIRLINES

▬ MILEAGE PLUS.
United Airlines

US AIRWAYS
DIVIDEND MILES

Hawaiian Crafts

Some visiting shoppers are determined to buy only what they can't get anywhere else. The arts and crafts native to Hawai'i can be just the thing. Such woods as koa and milo grow only in certain parts of the world, and because of their increasing scarcity, prices are rising. In Hawai'i, artisans turn the woods into bowls, trays, and jewelry boxes that will last for years. Look for them in galleries and museum shops as well as the places listed below.

The **Hāna Cultural Center** (⊠ Ukea St., Hāna, ☎ 808/248–8622) sells distinctive island quilts and other Hawaiian crafts.

Island Christmas (⊠ Kama'ole Shopping Center, 2463 S. Kīhei Rd., Kīhei, ☎ 808/874–1076; ⊠ Wailea Shopping Center, Wailea, ☎ 808/875–7418) specializes in locally crafted tree ornaments, Santas, angels, and other holiday-season goodies with a Hawaiian design.

John of Maui & Sons (⊠ 810 Ha'ikū Rd., B-6, Ha'ikū, ☎ 808/575–7402) turns out some of the most exacting wood products in the Islands.

A fun place to investigate is the **Kīhei Kalama Village Marketplace** (⊠ 1941 S. Kīhei Rd., Kīhei, ☎ 808/879–6610), a shaded collection of outdoor stalls selling everything from printed and hand-painted T-shirts and sundresses to jewelry, pottery, wood carvings, fruit, and gaudily painted coconut husks—all made by local craftspeople.

Quilters Corner (⊠ 283 Wili Ko Pl., Lahaina, ☎ 808/661–0944) has a huge selection of Hawaiian quilts and needlepoint, as well as plenty of tropical-print fabrics, silver jewelry, and other local craft and gift items.

Jewelry

Haimoff & Haimoff Creations in Gold (☎ 808/669–5213), at the Kapalua Resort, features the original work of several jewelry designers including the award-winning Harry Haimoff.

Jessica's Gems (⊠ Whalers Village, Kā'anapali, ☎ 808/661–4223) has a good selection of Hawaiian heirloom jewelry, and their **Lahaina** store (⊠ 858 Front St., ☎ 808/661–9200) specializes in black pearls.

You can buy brooches, rings, pendants, cuff links, tie tacks, and collectors items adorned with this intricately carved sailors' art from **Lahaina Scrimshaw** (⊠ 845A Front St., Lahaina, ☎ 808/661–8820; ⊠ Whalers Village, Kā'anapali, ☎ 808/661–4034).

Original Maui Divers (⊠ 640 Front St., Lahaina, ☎ 808/661–0988) is a company that has been crafting gold and coral into jewelry for more than 20 years.

Shopping Centers

Maui now has five major shopping centers: the Ka'ahumanu Center and Maui Marketplace in Kahului, Whalers Village in Kā'anapali, and the Lahaina Cannery Mall and Lahaina Center in Lahaina.

A $55 million expansion has turned **Ka'ahumanu Center** (⊠ 275 Ka'ahumanu Ave., Kahului, ☎ 808/877–3369), Maui's largest mall, into a showplace with more than 75 stores and a gorgeous glass-enclosed atrium entrance topped by an umbrella-shaded food court. Stop at **Camellia Seed Shop** for what the locals call "crack seed," a delicacy made from dried fruits, nuts, and sugar. Other interesting places to shop here include **Shirokiya**, a popular Japanese retailer; **Maui Hands**, purveyor of prints, paintings, woodwork, and jewelry by some of the island's finest artists; and such American standards as **Foot Locker,** **Mrs. Field's Cookies,** and **Kinney Shoes.**

A sure sign that Maui has come of age is the opening of the 20-acre **Maui Marketplace** (⊠ 270 Dairy Rd., Kahului, ☎ 808/873–0400), where several outlet stores and big retailers, such as **Eagle Hardware, Sports Authority, OfficeMax,** and **Borders Books & Music,** have made their first expansion to a Neighbor Island. The center couldn't have a better location to entice visitors as well as residents—it's at the busy intersection of Hāna Highway and Dairy Road, close to Kahului Airport.

Chic and trendy, **Whalers Village** (⊠ 2435 Kāʻanapali Pkwy., Kāʻanapali, ☎ 808/661–4567) has grown into a major West Maui shopping center, with a whaling museum and more than 50 restaurants and shops, including such upscale haunts as **Louis Vuitton, Prada, Ferragamo, Hunting World,** and **Chanel Boutique.** The recently expanded complex offers some interesting diversions: Hawaiian artisans display their crafts daily, hula dancers perform on an outdoor stage weeknights from 7 PM to 8 PM, and a free slide show spotlighting whales and other marine life takes place at the **Whale Center of the Pacific** on Tuesday and Thursday at 7 PM.

Lahaina Cannery Mall (⊠ 1221 Honoapiʻilani Hwy., Lahaina, ☎ 808/661–5304) is set in a building reminiscent of an old pineapple cannery. Unlike many shopping centers in Hawaiʻi, the Lahaina Cannery isn't open-air; it is air-conditioned. The center has 50 shops, including **Hawaiian Island Gems,** featuring striking Hawaiian heirloom jewelry and pearls; **Superwhale,** with a good selection of children's tropical wear; and **Kite Fantasy,** one of the best kite shops on Maui.

Lahaina Center (⊠ 900 Front St., Lahaina, ☎ 808/667–9216) has added to its roster of shops and to its attractiveness as a "shopping event." **World Cafe** and the **Hard Rock Cafe** are great for eats, while **Arabesque Maui, Banana Republic,** and **Waterwear** offer new clothing venues. Island department stores **Hilo Hattie** and **Liberty House** still anchor the center, which puts on a free hula show at 2 PM every Wednesday and Friday. An additional 10,000 square ft of parking lot space here have been transformed into an ancient Hawaiian village complete with three full-size thatch huts built with 10,000 linear ft of ʻōhiʻa wood from the Big Island, 20 tons of *pili* grass, and more than 4 mi of handwoven coconut *senit* (twine). Indoor entertainment is found at the four-screen cinema.

In East Maui, Kīhei offers the large and bustling **Azeka Place Shopping Center** (⊠ 1280 S. Kīhei Rd.). Maui residents favor the locally owned shops at the small **Kamaʻole Shopping Center** (⊠ 2463 S. Kīhei Rd.). Another place to rub elbows with Kīhei locals is **Rainbow Mall** (⊠ 2439 S. Kīhei Rd.). South of Kīhei, the Wailea Resort has the **Wailea Shopping Village** (⊠ Wailea Alanui Dr., Wailea), with 25 gift shops, boutiques, restaurants, and a general store.

8 Side Trip to Lāna'i

Lāna'i's only population center is Lāna'i City, smack in the middle of the island. The town is surrounded by natural wonders: Garden of the Gods, an eerie canyon strewn with colorful boulders, to the northwest; breathtaking Hulopo'e Beach to the south; and Lāna'ihale, the highest point on the island, to the east.

By Marty
Wentzel

FOR DECADES, LĀNA'I WAS KNOWN as the Pineapple Island, with hundreds of acres of fields filled with the golden fruit. Today this 140-square-mi island has been renamed "Hawai'i's Private Island," as developers replace its pineapple fields with sophisticated hotels in an effort to boost tourism. Once rarely visited, Lāna'i has joined most of its sister islands in the tourism business. Since 1990, Dole Foods Inc., which owns 98% of the island, has opened the luxurious 102-room Lodge at Kō'ele and the 250-room Mānele Bay Hotel, plus two championship golf courses. Despite these new additions, Lāna'i—the third smallest of the Islands— still remains the most remote and intimate visitor destination in Hawai'i.

Most of the island's population is centered in Lāna'i City, an old plantation town of 2,700 residents, whose tiny houses have colorful facades, tin roofs, and tidy gardens. Although the weather across much of the island is hot and dry, the Norfolk Island pines that line Lāna'i City's streets create a cool refuge. Here, you'll encounter some of the people who came from the Philippines in the 1920s to work in Lāna'i's pineapple fields. You'll also notice the many other nationalities of Hawai'i, from Korean, Chinese, and Japanese to transplanted mainland *haole* (Caucasians). Though Lāna'i City has a few family-run shops and stores, its options are limited. You'll find a couple of diner-style eateries, a restored theater, and the comfy old Hotel Lāna'i, an 11-room hostelry that serves as a gathering place for locals and tourists.

With its well-planned grid of paved roads with small businesses, the town adds a hint of civilization to a mostly wild island. However, Lāna'i City is not the primary reason for coming to Lāna'i. Among the island's unique outdoor attractions is the Garden of the Gods, where rocks and boulders are scattered across a crimson landscape as if some divine being had placed them there as a sculpture garden. The waters at Hulopo'e Beach are so clear that within a minute of snorkeling you can see fish the colors of turquoise and jade. And you can drive or hike to the top of Lāna'ihale, a 3,370-ft-high, windswept perch from which you can see nearly every inhabited Hawai'ian island.

Although today it is an island that welcomes visitors with its friendly, rustic charm, Lāna'i has not always been so amiable. The earliest Polynesians believed it to be haunted by evil ghosts who gobbled up unsuspecting visitors. In 1836 a pair of missionaries named Dwight Baldwin and William Richards came and went after failing to convert the locals to their Christian beliefs. In 1854 a group of Mormons tried to create the City of Joseph here, but they were forced to abandon their mission after a drought in 1857.

One of Lāna'i's more successful visitors was a man named Jim Dole (1877–1958). In 1922 Dole bought the island for $1.1 million and began to grow pineapples on it. He built Lāna'i City on the flatlands, where the crater floor is flanked by volcanic slopes. Then he planned the harbor at Kaumālapa'u, from which pineapples would be shipped. Four years later, as he watched the first harvest sail away to Honolulu, this enterprising businessman could safely say that Lāna'i's Dole Plantation was a success. Over the past decade, however, pineapples have ceased to be a profitable crop in Hawai'i because of global competition; thus the new thrust toward tourism.

A visit to Lāna'i can be either simple or elegant. Solitude is easily acquired, though you may encounter the occasional deer on the hillsides, the spirits that linger in the ancient fishing village of Kaunolū, and the playful dolphins of Mānele Bay. On the other hand, you can rub elbows with sophisticated travelers during a game of croquet at the Lodge at Kō'ele or a round of golf at one of the island's two championship courses. Bring casual clothes, because many of your activities will be laid-back, whether you're riding the unpaved roads in a four-wheel-drive vehicle or having a drink on the front porch of the Hotel Lāna'i. Come, take your time, and enjoy yourself before the island changes too much more.

Pleasures and Pastimes

Dining

Some call it Lāna'i Regional Cuisine. Others call it Private Island Palate. Either way, the menus at Lāna'i's two resorts reflect the fresh-flavored products provided by local farmers, hunters, and fishermen—everything from Mānele ahi (yellowfin tuna) to Lāna'i liliko'i (passion fruit). Lāna'i City's eclectic fare ranges from grilled cheese to eggplant creole. Pricing is straightforward: Hotel dining rooms are expensive, while family-run eateries are much more affordable. Picnic lunches are the best option for visitors on the go. Some outfitters include them in their packages, or you can head to either of the two grocery stores in Lāna'i City and concoct your own afternoon treat.

Hiking

Treks are distinctive, from a self-guided walk through Hawai'i's largest native dryland forest, to an 8-mi adventure over Lāna'ihale with ocean and island views from here to eternity. Before you go, fill a water bottle and arm yourself with provisions, in case you get a little off track. Also, look at Craig Chisholm's paperback, *Hawaiian Hiking Trails* (Touchstone Press, 1977), and Robert Smith's *Hawai'i's Best Hiking Trails* (Wilderness Press, 1987).

Lodging

Lāna'i offers a mixed bag of lodging options, though the number of properties is limited due to the island's small size. You'll pay top dollar for upscale digs at The Lodge at Kō'ele and Mānele Bay Hotel. If you're on a tight budget, seek out a bed-and-breakfast spot (the ones we've mentioned have particularly friendly hosts). House rentals are expensive, but they do give you a taste of what it's actually like to live on such a remote isle.

Snorkeling and Scuba Diving

With Cathedrals (pinnacle formations) for a dive site and marine life like angelfish, it's no wonder that snorkeling and scuba-diving buffs call the waters off Lāna'i a religious experience. For the best underwater viewing, try the south shore's Hulopo'e Beach, a marine-life conservation area, or go on a snorkeling/diving excursion with Trilogy Ocean Sports (☞ Outdoor Activities and Sports, *below*).

EXPLORING LĀNA'I

Most of Lāna'i's sights are out of the way; that is, you won't find them in Lāna'i City or along paved roads. You'll have to look to find them, but the search is worth it. Ask your hotel's concierge for a road and site map; it's a good resource. Bring along a cooler with drinks and snacks for your explorations, because there are no places to stop for refreshments along the way. Admission to all sights mentioned in this chapter is free.

Numbers in the text correspond to numbers in the margin and on the Lāna'i map.

Great Itineraries

Lāna'i is small enough to explore in a couple of days of leisurely travel, depending on how you want to experience it. Be selective with your time, for it goes by fast here.

IF YOU HAVE 1 DAY

If you can only tear yourself away from your lounge chair for one day of exploring, rent a four-wheel-drive vehicle and get to know the backroads of Lāna'i, where the power of the landscape is overwhelming. If you're staying at the Lodge at Kō'ele or Hotel Lāna'i, allow yourself enough time to see the **Garden of the Gods** ⑦ in the morning. After lunch in Lāna'i City, drive down to **Lu'ahiwa Petroglyphs** ② and **Kaunolū** ③, followed by a late-afternoon swim at **Hulopo'e Beach** ⑥. Guests of the Mānele Bay Hotel should reverse the itinerary, with the beach, petroglyphs, and Kaunolū in the morning and Garden of the Gods in the afternoon.

IF YOU HAVE 3 DAYS

Follow the one-day itinerary. Then on day two, take an adventurous tour of the undeveloped north and east shores. Start the day with a drive to **Shipwreck Beach** ⑨ for a morning walk and some sunbathing. Then drive along the bumpy coastal road to **Keōmuku** ⑩, **Kahe'a Heiau** ⑪, **Naha** ⑫, and Lōpā Beach, where you can eat that picnic you packed. After retracing your route and returning your rental vehicle, relive the day's adventures over tropical drinks at your hotel's lounge. Start your third day with a cool morning hike atop Lāna'ihale, stopping mid-way for a picnic. In the afternoon, relax those tired muscles with an afternoon spa treatment or some time in the swimming pool and hot tub.

IF YOU HAVE 5 DAYS

Follow the three-day itinerary then dedicate day four to the sport of choice, be it golf on one of the island's two championship courses, tennis at Mānele or Kō'ele, horseback riding from Kō'ele Stables, or sporting clays in the highlands; or sign up for a lesson and learn a new sport. On day five, see the island from the sea by going on a half-day fishing trip or snorkeling/scuba diving expedition. In the afternoon, stroll around Lāna'i City, chat with the residents and shop owners, and pick up some island souvenirs, like Lāna'i T-shirts and hand-carved pine bowls.

When to Tour Lāna'i

The weather on Lāna'i is warm and clear throughout the year. It's sunniest at sea level, while in upcountry Lāna'i City, the nights and mornings can feel chilly and the fog can settle in on the tops of the pine trees. As in all of Hawai'i, winter weather is cooler and less predictable. For a taste of local arts, crafts, and entertainment, time your trip with an island event such as autumn's Aloha Festivals.

South and West Lāna'i

Pineapples once blanketed the Pālāwai Basin, the flat area south of Lāna'i City. Today it is used primarily for agriculture and grazing, but it does hold historic and natural treasures worth exploring.

In the Islands, the directions *mauka* (toward the mountains) and *makai* (toward the ocean) are often used. We've included them in the text here as well.

A Good Drive

From Lāna'i City, drive south on Highway 440 a few blocks until you reach a major intersection. Go straight, following the highway west to **Kaumālapa'u Harbor** ①, the island's main seaport. Backtrack to the intersection, turn right, and take Highway 440 south (also called Mānele

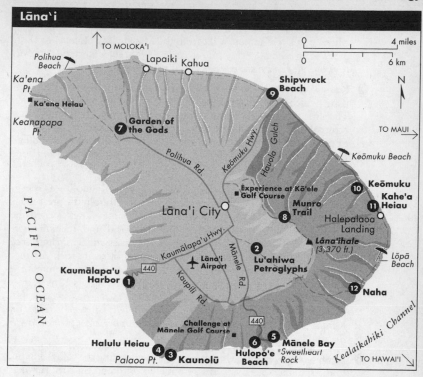

Lāna'i

TO MOLOKA'I

Polihua Beach
Ka'ena Pt.
■ Ka'ena Heiau
Keanapapa Pt.

Lapaiki Kahua

Shipwreck Beach **9**

7 Garden of the Gods

Polihua Rd.

Keōmuku Hwy.

Hauola Gulch

Keōmuku Beach

TO MAUI

PACIFIC OCEAN

Experience at Kō'ele ■ Golf Course

Lāna'i City

Kaumālapa'u Hwy.

Lāna'i Airport

Munro **8** Trail

Mānele Rd.

Keōmuku **10**
11 Kahe'a Heiau

Halepalaoa Landing

2 Lu'ahiwa Petroglyphs

▲ Lāna'ihale (3,370 ft.)

Lōpā Beach

Kaumālapa'u Harbor **1**

Kaupili Rd.

12 Naha

440

Challenge at Mānele Golf Course

440

Halulu Heiau

6 **5** Mānele Bay

4 **3** Kaunolū

Palaoa Pt.

Hulopo'e Beach

Sweetheart Rock

Kealaikahiki Channel

TO HAWAI'I

N

0 — 4 miles
0 — 6 km

Road). After about a mile you'll see a dirt road on your left, which will lead you to **Lu'ahiwa Petroglyphs** ② and its ancient rock carvings.

Return to Highway 440 and drive another 2 mi south until the road veers left. Here, go straight on bumpy and unpaved Kaupili Road, then take the fourth left onto another unnamed dirt road. All of this four-wheeling pays off when you reach your destination: the well-preserved archaeological sites of **Kaunolū** ③ and **Halulu Heiau** ④.

Back on Highway 440, drive down the long steep hill. At the bottom awaits **Mānele Bay** ⑤, with its boat harbor. Take a look at **Sweetheart Rock** and its sheer 50-ft-high cliffs. The road ends at the island's only true swimming area, **Hulopo'e Beach** ⑥ (☞ Beaches, *below*).

TIMING

Although it's a small area, south and west Lāna'i deserves a full day of exploration. If you're a fan of water sports, you'll want to spend half the day at Hulopo'e Beach and use the rest for visiting the other attractions. The south is almost always sunny, clear, and warm, so wear sunscreen and head for shade in the middle of the day.

Sights to See

❹ **Halulu Heiau.** The carefully excavated remains of an impressive stone *heiau* (outdoor shrine) attest to the sacred history of this spot, which was actively used as a place of worship by the earliest residents of Lāna'i. As late as 1810, this hilltop sight was also considered a place of refuge for wayward islanders. ☒ *From Lāna'i City, follow Hwy. 440 (Mānele Rd.) south; when road makes sharp left, continue straight on Kaupili Rd., which leads you through pineapple fields; turn onto 4th dirt road in makai direction.*

❻ **Hulopo'e Beach.** Lāna'i's only swimming beach, Hulopo'e beckons with its perennially clear waters, great snorkeling reefs, and views of spinner dolphins at play. Shady trees and grassy expanses make it a good picnic spot, and there are showers, rest rooms, and changing facilities. It's a five-minute walk from the Mānele Bay Hotel via a short path. ⊠ *From Lāna'i City, follow Hwy. 440 (Mānele Rd.) south to bottom of hill; road dead-ends at beach's parking lot.*

❶ Kaumālapa'u Harbor. Built in 1926 by the Hawaiian Pineapple Company (which later became Dole), this is the principal seaport for Lāna'i. The cliffs flanking the western shore are as much as 1,000 ft tall. Since Kaumālapa'u is actively used for shipping, no swimming, snorkeling, or other water activities are allowed here. ⊠ *From Lāna'i City, follow Hwy. 440 (Kaumālapa'u Hwy.) west as far as it goes; turn left and drive about 7 mi to ocean.*

❸ Kaunolū. Set atop the island's highest sea cliffs, Kaunolū was a fishing village in precontact times. A team from Honolulu's prestigious Bishop Museum (☞ Exploring O'ahu *in* Chapter 2) excavated the ruins of this important Hawaiian archaeological find, including terraces, stone floors, and platforms where 86 houses and 35 shelters once stood. You'll also see petroglyphs, a series of intricate rock carvings that have been preserved in tribute to the once-thriving community. Kaunolū has additional significance because Hawai'i's King Kamehameha I sometimes lived here. ⊠ *From Lāna'i City, follow Hwy. 440 (Mānele Rd.) south; when road makes sharp left, continue straight on Kaupili Rd., which leads you through pineapple fields; turn onto 4th dirt road, in makai direction.*

❷ Lu'ahiwa Petroglyphs. On a steep slope overlooking the Pālāwai Basin, in the flatlands of Lāna'i, are 34 boulders with ancient rock carvings inscribed on them. Drawn in a mixture of ancient and historic styles by the Hawaiians of the early 19th century, the simple stick-figure drawings represent humans, nature, and life on Lāna'i. ⊠ *From Lāna'i City, follow Hwy. 440 (Mānele Rd.) south for 1 mi until you see an unmarked dirt road that leads left through pineapple fields; at end of that road, walk up unmarked trail to petroglyphs.*

❺ Mānele Bay. Flanked by lava cliffs that are hundreds of feet high, Mānele Bay is the only public boat harbor on Lāna'i, and it was the location of most post-contact shipping until Kaumālapa'u Harbor was built in 1926. Today it hosts a regular influx of small boats whose owners are generally from other Neighbor Islands. The ferry to and from Maui also pulls in here. To the right of the harbor are the foundations of some old Hawaiian houses; in fact, this was the site of ancient Hawaiian villages dating back to AD 900.

Just offshore you can catch a glimpse of **Sweetheart Rock.** Called Pu'u Pehe in Hawaiian, the rock is an isolated 50-ft-high formation that carries a sad Hawaiian legend—to make a long story short, a man hid his sweetheart there, and later she drowned. ⊠ *From Lāna'i City, follow Hwy. 440 (Mānele Rd.) south to bottom of hill, and look for harbor on your left.*

North and East Lāna'i

With a ghost town and heiau to its credit, the north and east sections of Lāna'i are wild and untamed. The best way to explore the area's distinctive beauty is by hiking or four-wheel driving, since most of its attractions are accessible only by rugged dirt roads.

A Good Drive

From Lāna'i City, take Keōmuku Highway north. Turn left on the road that runs between the Kō'ele Stables and tennis courts. This leads you

HAWAIIAN MYTHS AND LEGENDS

THE MOST WELL-KNOWN DEITY in Hawaiian lore is Pele, the volcano goddess. Although visitors are warned not to remove lava rocks from Pele's domain without her permission, some do and find themselves dogged by bad luck until they return the stolen items. The Hawai'i Volcanoes National Park Service often receives packages containing chunks of lava along with letters describing years of misfortune.

Tales of Pele's fiery temper are legion. She battled Poli'ahu, ruler of snow-capped Mauna Ke'a on the Big Island, in a fit of jealousy over the snow goddess's extraordinary beauty. She picked fights with her peace-loving sister, Hi'iaka, turning the younger goddess's friends into pillars of stone. And her recurring lava-flinging spats with suitor Kamapua'a, a demigod who could change his appearance at will, finally drove him into the sea where he turned into a fish to escape from her wrath.

But Pele can be kind if the mood suits her. It is said that before every major eruption, she appears in human form as a wrinkled old woman walking along isolated back roads. Those who pass her by find their homes devastated by molten lava. Those who offer her a ride home return home to find a river of boiling magma abruptly halted inches from their property or diverted around their houses. Many hula *hālau* (schools) still make pilgrimages to the rim of Kīlauea—Pele's home—where they honor the fickle goddess with prayers, chants, and offerings of gin and flower leis.

A less volatile but equally intriguing figure in Hawaiian lore is Māui, a demigod who is credited with pulling the Hawaiian Islands up from the bottom of the sea with a magic fishhook, pushing the sky away from the treetops because it had flattened all the leaves, and his most prestigious feat—lassoing the sun as it came up over the top of Haleakalā and demanding that it move more slowly across the sky in summer so that Māui's mother would have longer daylight hours to dry her *kapa* (cloth made from bark).

In addition to battling the elements and each other, gods were thought to have intervened in the daily lives of early Hawaiians. Storms that destroyed homes and crops, a fisherman's poor catch, or a loss in battle were blamed on the wrath of angry gods. And, according to legend, an industrious race of diminutive people called *menehune* built aqueducts, fishponds, and other constructs requiring advanced engineering knowledge unavailable to early Hawaiians. Living in remote hills and valleys, these secretive workers toiled only in darkness and completed complex projects in a single night. Their handiwork can still be seen on all the islands.

Also at night, during certain lunar periods, a traveler might inadvertently come across the Night Marchers—armies of dead warriors, chiefs, and ancestral spirits whose feet never touch the ground as they tread the ancient highways, chanting and beating their drums, and pausing only to claim the spirits of their brethren who died that night. It was believed that such an encounter would mean certain death unless a relative among the marchers pleaded for the victim's life.

The moral? Leave the lava rocks as they are and pick up any elderly hitchikers you might come across. Straightforward enough. But I'd still hightail it in the other direction if I heard mysterious chanting or drum beating.

to a dirt road, which cuts through hay fields for a couple of miles. At the crossroad, turn right. This road heads upward through an ironwood forest and, 1½ mi beyond, to the **Garden of the Gods** ⑦. Red and black lava rocks are scattered across this unique landscape; beyond is a crystal-blue seascape.

Return to Keōmuku Highway, turn left, and drive toward the top of the hill. Make a right onto the only major dirt road in sight, and you're on your way to the **Munro Trail** ⑧, an 8-mi route that runs over the top of Lāna'ihale, the mountain that rises above Lāna'i City.

Keōmuku Highway makes its long descent down Lāna'ihale and then heads north to **Shipwreck Beach** ⑨ (☞ Beaches, *below*), an 8-mi expanse of sand where you can stretch your legs and look for glass balls (used as flotation devices for fishing nets) and other washed-up treasures.

There's more excitement if you feel adventurous. A word of caution: Do not continue unless you have a four-wheel-drive vehicle. The going is rough and often muddy.

From the end of the paved road (Keōmuku Hwy., which dead ends at Shipwreck Beach), head southeast (the opposite direction from Shipwreck Beach) along the very bumpy dirt road. Five miles later you will see dozens of tall coconut trees and an old, run-down church. This is **Keōmuku** ⑩, an abandoned town where 2,000 people once lived.

A mile and a half farther down the road, you can see the ruins of a shrine called **Kahe'a Heiau** ⑪. The road ends 3 mi later at the remnants of an old Hawaiian fishpond at **Naha** ⑫ and the often-deserted Lōpā Beach. To get back to Keōmuku Highway, retrace your route.

TIMING

Give yourself a day to tour the north and east reaches of the island. You can visit all of the following sights any day of the year, but keep your eye on the sky; it's more apt to rain in the highlands than in Lāna'i City. If you're a hiker, you'll want a day just to enjoy the splendors of Lāna'ihale. Bring a jacket; it gets cool up there. A walk along Shipwreck Beach makes a nice morning outing, with stops for shell-collecting, picture-taking, and picnicking.

Since most of the driving is on rugged roads, it takes more time to reach such places as the Garden of the Gods and Keōmuku than it does to actually experience them. Relax; on Lāna'i, getting there is half the fun.

Sights to See

❼ **Garden of the Gods.** This heavily eroded landscape is scattered with boulders of different sizes, shapes, and colors that seem to have been placed here for some divine purpose. Stop and enjoy this inspiring scenery for a while, for its lunar appearance is unmatched in Hawai'i. Anyone who's a geology buff will want to photograph the area, which presents magnificent views of the Pacific Ocean, Moloka'i, and on clear days, O'ahu. Stand quietly and you might spot a deer here. ⊠ *From Kō'ele Stables, follow dirt road that cuts through hay fields; 2 mi later, turn right at crossroads and head through ironwood forest for 1½ mi.*

⓫ **Kahe'a Heiau.** This ancient temple was once a place of worship for the people of Lāna'i. Today you must look hard to find its stone platforms and walls, for they have succumbed to an overgrowth of weeds and bushes. ⊠ *6½ mi southeast from where Keomuku Hwy. dead ends at Shipwreck Beach, on dirt road running along island's north shore.*

⓾ **Keōmuku.** During the late 19th century, this busy Lāna'i community of some 2,000 residents served as the headquarters of the Maunalei Sugar Company. When the sugar company failed, Keōmuku shut down in 1901. For a while the land was used for cattle and sheep ranching, but by 1954 the area was abandoned. You can still go into its ramshackle church, the oldest on the island. There's an eerie beauty about Keōmuku, with its once-stately homes now reduced to weed-infested ruins and crumbling stone walls. There are dozens of tall coconut trees. ⊠ *5 mi along unpaved road southeast of Shipwreck Beach.*

★ ⑧ **Munro Trail.** This 8-mi path winds through a lush tropical rain forest. It was named after George Munro, ranch manager of the Lāna'i Ranch Co., who began a reforestation program in the 1950s. Use caution if it has been raining, as the roads get very muddy.

The trail winds over the top of **Lāna'ihale.** This is the highest point of the island, at 3,370 ft. Its peak delivers spectacular views of nearly all the Hawaiian Islands. From here, you can see 2,000 ft down into Lāna'i's deepest canyon, Hauola Gulch. ⊠ *From Lodge at Kō'ele head north on Keōmuku Hwy. for about 1¼ mi, then turn right onto tree-lined dirt road; trailhead is ½ mi past cemetery on right.*

⑫ **Naha.** An ancient rock-walled fishpond can be seen clearly here at low tide, where the sandy shorelines end and the cliffs begin their rise along the south, west, and north shores of the island. Local fishermen come here to fish, but the treacherous tide and currents make this a dangerous place for swimming. ⊠ *East side of Lāna'i, at end of dirt road that runs from the end of Keomuku Hwy. along the eastern shore.*

★ ⑨ **Shipwreck Beach.** Beachcombers come for its shells and washed-up treasures, photographers love the spectacular view of Moloka'i across the channel, and walkers enjoy ambling along this broad stretch of sand—in all a beach with great allure. It's not for swimmers, however. Have a look at the tanker rusting offshore and you'll see that these are not friendly waters. ⊠ *End of Keōmuku Hwy. heading north.*

BEACHES

Only a few beaches on Lāna'i are worth seeking out, and only one of them has good swimming in protected waters. None has a phone number, so if you need more information, try **Destination Lāna'i** (⊠ Box 700, Lāna'i City 96763, ☎ 808/565–7600) or ask at your hotel desk. The beaches below are listed clockwise from the south.

Hulopo'e Beach. A sparkling crescent, this marine-life conservation area is also Lāna'i's only easily accessed white-sand beach. One of the best beaches in all of Hawai'i, it's an ideal spot for a picnic lunch, a dip in the water, and a nap under the trees. The waves are gentle enough for beginning bodysurfers, and the waters are full of fish that are easily visible to snorkelers. There are no lifeguards. ⊠ *Mānele Rd., south shore of Lāna'i, 10 mi south of Lāna'i City.*

Polihua Beach. Due to its more obscure location and frequent high winds, this beach is often deserted, except for the turtles that nest here. That makes it all the more spectacular, with its long white-sand beach and glorious views of Moloka'i. Because of strong currents, swimming is dangerous here. To find it, you need four-wheel drive—and a map. ⊠ *Northwest shore, 11 mi from Lāna'i City, past Garden of the Gods.*

Shipwreck Beach. A nice beach for walking, but not swimming, Shipwreck is an 8-mi stretch of sand on the Kalohi Channel between Lāna'i and Moloka'i. The beach has no lifeguards, no changing rooms, and no outdoor showers. ⊠ *North shore, 10 mi north of Lāna'i City at end of Keōmuku Hwy.*

DINING

Although Lāna'i's restaurant choices are limited, the menus are wide-ranging. If you dine at the Lodge at Kō'ele or Mānele Bay Hotel, you'll be treated to unique preparations of ingredients harvested or caught locally and served in upscale surroundings. Dining in Lāna'i City is a different story; its restaurants have simple fare, homey atmospheres, and nondescript service. For an explanation of price categories, *see* On the Road with Fodor's in the beginning of the book.

South and West Lāna'i

$$$-$$$$ ✕ **'Ihilani.** The Mānele Bay Hotel's specialty dining room shimmers with crystal and silver and lace-trim tables. The executive chef uses fresh local ingredients to create a cuisine called "Mediterranean French Gourmet." Menus change nightly and include such dishes as sautéed fresh-caught prawns atop local greens, and fillet of sea bass in saffron sauce. There are 14 desserts, including concoctions made from Hawai'i-grown cocoa beans. ⊠ *Mānele Bay Hotel,* ☎ *808/565–7700. Reservations essential. AE, DC, MC, V.* ⊙ *No lunch.*

North and East Lāna'i

$$$-$$$$ ✕ **Formal Dining Room.** Reflecting the elegant country atmosphere of the Lodge at Kō'ele, the hotel's main restaurant has hefty wood beams, gleaming crystal, a roaring fireplace, and hand-stenciled walls. Inventive Island cuisine is created by a chef who works closely with local farmers and fishermen to keep the ingredients fresh. Try the Lāna'i venison carpaccio with shaved reggiano cheese or the smoked salmon with potato salad for an appetizer. Entrées include grilled mahimahi (dolphinfish) with rock shrimp succotash and buttermilk mashed potatoes. ⊠ *Lodge at Kō'ele,* ☎ *808/565–7300. Reservations essential. Jacket required. AE, DC, MC, V.* ⊙ *No lunch.*

$$-$$$ ✕ **Henry Clay's Rotisserie.** Don't overlook this charming, popular spot at the Hotel Lāna'i. You'll find much to choose from, including Cajun-style spit-roasted meats and fish, gourmet pizzas, and salads. Chef Henry Clay Richardson calls his menu "American Country," and spices it up with such fresh local ingredients as axis deer, Hawaiian-caught seafood, and island produce. Late-night snacks are served at the bar. ⊠ *828 Lāna'i Ave.,* ☎ *808/565–7211. AE, MC, V.*

$ ✕ **Blue Ginger Cafe.** This small, no-frills eatery may look run-down, but the menu is diverse. There's even some art on the walls. At breakfast enjoy a three-egg omelet with rice or a big plate of French toast. The only bakery in town, Blue Ginger also has fresh pastries each morning. Lunchtime selections include burgers, chef's salad, pizza, and *saimin* (noodle soup). Try the stir-fry fish for dinner. There are no waiters here: You simply order at the counter and dine with mismatched silverware on Formica tables. ⊠ *409 7th Ave.,* ☎ *808/565–6363. Reservations not accepted. No credit cards.*

$ ✕ **Pele's Other Garden.** Call it a juice bar, a deli, or a pizza parlor. By any name, this white building with the blue trim adds a healthy twist to the Lanai City dining scene, with its mile-high sandwiches, vegetarian dishes, and fresh-baked pastries. The 16-inch whole wheat–crust pizza with four types of cheese, organic tomatoes, and garlic is a great reward after an arduous hike. Though it's cramped, there are two tables if you want to eat inside. It's better to have a seat on the porch or carry out. ⊠ *811 Houston St.,* ☎ *808/565–9628. Reservations not accepted. No credit cards.*

LODGING

In years past the only accommodation on the island was the no-frills Hotel Lāna'i in Lāna'i City. Today you can choose among two classy resorts, pleasant bed-and-breakfasts, and a few house rentals. Let your tastes and your budget determine which place you choose. For an explanation of price categories, *see* On the Road with Fodor's in the beginning of the book.

South and West Lāna'i

$$$$ ⊞ **Mānele Bay Hotel.** Rooms with views of Hulopo'e Bay, the coastline, and the island of Maui attract daydreamers to this elaborate beachfront property. Its design is reminiscent of traditional Hawaiian architecture, with lots of open-air lānai. Three two-story buildings overlook a courtyard; a reception building houses the lobby and specialty boutiques. ⊠ *Box 310, Lāna'i City 96763,* ☎ *808/565–7700 or 800/321–4666,* FAX *808/565–3868. 222 rooms, 28 suites. 3 restaurants, bar, pool, spa, 18-hole golf course, 6 tennis courts, health club, shops. AE, DC, MC, V.*

North and East Lāna'i

$$$$ ⊞ **Captain's Retreat.** Single-room bookings are not available, but split between four couples, this two-story private home turns out to be a reasonably priced lodging alternative. Within walking distance of town, it's the ultimate group getaway, with 3,000 square ft, four bedrooms, a redwood deck, an outside shower, and a roomy kitchen. ⊠ *Okamoto Realty, 730 Lāna'i Ave., Lāna'i City 96763,* ☎ *808/565–7519. No credit cards.*

$$$$
★ ⊞ **Lodge at Kō'ele.** The feeling here—on 21 acres in the highlands on the edge of Lāna'i City—is of a luxurious private mountain retreat: The temperature is cool and the pine trees are plentiful. There's a generous porch with a relaxing view; interiors have high beam ceilings, natural stone fireplaces, and island artwork. More than 1½ mi of pathways wind through the property's orchid gardens and palms. Don't be surprised to see wild turkeys strolling across the back lawn. ⊠ *Box 310, Lāna'i City 96763,* ☎ *808/565–7300 or 800/321–4666,* FAX *808/565–3868. 92 rooms, 10 suites. 2 restaurants, bar, lobby lounge, pool, 18-hole golf course, 3 tennis courts, croquet, exercise room, horseback riding, shops. AE, DC, MC, V.*

$$$ ⊞ **Jasmine Garden.** The Hunters, who run the Dreams Come True B&B (☞ *below*), also rent out a three-bedroom house. In the older section of Lāna'i City, it sleeps six, so three couples can share it for a relatively low price. ⊠ *547 12th St., Lāna'i City 96763,* ☎ *808/565–6961,* FAX *808/565–7056. No credit cards.*

$$–$$$ ⊞ **Hotel Lāna'i.** Built in 1923 to house visiting plantation executives, this quaint 11-room inn was once the only accommodation on the island. Today, even though two luxury hotels may tempt you, you shouldn't overlook this Lāna'i institution. The old front porch with the big wicker chairs has long been a meeting place for residents and locals, who gather to read the paper, order a drink, and "talk story" (chat). The rooms, simple with single or twin beds and flowered wallpaper, make you feel like you're in a great-aunt's country home. ⊠ *Box 520, Lāna'i City 96763,* ☎ *808/565–7211 or 800/795–7211,* FAX *808/565–6450. 11 rooms. Restaurant. CP. AE, MC, V.*

$$ ⊞ **Blue Ginger Bed and Breakfast.** Georgia Abilay of Blue Ginger Cafe (☞ *Dining, above*) fame invites guests into her home, in a newer neighborhood of Lāna'i City. Grounds are landscaped with tropical plants and roses and room decor is modern and light-colored but not distinctive. One of the bedrooms has a double bed, the other has twin beds, and the living room's overstuffed couch converts to a bed. ⊠ *421 Lama St., Lāna'i City 96763,* ☏ *808/565–6363 or 808/565–7016. 2 rooms. Full breakfast. No credit cards.*

$$ 🏠 **Dreams Come True.** Michael and Susan Hunter's bed-and-breakfast in the heart of Lāna'i City has canopy beds, antique furnishings, and memorabilia from their many years in Asia and on Lāna'i. Fresh fruit from their own trees enhances the big morning meal. A trained massage therapist, Susan provides in-house massage for $35 an hour. Vehicle rental is available. ⊠ *547 12th St., Lāna'i City 96763,* ☏ *808/ 565–6961,* ℻ *808/565–7056. 3 rooms, 2 with bath. Full breakfast. No credit cards.*

NIGHTLIFE AND THE ARTS

Locals entertain themselves by gathering on the front porch of the **Hotel Lāna'i** (☏ 808/565–7211) for drinks and conversation. Each evening the classy billiards room at the **Mānele Bay Hotel** (☏ 808/565–7700) attracts a young crowd in search of some friendly competition. The cozy cocktail lounge at the **Lodge at Kō'ele** (☏ 808/565–7300) stays open until 11 PM. The lodge also features music in its Great Hall. Entertainment is offered by Lāna'i residents who share songs, dances, and chants of the island. In addition, there are occasionally outside entertainers in the Music Room.

The 153-seat **Lāna'i Theater and Playhouse** (☏ 808/565–7500), a '30s landmark, presents first-run movies, occasional plays, and special events.

Lāna'i's **Visiting Artist Program** brings world-renowned authors and musicians to the island once a month for free, informal presentations. Past visitors have included humorist Garrison Keillor, author William Styron, and pianist Awadagin Pratt. These events take place at either the Lodge at Kō'ele or Mānele Bay Hotel.

OUTDOOR ACTIVITIES AND SPORTS

Golf

Cavendish Golf Course is a 9-hole course in the pines. Though it's free to the public, a donation for upkeep is requested. Call the Lodge at Kō'ele concierge (☏ 808/565–7300) for information and directions. Bring your own clubs.

The **Challenge at Mānele** is an 18-hole course designed by Jack Nicklaus. ⊠ *Mānele Bay Hotel,* ☏ *808/565–2222 or 800/321–4666.* 🏌 *Greens fee $125 guests of the Lodge at Kō'ele or Mānele Bay Hotel, $175 nonguests, including cart.*

Experience at Kō'ele is an 18-hole championship course designed by Greg Norman, with Ted Robinson as architect. The lodge also has an 18-hole executive putting course, free for guests but not accessible to nonguests.⊠ *Lodge at Kō'ele,* ☏ *808/565–4653.* 🏌 *Greens fee $125 guests, $175 nonguests, including cart.*

Hiking

The most popular Lāna'i hike is the **Munro Trail,** a strenuous 8-mi trek that takes about eight hours. There is an elevation gain of 1,400 ft, leading you to the lookout at Lāna'i's highest point, Lāna'ihale. No permission is necessary to hike this route.

Horseback Riding

The **Stables at Kō'ele** (☏ 808/565–4424) takes you to scenic high-country trails. They have a corral full of well-groomed horses for riders of all ages and skill levels. Rides cost $35 for one hour, $65 for two hours, and $90 for one that includes lunch. Need a lesson? This is your place.

Mountain Biking

Lāna'i City Service (☎ 808/565–7227) rents sturdy mountain bikes for $20 a day. The **Lodge at Kō'ele** (☎ 808/565–7300) rents mountain bikes only to guests of the lodge and of the Mānele Bay Hotel for $8 per hour.

Sporting Clays

Take aim on your target-shooting skills at **Lāna'i Pine Sporting Clays Range,** the only resort course of its kind in Hawai'i. The rustic 14-station course is in a pine-wooded valley overlooking the sea. A single shooter can complete the course in an hour. Cost is $125 for 100 targets and $65 for 50 targets. There's no phone at the sporting clays headquarters. Instead, you may arrange to play the course through the concierge of your hotel.

Water Sports

SCUBA DIVING

Trilogy Ocean Sports (☎ 808/667–7721) offers introductory and one-tank dives. There's a free diving session for novices at the **Mānele Bay Hotel** pool; you can book any of their offerings through the hotel concierge (☎ 808/565–7700). The intro dive costs $130; breakfast, lunch, and gear are included. The one-tank dive costs $120. Scuba diving is also available on Trilogy's daily snorkel/sail (☞ Snorkeling, *below*).

What follows are two dive sites. **Cathedrals,** off the south shore, gets its name from the numerous pinnacles that rise from depths of 60 ft to just below the water's surface. Its spacious caverns create a cathedral effect. In these beautiful chambers live friendly spotted moray eels, lobster, and ghost shrimp. **Sergeant Major Reef,** on the south shore, is made up of three parallel lava ridges, a cave, and an archway, with rippled sand valleys between the ridges. Several large schools of sergeant major fish that live here give the site its name. Depths range from 15 ft to 50 ft. Other nearby sites include Lobster Rock; Menpachi Cave; Grand Canyon; Sharkfin Rock; and Monolith, home to Stretch, a 5-ft-long moray eel.

SNORKELING

Trilogy Ocean Sports (☎ 808/667–7721) presents a daily five-hour morning snorkel/sail on a 51-ft sailing catamaran for $85. Continental breakfast, lessons, equipment, and lunch are included. You can make arrangements with the concierge at the Mānele Bay Hotel (☎ 808/565–7700). The boat leaves at 9 AM.

Hulopo'e Beach is one of the most outstanding snorkeling destinations in all of Hawai'i. It attracts brilliantly colored fish to its protected cove, in which you can also marvel at underwater coral and lava formations. Ask your hotel's concierge about renting equipment.

SHOPPING

Except for the boutiques at the Lodge at Kō'ele and Mānele Bay Hotel, Lāna'i City is the island's only place to buy what you need. Its main streets, 7th and 8th avenues, have a small scattering of shops straight out of the '20s. In the most literal sense, the main businesses in town are what you would call general stores. They do offer personal service and congenial charm.

Stores open their doors Monday through Saturday between 8 and 9 and close between 5 and 6. Some shops are closed on Sunday and between noon and 1:30 on weekdays.

General Stores

You can get everything from cosmetics to canned vegetables at **Pine Isle Market** (⊠ 356 8th Ave., ☎ 808/565–6488), one of Lāna‘i City's two supermarkets. It's a great place to buy fresh fish.

In 1946, Richard Tamashiro founded **Richard's Shopping Center** (⊠ 434 8th Ave., ☎ 808/565–6047), and the Tamashiro clan continues to run the place. Along with groceries, the store has a fun selection of Lāna‘i T-shirts, which make great souvenirs.

You may not find everything the name implies at **International Food and Clothing Center** (⊠ 833 ‘Ilima Ave., ☎ 808/565–6433). However, this old-fashioned emporium, founded in 1952, does stock many items for your everyday needs.

Lāna‘i City Service (⊠ 1036 Lāna‘i Ave., ☎ 808/565–7227) is more than a gas station and car-rental operation. It also sells microwave pizzas and burritos, sodas, sundries, paperbacks, T-shirts, and island crafts. It even rents cellular phones.

Specialty Stores

Crafts

Akamai Trading & Gifts (⊠ 408 8th Ave., ☎ 808/565–6587) sells such unique Lāna‘i crafts as pine-tree bowls and flower-dyed gourds alongside its Lāna‘i posters, T-shirts, and tropical jellies and jams.

At **Heart of Lāna‘i** (⊠ 363 7th Ave., ☎ 808/565–6678) you'll find local crafts like Norfolk pine bowls, fiber-woven mats, quilts, and jewelry.

Lāna‘i Art Studio (⊠ 339 7th Ave., ☎ 808/565–7503) is the home of the Lāna‘i Art Program, which offers art classes to residents and visitors. Its gift shop sells unique Lāna‘i handicrafts, from painted silk scarves to beaded jewelry.

Hotel Shops

The **Lodge at Kō‘ele** (☎ 808/565–7300) and **Mānele Bay Hotel** (☎ 808/565–7700) have sundries shops that are handy for guests who need to stock up on suntan lotion, aspirin, and other vacation necessities. They also carry classy logo wear, resort clothing, books, and jewelry.

LĀNA‘I A TO Z

Arriving and Departing

By Plane

The small **Lāna‘i Airport** (☎ 808/565–6757) is centrally located in the southwest area of the island. There's a gift shop, food concession, plenty of parking, and a federal agricultural inspection station so that departing guests can check luggage directly to the mainland.

In order to reach Lāna‘i from the mainland United States, you must first stop at O‘ahu's Honolulu International Airport; from there it takes about a half hour to fly to Lāna‘i. **Hawaiian Airlines** (☎ 800/367–5320) offers two round-trip flights daily between Honolulu and Lāna‘i. A round-trip on one of its DC-9 jets costs $162. **Island Air** (☎ 800/323–3345) has 12 round-trip flights daily on its 18-passenger Twin Otters and its Dornier 228s, at a cost of $164.

BETWEEN THE AIRPORT AND HOTELS

Lāna‘i Airport is a 10-minute drive from Lāna‘i City. If you're staying at the Hotel Lāna‘i, the Lodge at Kō‘ele, or the Mānele Bay Hotel, you will be met by a complimentary shuttle. Don't expect to see any public buses at the airport, because there aren't any on the island.

By Car. There is a distinct advantage to renting your own vehicle on Lāna'i: Public transportation is virtually nonexistent and attractions are far apart. Make your car- or four-wheel-drive-rental reservation way in advance of your trip, because Lāna'i is small and its fleet of vehicles limited (☞ Car and Four-Wheel-Drive Rentals, *below*).

By Taxi. Taxi transfers between Lāna'i City and the airport are handled by **Lāna'i City Service** (☎ 808/565–7227 or 800/533–7808). One-way charges are $5 per person.

Getting Around

Private transportation is advised on Lāna'i, unless you plan to stay in one place during your entire visit. Avoid that urge, because the island has natural splendors from one end to the other.

By Bike
☞ Mountain Biking *in* Outdoor Activities and Sports, *above*.

By Car
Driving around Lāna'i isn't as easy as on other islands—most roads aren't marked. But renting a car can be fun (☞ Car and Four-Wheel-Drive Rentals, *below*). From town, the streets extend outward as paved roads with two-way traffic. Keōmuku Highway runs north to Shipwreck Beach, while Highway 440 leads south down to Mānele Bay and Hulopo'e Beach and west to Kaumālapa'u Harbor. The rest of your driving takes place on bumpy and muddy dirt roads, best navigated by a four-wheel-drive vehicle or van.

The island doesn't have traffic lights, and you'll never find yourself in a traffic jam. However, heed these words of caution: before heading out on your explorations, ask at your hotel desk for a road and site map, and ask them to confirm that you're headed in the right direction. Some of the major attractions don't have signs, and it's easy to get lost.

By Moped
Lāna'i City Service (☎ 808/565–7227 or 800/533–7808) will set you up with a moped for $30 a day. Pay $5 extra and they'll give you lunch to take along on your explorations.

By Taxi
It costs about $5 per person for a cab ride from Lāna'i City to almost any point on the paved roads of the island. Call **Lāna'i City Service** (☎ 808/565–7227 or 800/533–7808).

Contacts and Resources

Car and Four-Wheel-Drive Rentals
Two companies on Lāna'i rent vehicles to visitors. **Lāna'i City Service** (✉ Box N, Lāna'i City, ☎ 808/565–7227 or 800/533–7808) is the Dollar Rent-a-Car affiliate on the island. You'll pay $60 a day for a compact car, from $129 a day for a seven-passenger minivan, and from $119 to $129 a day for a four-wheel-drive Jeep Wrangler. The company offers complimentary airport pickup and drop-off.

Red Rover (✉ Lāna'i Ave. at 15th St., Lāna'i City, ☎ 808/565–7722) specializes in Land Rovers. Their fleet ranges from a two-passenger softtop for $139 a day to a nine-person African safari vehicle for $159 a day. You get a CB radio for emergencies, and cell phones and cassette tapes are available. Snorkeling masks, fins, and boogeyboards are gratis, and a staff member will meet you at the airport with your vehicle.

Emergencies

Police, fire, or **ambulance** (☎ 911).

HOSPITAL

The **Lāna'i Community Hospital** (✉ 628 7th Ave., Lāna'i City, ☎ 808/
565–6411) is the health-care center for the island. It has 24-hour ambulance service and a pharmacy.

Guided Tours

HIKING TOURS

A trained docent from the **Nature Conservancy of Hawai'i** (☎ 808/
537–4508) leads a free hike once a month through Kānepu'u, a 590-
acre preserve northwest of Lāna'i City, on the island's western plateau.
Kānepu'u contains the state's largest remnant of native dryland forest,
hosting 48 plant species unique to Hawai'i, such as *'iliahi* (sandalwood).
Call for reservations. You can also go on a self-guided hike here by
following the interpretive signs.

HORSE-DRAWN CARRIAGE TOURS

For an old-fashioned way to tour the town, take a horse-drawn carriage ride around Lāna'i City courtesy of the **Stables at Kō'ele** (☎ 808/
565–4424). A one-hour ride costs $75 for two people.

OFF-ROAD TOURS

Many sites are accessible only from the island's unpaved back roads.
On a tour you can leave the navigation to a driver, while you simply
hang on and enjoy the ride in a Geo Tracker. Along the way you will
see petroglyphs, the Garden of the Gods, Shipwreck Beach, and the
Munro Trail. Tours are about five hours long, require a minimum of
four people, and cost $80 per person. **Lāna'i City Service** (☎ 808/565–
7227 or 800/533–7808) offers such tours throughout the week.

PROPERTY TOURS

Tours of the island's two major hotels are free and open to the public. **Mānele Bay Hotel** (☎ 808/565–7700) offers daily free one-hour
tours of the hotels and grounds. Check with the concierge desk for a
Lodge at Kō'ele tour (☎ 808/565–7300).

Visitor Information

You can write ahead of time to **Destination Lāna'i** (✉ Box 700, Lāna'i
City 96763, ☎ 808/565–7600) for brochures and maps; the office is
not open to visitors. The **Maui Visitors Bureau** (✉ 1727 Wili Pa Loop,
Wailuku, Maui 96793, ☎ 808/244–3530, FAX 808/244–1337) has information about Lāna'i as well as Maui.

Once on the island, the information desks of two major hotels—the
Lodge at Kō'ele and the Mānele Bay Hotel—are useful sources for guests
of those properties.

9 Portraits of Maui

Heavenly Hana! Greener than Eden!
Watered and warmed by our God above!
What shall we grow here?
What shall we show here?
The trees of Truth, Faith,
Hope and Love.*

Second verse of the "Hanna Hymn," as translated from the Hawaiian

HAWAIIAN HISTORY AT A GLANCE: A CHRONOLOGY

ca. AD 800　The first human beings to set foot on Hawaiian shores are Polynesians, who travel 2,000 miles in 60- to 80-ft canoes to the islands they name *Havaiki* after their legendary homeland. Researchers today believe they were originally from Southeast Asia, and that they discovered the South Pacific Islands of Tahiti and the Marquesas before ending up in Hawai'i.

ca. 1758　Kamehameha, the Hawaiian chief who unified the Islands, is born.

1778　In January, British Captain James Cook, commander of the HMS *Resolution* and the consort vessel HMS *Discovery,* lands on the island of Kaua'i and "discovers" it for the Western world. He names the archipelago the Sandwich Islands after his patron, the Earl of Sandwich. In November, he returns to the Islands for the winter, anchoring at Kealakekua Bay on the Big Island.

1779　In February, Cook is killed in a battle with Hawai'i's indigenous people at Kealakekua.

1785　The isolation of the Islands ends as British, American, French, and Russian fur traders and New England whalers come to Hawai'i. Tales spread of thousands of acres of sugarcane growing wild, and farmers come in droves from the United States and Europe.

1790　Kamehameha begins his rise to power through a series of bloody battles to unify the Islands of Hawai'i.

1791　Kamehameha builds Pu'ukoholā *Heiau* (temple) and dedicates it by sacrificing a rival chief.

1795　Using Western arms, Kamehameha fights a decisive campaign on O'ahu to unite the Islands. Except for Kaui'a (which he tries to invade in 1796 and 1804) this completes his military conquest of the Islands.

1810　The chief of Kaua'i acknowledges Kamehameha's rule, giving him suzerainty over Kaua'i and Ni'ihau and uniting the Islands under one chief. Kamehameha becomes known as King Kamehameha I, and he rules the unified Kingdom of Hawai'i with an iron hand.

1819　Kamehameha I dies, and his eldest son, Liholiho, becomes Kamehameha II, beginning his short reign with Ka'ahumanu, Kamehameha I's favorite wife, as co-executive. Ka'ahumanu persuades the new king to abandon old religious taboos, including those that forbade women to eat with men or to hold positions of power. The first whaling ships land at Lahaina on Maui.

1820　By the time the first missionaries arrive from Boston, Hawai'i's social order is beginning to break down. First, Ka'ahumanu and then Kamehameha II defy *kapu* (taboo) after kapu without attracting divine retribution. Hawaiians, disillusioned with their own gods, are receptive to the ideas of Christianity. The influx of Western culture also introduces Hawai'i to Western disease, liquor, and what some view as moral decay.

1824　King Kamehameha II and his favorite wife die of measles during a visit to England. Honolulu missionaries gave both royals a Christian burial outside Kawaiaha'o Church, inspiring many Hawaiians to convert to the Protestant faith. His younger brother, Kau'ikea'ouli, becomes King Kamehameha III, a wise and gentle sovereign who reigns for 30 years with Ka'ahumanu as regent.

1832 Ka'ahumanu is baptized and dies a few months later.

1840 The Wilkes Expedition, sponsored by the U.S. Coast and Geodetic Survey, pinpoints Pearl Harbor as a potential Naval Base.

1845 Kamehameha III and the legislature move Hawai'i's seat of government from Lahaina, on Maui, to Honolulu, on O'ahu.

1849 Kamehameha III turns Hawai'i into a constitutional monarchy and wins official recognition of Hawai'i as an independent country by the United States, France, and Great Britain.

1850 The Great Mahele, a land commission, reapportions land among crown, government, chiefs, and commoners, thus introducing for the first time the Western principle of private ownership. Commoners now were able to buy and sell land, but this great division becomes the great dispossession: By the end of the 19th century white men owned four acres for every one owned by a native. Even today, current land disputes originate from this division of property.

1852 As Western diseases depopulate the Islands, a labor shortage occurs in the sugarcane fields. For the next nine decades, a steady stream of foreign labor pours into Hawai'i, beginning with the Chinese. The Japanese begin arriving in 1868, followed by Filipinos, Koreans, Portuguese, and Puerto Ricans.

1872 Kamehameha V dies without heirs, ending the direct descendants of the first king. A power struggle ensues between the adherents of David Kalākaua and William Lunalilo.

1873 Lunalilo is elected Hawai'i's sixth king in January. The bachelor rules only 13 months before dying of tuberculosis.

1874 Kalākaua vies for the throne with the Dowager Queen Emma, half-Caucasian widow of Kamehameha IV. Kalākaua is elected by the Hawai'i Legislature, against protests by supporters of Queen Emma. American and British marines are called in to restore order, and Kalākaua begins his reign as the "Merrie Monarch."

1875 The United States and Hawai'i sign a treaty of reciprocity assuring Hawai'i a duty-free market for sugar in the United States.

1882 King Kalākaua builds 'Iolani Palace, an Italian Renaissance–style structure, on the site of the previous royal palace.

1887 The reciprocity treaty of 1875 is renewed, giving the United States the exclusive use of Pearl Harbor as a coaling station. Coincidentally, successful importation of Japanese laborers begins in earnest (after a false start in 1868).

1891 King Kalākaua dies and is succeeded by his sister, Queen Lili'uokalani, the last monarch of Hawai'i.

1893 After reigning only two years, Lili'uokalani is removed from the throne by American business interests led by Lorrin A. Thurston (grandson of missionary and newspaper founder Asa Thurston). Lili'uokalani is imprisoned in 'Iolani Palace for nearly eight months.

1894 The provisional government converts Hawai'i into a republic and proclaims Sanford Dole president.

1898 The outbreak of the Spanish-American War and Hawai'i's strategic military importance in the Pacific lead the next U.S. president, William McKinley, to move toward Hawai'i's annexation. On August 12, Hawai'i is officially annexed by a joint resolution of Congress.

1901   Sanford Dole is appointed first governor of the territory of Hawai'i.
The first major tourist hotel, the Moana (now called the Sheraton
Moana Surfrider), is built on Waikīkī Beach.

1903   James Dole (a cousin of Sanford Dole) produces nearly 2,000 cases
of pineapple, marking the beginning of Hawai'i's pineapple
industry. Pineapple eventually surpasses sugar as Hawai'i's number-
one crop.

1907   Fort Shafter Base, headquarters for the U.S. Army, becomes the first
permanent military post in the Islands.

1908   Dredging of the channel at Pearl Harbor begins.

1919   Pearl Harbor is formally dedicated by the U.S. Navy. Prince Jonah
Kūhiō Kalaniana'ole (the adopted son of Kalākaua's wife,
Kapi'olani, and with his brother an heir designated by the childless
Lili'uokalani to her throne), representing the Territory of Hawai'i in
the U.S. House of Representatives, introduces the first bill proposing
statehood for Hawai'i.

1927   Army Lieutenants Lester Maitland and Albert Hegenberger make
the first successful nonstop flight from the mainland to the Islands.
Hawai'i begins to increase efforts to promote tourism, the industry
that eventually dominates development of the Islands. The Matson
Navigation Company builds the Royal Hawaiian Hotel as a
destination for its cruise ships.

1929   Hawai'i's commercial interisland air service begins.

1936   Pan American World Airways makes history as the first to start
regular commercial passenger flights to Hawai'i from the mainland.

1941   Pearl Harbor becomes a tragic part of U.S. history when the U.S.
Pacific Fleet is attacked by the Japanese, causing the U.S. to enter
World War II. Nearly 4,000 casualties result from the surprise
attack.

1942   James Jones, with thousands of others, trains at Schofield Barracks
on O'ahu. He later writes about his experience in *From Here to
Eternity*.

1959   Congress passes legislation granting Hawai'i statehood. In special
elections the new state sends to the U.S. House of Representatives its
first American of Japanese ancestry, Daniel Inouye, and to the U.S.
Senate its first American of Chinese ancestry, Hiram Fong. Later in
the year, the first Boeing 707 jets make the flight from San Francisco
in a record five hours. By year's end 243,216 tourists visit Hawai'i,
and tourism becomes Hawai'i's major industry. Today the Islands
draw more than 6 million visitors a year.

1986   Hawai'i elects its first native Hawaiian governor, John Waihe'e.

1993   After Native Hawaiians commemorate the 100th anniversary of the
overthrow of Queen Lili'uokalani with a call for sovereignty,
Congress issues an apology to the Hawaiian people for the
annexation of the Islands.

HIGHWAY TO HANA

THE ROAD TO HANA is paved, I was told, with rude inventions. For starters, its 44 spine-tingling miles were said to contain 56 one-lane bridges—guaranteed to elevate adrenaline to levels associated with such activities as gladiatorial combat—along with precisely 617 whirligig curves, several stretches of one-way traffic, innumerable potholes, much evidence of recent washouts, a few crumbled cliffsides, and significant numbers of pinprick-pupiled tourists whose fingers would have to be removed surgically from the steering wheels of their rental cars.

This run of fabled highway along Maui's wild, windward, sparsely populated, and stunningly scenic northeast coast seemed to have been the scene of countless cases of cracked nerves and hair-raising mishaps, dreadful weather, and backed-up traffic. "I just *hate* that drive," said the waitress at Mama's Fish House outside Paia (usually cited as the beginning point for the journey) as she cleaned up the remains of my *ahi* sandwich just before I hit the road. "Something *always* happens."

I knew better. During three previous trips on the Hana Highway nothing particularly untoward had occurred, except a bit of hesitant traffic and some light rain, along with plenty of gorgeous scenery. And travel time was well below the 2½-hour minimum quoted to timid tourists. On the last run, in fact, I had established a personal best of less than 1½ hours from Hana to Paia—in an open Jeep, to boot. Sure, occasional mists descended to dampen my baseball cap, tires sometimes squealed around some of the more serious switchbacks, and a backseat passenger emerged at the end dazed and hobbling but grinning happily.

The mostly two-lane road—ancient footpaths widened by convict gangs in 1926, paved in 1962 and upgraded into passable shape for normal traffic only in 1982—is in fairly good shape. But all that weather and those winter washouts tend to age the road quickly in its more vulnerable spots,

so don't expect smooth sailing for the entire length. The two slowest stretches have many places where 10 mph is the norm, and careful drivers inch around the hairpins much more slowly than that.

But what a small price to pay for such a spectacular journey—through rain forest and jungle, past streams and waterfalls, with postcard vistas of windswept peninsulas, deep bays, and green valleys. Tiny villages, each centered by a steepled church, pop up unexpectedly in the midst of all this natural grandeur. The sprinkling of people, most with a high percentage of Polynesian blood, live simply, farming taro, bananas, and other crops. It's not hard to see why this part of Maui is called the true Hawaii, away from any sign of tourism or commerce.

Easily distracted from missions of most sorts, I made it only a couple of miles past Mama's to Hookipa Beach Park, situated on a windy bluff overlooking the most famous wind-surfing waters in the world. Usually, one quick look at the scores of boards with brightly colored sails skipping through and flipping over the churning waves is fortifying enough to make the most harrowing drive seem dull and uneventful. Not today, though. It was so rough and windy that even the notoriously devil-may-care windsurfers had furled their sails and slunk back to the saloons of Paia. No matter. Hana, ho.

The drive was actually fun as well as beautiful, and the one-way bridges over steep gullies were welcome opportunities to slow and even pause to gaze at the rain forest and stream-fed waterfalls. The wonder of Hawaii's renowned microclimates becomes gradually evident as the drive unfolds from rolling pastureland to jungled cliffs sliced by narrow valleys and then level tropical upland.

The modest tongue of flatland that is the Keanae Peninsula materializes suddenly, its simple weathered church and taro patches a shock after miles of rain forest. Just beyond, spread far below the road, is the community of Wailua, its white-steeple church boldly visible from the great distance. Then the jungle closes in to swallow a road that once more plunges in cramped surrender. During previous drives I had been fascinated by a tree whose spade-shape leaves shimmered so filmily from above that the jungle below appeared like a sea of glistening white. I stopped to follow a stream a short distance until I found one of those trees and picked a leaf. A gardener at the Hotel Hana-Maui later identified it as from the Kukui tree—one of the few native trees able to compete with such imported varieties as guava, mango, eucalyptus, and bamboo that now dominate the forest. Even the wild white and torch ginger that bloom along the roadside are imports.

Toward the end, just a few miles outside Hana and giddy with the pleasant vertigo of it all, I began drifting into some other road-warrior dimension. Here as the highway begins to untwist, drivers are lulled into thinking they can relax, but another series of one-lane bridges appears. By then I was making up stories for each bridge, at one noting mynah birds standing guard "like tiny Horatios." Ninety minutes after stopping at Hookipa to look for windsurfers, the drive was over.

I thought that was *hauling* until Clyde Min, who manages the Hotel Hana-Maui, casually mentioned that his best-ever time was at night after dinner at Mama's. No traffic. No sightseeing. And all in 50 minutes flat. He swears.

— Richard J. Pietschmann

Freelance writer Richard J. Pietschmann contributes regularly to many national publications, including *Travel Holiday* and *Outside* magazines. A Los Angeles resident, he is also the West Coast and Mexico editor of *Departures* magazine.

HEAVENLY HANA

HYMNS SUNG IN Hawaiian filter from two nearby churches through fragrant butter-yellow and magenta plumeria blossoms. I slump in the slanting morning sunlight on my lanai at the Hotel Hana-Maui, dissipating my morning torpor with a cup of Kona's finest, made moments ago in my plantation-posh room. Silent thanks are offered to the management for supplying whole coffee beans, a machine to grind them and another to brew them. Such welcome surprises in such a removed, ethereal place.

It is odd but fascinating to hear familiar hymns transmuted into Polynesian dialect, and I actually heave myself up in curiosity and stumble with cup in hand across the hotel's broad central lawn to squint through an archway at the 150-year-old Wananalua Congregational Church. The singing swells dramatically through the old church's open doors and then fades into the rustle of palm fronds and the faint slapping of swells against a rocky shoreline. Not even the shrill cry of an annoyed mynah can break the reflective spell.

As the hymn ends I head back to my lanai, mostly awake but lost in the kind of dreamy contemplation that Hana often induces. I had read that the church's walls, 2½ feet thick at the base, were constructed in 1842 by local volunteers directed by a Yankee *kahu* (shepherd or pastor), the Rev. Daniel Conde. The walls were built of volcanic stone, much of it scavenged from the ruins of the many ancient and highly sacred *heiaus* (shrines or temples) dotting this once heavily populated coastline. The mortar was made from coral brought up from depths of two or three fathoms by pure-blooded Hawaiians diving from ancestral canoes.

The church, like everything else along this storied eastern coast, is interwoven with the legends, history, and people of the remote, rainy area. The way things interconnect here is frequently so eerie that the strains of the *Twilight Zone* theme begin playing unbidden in the back of your mind. A heightened sense of the physical and the spiritual binds the inhabitants of this extraordinary place into a dedicated community of protectors of its legend, superstition, and beauty.

Even the Hotel Hana-Maui, first opened in 1946 (and ever since the sophisticated centerpiece of this otherwise rural area) is inexorably intertwined with the community. Along with the surrounding 4,500-acre Hana Ranch, it was rescued from decrepitude in 1984 by Texas oil heiress Caroline Rose Hunt's Rosewood Corporation. It is certainly one of the most casually luxurious—and expensive—hotels in Hawaii.

Guests have been surprised that the hotel is set in the midst of the modest town of Hana rather than plunked on some pristine beach, as its cachet and price might suggest. Traffic from the one main road chugs by just feet from many of the rooms, and the most expensive accommodations in the Sea Ranch Cottages are a considerable stroll away, across another well-used public road. The community tennis courts and ball field lie adjacent, a lob away between Hana Bay and the hotel. This is no remote hideaway, at least not in the Robinson Crusoe sense.

Visitors to Hana have little choice, for example, but to join the estimated 1,500 sightseers who come daily in rental cars or on van tours to rubberneck through town, pause for lunch, lurch out to see the Seven Pools of Oheo Gulch, perhaps search futilely for Lindbergh's grave in Kipahulu and then turn around for the long drive back. If they want to stay overnight, alternatives to the Hotel Hana-Maui are the decidedly funky little Heavenly Hana Inn, the nice but few condo units of the Hana Kai-Maui Resort, or one of the private houses that can be booked through Hana Bay Vacation Rentals. Added together, there are only about 100 rooms for rent at Hana.

It rains a lot here: in the average year, 70 to 100 inches, and more than that just up the slope of 2-mi-high Haleakala, whose largely unseen bulk looms over the rugged coastline its eruptions created. All of Hawaii's islands have a wet and a dry side, created by the convergence of steady trade winds and high mountains. On Maui, resort areas like Kaanapali Beach are on the arid leeward coasts, which have better beaches and a reliably sunny climate. Not so with lush, green Hana. The rain comes year-round, though much of it falls at night and in the early morning, and the most popular months of December and January, along with November, February, and March, are the rainiest of all. Then it comes at any time and in frequent downpours, causing visitors to seek indoor entertainment that largely does not exist here. Scenic drives, beach barbecues, horseback rides, hiking, jogging, bicycling and the other normally wonderful outdoor diversions popular at Hana do not tend to be successful in wet weather. And the limited undercover activities, such as a visit to the Hana Cultural Center, seem to use up minutes instead of hours. The Hotel Hana-Maui has a well-stocked library but no television or radio in the rooms.

BUT, OF COURSE, unending activity and utter comfort are not the things that have made Hana so alluring for so long to so many different people. Ex-Beatle George Harrison, Jim Nabors, and other celebrities chose to live part-time in the Hana area because of the seclusion and the deep sense of physical and spiritual wonder. At Henry Kahula's Chevron station the windows are signed in grease pencil by entertainers like Kris Kristofferson and Steve Forrest.

The real Hana takes a while to work its peculiar magic on visitors. It is in the air all around, in this place where cultures gracefully glance off one another and legends mix as freely with facts as the broad-faced Hawaiians intermingle with the town's anachronistic contingent of backwoods hippies. One moment you will see two Hawaiians peacefully lounging in a pickup truck parked at the end of the old sugarcane-loading wharf that juts into Hana Bay quietly smoking *pakalolo* (marijuana), and the next, there is a placid blond, barefoot haole padding happily along Hana Highway as calves packed against a fence moo and eye her curiously. It is the sort of place where the Bank of Hawaii—the only bank—opens for 1½ hours every weekday except Friday (clearly the big day of the week), when it's open for three hours.

Sitting in the hotel's airy dining room eating banana waffles with ginger syrup—a breakfast as trendily correct as it is jarring and unlikely in such a determinedly retro place—my gaze rises from the torch ginger in the gardens to the modest mound of Kauiki Hill standing at one arm of Hana Bay. Clouds brush over the low ironwood-covered cinder cone, stirring up stories from the past.

In legend, it was here that the lovers Kauiki and Noenoe were forever united by the demigod Maui, who changed them into a hill and the mist that clings to it. In reality, it was the birthplace in 1768 of Queen Kaahumanu, Kamehameha the Great's favorite wife and later the regent, who turned Hawaii away from the past by fostering the breaking of the old *kapus* (taboos) and converting to Christianity. And it was around this ancient natural fortress that bloody battles raged for control of the coveted region.

Hana has always been cherished and important. Before the arrival of the first European ships offshore in the mid-1700s, Hana's rich agricultural lowland and forested upper reaches supported an estimated 45,000 to 75,000 people. The population had dropped to about 11,000 by 1831, and despite the importation of contract labor from China, Japan, and other countries during the sugarcane boom that started in 1864, it's dwindled steadily ever since. In the 1930s, when the plantations began to close and various agricultural experiments failed, people began leaving at an even greater rate. A stabilized population of about a thousand people occupies the district today, many of predominantly Hawaiian blood, others bliss-seeking haole or the descendants of Chinese, Japanese, and Portuguese workers.

In Hana, the issues of growth and tourism are as hotly debated and uses of the land are as fiercely contested as when armies fought over it in past centuries. Isolation and attitude discourage development and, sometimes, even curiosity here. Residents are fiercely protective of the land, chary of change. They will not hear of plans to expand the tiny airport so it can accommodate jets.

In this place of almost-mesmerizing tranquillity, the most peaceful, serene spot touched by man must be Palapala Hoomau Congregational Church, a place I find purely by instinct and have visited four times without encountering another human being. You drive out past Hana about 10 miles on a road far worse and more tortuous than the serpentine highway to the town, past the place called Seven Pools that is the terminus of most day tours, past the scattered ramshackle and grand houses of Kipahulu, past tiny St. Paul's Church and, on the right, the nearly hidden massive chimney of a ruined sugar mill.

Just past the mill, on the left side of the road, is a pasture and then a galvanized-steel gate swung permanently open on a rutted track that heads toward the sea. The road goes to the Palapala Hoomau Congregational Church, a few hundred yards away, mostly hidden behind thick vegetation. There is no sign on the road and nothing at all to indicate that anything lies down this country lane, but unlike the other gates in the area this one has no "kapu," or "keep out," sign. Founded in 1857 and built in 1864, the simple one-room church sits on a bluff over the sea, with a small graveyard on the ocean side.

It is a place of such healing aura and calming silence that the temptation is overwhelming to linger, to sit in the quiet, musty church reading the program from the last service—the call to worship, doxology, and three hymns in Hawaiian—and then to stroll around the grounds. It is small wonder that Charles A. Lindbergh loved it so that he wanted his grave here. There it is, dated 1974, with three tiny American flags planted in the soil. Almost no one ever finds it.

At dusk on the way back to Hana, just after passing a grinning Hawaiian with his handsome small son, and driving cautiously along the bad road, I glanced up to see a small snow-white owl perched on a wire, gazing down at me. It was a *pueokea,* the rarely seen and endangered Hawaiian owl, a sighting some locals later told me was fraught with good fortune, for it is a blessing promising a safe journey. Minutes later I saw a second, also curiously watching me. This, I was told, was almost unprecedented. I was regarded with new respect in Hana. I might be home.

— Richard J. Pietschmann

THE HOUSE OF THE SUN

THERE ARE HOSTS of people who journey like restless spirits round and about this earth in search of seascapes and landscapes and the wonders and beauties of nature. They overrun Europe in armies; they can be met in droves and herds in Florida and the West Indies, at the pyramids, and on the slopes and summits of the Canadian and American Rockies; but in the House of the Sun they are as rare as live and wriggling dinosaurs. Haleakala is the Hawaiian name for "the House of the Sun." It is a noble dwelling situated on the island of Maui; but so few tourists have ever peeped into it, much less entered it, that their number may be practically reckoned as zero. Yet I venture to state that for natural beauty and wonder the nature lover may see dissimilar things as great as Haleakala, but no greater, while he will never see elsewhere anything more beautiful or wonderful. Honolulu is six days' steaming from San Francisco; Maui is a night's run on the steamer from Honolulu, and six hours more, if he is in a hurry, can bring the traveler to Kolikoli, which is 10,032 feet above the sea and which stands hard by the entrance portal to the House of the Sun. Yet the tourist comes not, and Haleakala sleeps on in lonely and unseen grandeur.

Not being tourists, we of the *Snark* went to Haleakala. On the slopes of that monster mountain there is a cattle ranch of some 50,000 acres, where we spent the night at an altitude of 2,000 feet. The next morning it was boots and saddles, and with cowboys and pack horses we climbed to Ukulele, a mountain ranch house, the altitude of which, 5,500 feet, gives a severely temperate climate, compelling blankets at night and a roaring fireplace in the living room. Ukulele, by the way, is the Hawaiian for "jumping flea," as it is also the Hawaiian for a certain musical instrument that may be likened to a young guitar. It is my opinion that the mountain ranch house was named after the young guitar.

We were not in a hurry, and we spent the day at Ukulele, learnedly discussing altitudes and barometers and shaking our particular barometer whenever anyone's argument stood in need of demonstration. Our barometer was the most graciously acquiescent instrument I have ever seen. Also, we gathered mountain raspberries, large as hen's eggs and larger, gazed up the pasture-covered lava slopes to the summit of Haleakala, 4,500 feet above us, and looked down upon a mighty battle of the clouds that was being fought beneath us, ourselves in the bright sunshine.

Every day and every day this unending battle goes on. Ukiukiu is the name of the trade wind that comes raging down out of the northeast and hurls itself upon Haleakala. Now Haleakala is so bulky and tall that it turns the northeast trade wind aside on either hand, so that in the lee of Haleakala no trade wind blows at all. On the contrary, the wind blows in the counter direction, in the teeth of the northeast trade. This wind is called Naulu. And day and night and always Ukiukiu and Naulu strive with each other, advancing, retreating, flanking, curving, curling, and turning and twisting, the conflict made visible by the cloud masses plucked from the heavens and hurled back and forth in squadrons, battalions, armies, and great mountain ranges. Once in a while, Ukiukiu, in mighty gusts, flings immense cloud masses clear over the summit of Haleakala; whereupon Naulu craftily captures them, lines them up in new battle formation, and with them smites back at his ancient and eternal antagonist. Then Ukiukiu sends a great cloud army around the eastern side of the mountain. It is a flanking movement, well executed. But Naulu, from his lair on the leeward side, gathers the flanking army in, pulling and twisting and dragging it, hammering it into shape, and sends it charging back against Ukiukiu around the western side of the mountain. And all the while, above and below the main battlefield, high up the slopes toward the sea,

---

Although it was written in the early 20th century, before Haleakalā became a popular tourist attraction, Jack London's account of camping among the crater's cinder cones is still fascinating to read today.

Ukiukiu and Naulu are continually sending out little wisps of cloud, in ragged skirmish line, that creep and crawl over the ground, among the trees and through the canyons, and that spring upon and capture one another in sudden ambuscades and sorties. And sometimes Ukiukiu or Naulu, abruptly sending out a heavy charging column, captures the ragged little skirmishers or drives them skyward, turning over and over, in vertical whirls, thousands of feet in the air.

BUT IT IS ON the western slopes of Haleakala that the main battle goes on. Here Naulu masses his heaviest formation and wins his greatest victories. Ukiukiu grows weak toward late afternoon, which is the way of all trade winds, and is driven backward by Naulu. Naulu's generalship is excellent. All day he has been gathering and packing away immense reserves. As the afternoon draws on, he welds them into a solid column, sharp-pointed, miles in length, a mile in width, and hundreds of feet thick. This column he slowly thrusts forward into the broad battle front of Ukiukiu, and slowly and surely Ukiukiu, weakening fast, is split asunder. But it is not all bloodless. At times Ukiukiu struggles wildly, and with fresh accessions of strength from the limitless northeast smashes away half a mile at a time at Naulu's column and sweeps it off and away toward West Maui. Sometimes, when the two charging armies meet end-on, a tremendous perpendicular whirl results, the cloud masses, locked together, mounting thousands of feet into the air and turning over and over. A favorite device of Ukiukiu is to send a low, squat formation, densely packed, forward along the ground and under Naulu. When Ukiukiu is under, he proceeds to buck. Naulu's mighty middle gives to the blow and bends upward, but usually he turns the attacking column back upon itself and sets it milling. And all the while the ragged little skirmishers, stray and detached, sneak through the trees and canyons, crawl along and through the grass, and surprise one another with unexpected leaps and rushes; while above, far above, serene and lonely in the rays of the setting sun, Haleakala looks down upon the conflict. And so, the night. But in the morning, after the fashion of trade winds, Ukiukiu gathers strength and sends the hosts of Naulu rolling back in confusion and rout. And one day is like another day in the battle of the clouds, where Ukiukiu and Naulu strive eternally on the slopes of Haleakala.

Again in the morning, it was boots and saddles, cowboys and pack horses, and the climb to the top began. One pack horse carried 20 gallons of water, slung in five-gallon bags on either side; for water is precious and rare in the crater itself, in spite of the fact that several miles to the north and east of the crater rim more rain comes down than in any other place in the world. The way led upward across countless lava flows, without regard for trails, and never have I seen horses with such perfect footing as that of the 13 that composed our outfit. They climbed or dropped down perpendicular places with the sureness and coolness of mountain goats, and never a horse fell or balked.

There is a familiar and strange illusion experienced by all who climb isolated mountains. The higher one climbs, the more of the earth's surface becomes visible, and the effect of this is that the horizon seems uphill from the observer. This illusion is especially notable on Haleakala, for the old volcano rises directly from the sea, without buttresses or connecting ranges. In consequence, as fast as we climbed up the grim slope of Haleakala, still faster did Haleakala, ourselves, and all about us sink down into the center of what appeared a profound abyss. Everywhere, far above us, towered the horizon. The ocean sloped down from the horizon to us. The higher we climbed, the deeper did we seem to sink down, the farther above us shone the horizon, and the steeper pitched the grade up to that horizontal line where sky and ocean met. It was weird and unreal, and vagrant thoughts of Simm's Hole and of the volcano through which Jules Verne journeyed to the center of the earth flitted through one's mind.

And then, when at last we reached the summit of that monster mountain, which summit was like the bottom of an inverted cone situated in the center of an awful cosmic pit, we found that we were at neither top nor bottom. Far above us was the heaven-towering horizon, and far beneath us, where the top of the mountain should have been, was a deeper deep, the great crater, the House of the Sun. Twenty-three miles around stretched the dizzy walls of the crater. We stood on the edge of the nearly vertical western wall, and the floor of the crater lay nearly half a mile beneath. This floor, broken by lava flows and cinder cones, was as red and fresh and uneroded as if it were but yesterday that the fires went out. The cinder cones, the smallest over 400 feet in height and the largest over 900, seemed no more than puny little sand hills, so mighty was the magnitude of the setting. Two gaps, thousands of feet deep, broke the rim of the crater, and through these Ukiukiu vainly strove to drive his fleecy herds of trade-wind clouds. As fast as they advanced through the gaps, the heat of the crater dissipated them into thin air, and though they advanced always, they got nowhere.

IT WAS A SCENE OF vast bleakness and desolation, stern, forbidding, fascinating. We gazed down upon a place of fire and earthquake. The tie-ribs of earth lay bare before us. It was a workshop of nature still cluttered with the raw beginnings of world-making. Here and there great dikes of primordial rock had thrust themselves up from the bowels of earth, straight through the molten surface ferment that had evidently cooled only the other day. It was all unreal and unbelievable. Looking upward, far above us (in reality beneath us) floated the cloud battle of Ukiukiu and Naulu. And higher up the slope of the seeming abyss, above the cloud battle, in the air and sky, hung the islands of Lanai and Molokai. Across the crater, to the southeast, still apparently looking upward, we saw ascending, first, the turquoise sea, then the white surf line of the shore of Hawaii; above that the belt of trade clouds, and next, 80 miles away, rearing their stupendous bulks out of the azure sky, tipped with snow, wreathed with cloud, trembling like a mirage, the peaks of Mauna Kea and Mauna Loa hung poised on the wall of heaven.

It is told that long ago, one Maui, the son of Hina, lived on what is now known as West Maui. His mother, Hina, employed her time in the making of kapas. She must have made them at night, for her days were occupied in trying to dry the kapas. Each morning, and all morning, she toiled at spreading them out in the sun. But no sooner were they out than she began tak-

ing them in, in order to have them all under shelter for the night. For know that the days were shorter then than now. Maui watched his mother's futile toil and felt sorry for her. He decided to do something—oh, no, not to help her hang out and take in the kapas. He was too clever for that. His idea was to make the sun go slower. Perhaps he was the first Hawaiian astronomer. At any rate, he took a series of observations of the sun from various parts of the island. His conclusion was that the sun's path was directly across Haleakala. Unlike Joshua, he stood in no need of divine assistance. He gathered a huge quantity of coconuts, from the fiber of which he braided a stout cord, and in one end of which he made a noose, even as the cowboys of Haleakala do to this day. Next he climbed into the House of the Sun and laid in wait. When the sun came tearing along the path, bent on completing its journey in the shortest time possible, the valiant youth threw his lariat around one of the sun's largest and strongest beams. He made the sun slow down some; also, he broke the beam short off. And he kept on roping and breaking off beams till the sun said it was willing to listen to reason. Maui set forth his terms of peace, which the sun accepted, agreeing to go more slowly thereafter. Wherefore Hina had ample time in which to dry her kapas, and the days are longer than they used to be, which last is quite in accord with the teachings of modern astronomy.

We had a lunch of jerked beef and hard poi in a stone corral, used of old time for the night impounding of cattle being driven across the island. Then we skirted the rim for half a mile and began the descent into the crater. Twenty-five hundred feet beneath lay the floor, and down a steep slope of loose volcanic cinders we dropped, the sure-footed horses slipping and sliding, but always keeping their feet. The black surface of the cinders, when broken by the horses' hoofs, turned to a yellow ocher dust, virulent in appearance and acid of taste, that arose in clouds. There was a gallop across a level stretch to the mouth of a convenient blowhole, and then the descent continued in clouds of volcanic dust, winding in and out among cinder cones, brick-red, old rose, and purplish black of color. Above us, higher and higher, towered the crater walls, while we journeyed on across innumerable lava flows, turning and twisting a devious way among the adamantine billows of a petrified sea. Saw-toothed waves of lava vexed the surface of this weird ocean, while on either hand rose jagged crests and spiracles of fantastic shape. Our way led on past a bottomless pit and along and over the main stream of the latest lava flow for 7 miles.

At the lower end of the crater was our camping spot, in a small grove of olapa and kolea trees, tucked away in a corner of the crater at the base of walls that rose perpendicularly 1,500 feet. Here was pasturage for the horses, but no water, and first we turned aside and picked our way across a mile of lava to a known water hole in a crevice in the crater wall. The water hole was empty. But on climbing 50 feet up the crevice, a pool was found containing half a dozen barrels of water. A pail was carried up, and soon a steady stream of the precious liquid was running down the rock and filling the lower pool, while the cowboys below were busy fighting the horses back, for there was room for one only to drink at a time. Then it was on to camp at the foot of the wall, up which herds of wild goats scrambled and blatted, while the tent rose to the sound of rifle firing. Jerked beef, hard poi, and broiled kid was the menu. Over the crest of the crater, just above our heads, rolled a sea of clouds, driven on by Ukiukiu. Though this sea rolled over the crest unceasingly, it never blotted out nor dimmed the moon, for the heat of the crater dissolved the clouds as fast as they rolled in. Through the moonlight, attracted by the camp fire, came the crater cattle to peer and challenge. They were rolling fat, though they rarely drank water, the morning dew on the grass taking its place. It was because of this dew that the tent made a welcome bedchamber, and we fell asleep to the chanting of hulas by the unwearied Hawaiian cowboys, in whose veins, no doubt, ran the blood of Maui, their valiant forebear.

The camera cannot do justice to the House of the Sun. The sublimated chemistry of photography may not lie, but it certainly does not tell all the truth. The Koolau Gap [may be] faithfully reproduced, just as it impinged on the retina of the camera, yet in the resulting picture the gigantic scale of things is missing. Those walls that seem several hundred feet in height are almost as many thousand; that entering wedge of cloud is a mile and a half wide in the gap itself, while beyond the gap it is a veritable ocean; and that foreground of cinder cone and volcanic ash, mushy and colorless in appearance, is in truth gorgeous-hued in brick-red, terra cotta, rose, yellow, ocher, and purplish black. Also, words are a vain thing and drive to despair. To say that a crater wall is 2,000 feet high is to say just precisely that it is 2,000 feet high; but there is a vast deal more to that crater wall than a mere statistic. The sun is 93 million miles distant, but to mortal conception the adjoining county is farther away. This frailty of the human brain is hard on the sun. It is likewise hard on the House of the Sun. Haleakala has a message of beauty and wonder for the human soul that cannot be delivered by proxy. Kolikoli is six hours from Kahului; Kahului is a night's run from Honolulu; Honolulu is six days from San Francisco; and there you are.

WE CLIMBED THE CRATER walls, put the horses over impossible places, rolled stones, and shot wild goats. I did not get any goats. I was too busy rolling stones. One spot in particular I remember, where we started a stone the size of a horse. It began the descent easy enough, rolling over, wobbling, and threatening to stop; but in a few minutes it was soaring through the air 200 feet at a jump. It grew rapidly smaller until it struck a slight slope of volcanic sand, over which it darted like a startled jack rabbit, kicking up behind it a tiny trail of yellow dust. Stone and dust diminished in size, until some of the party said the stone had stopped. That was because they could not see it any longer. It had vanished into the distance beyond their ken. Others saw it rolling farther on—I know I did; and it is my firm conviction that that stone is still rolling.

Our last day in the crater, Ukiukiu gave us a taste of his strength. He smashed Naulu back all along the line, filled the House of the Sun to overflowing with clouds, and drowned us out. Our rain gauge was a pint cup under a tiny hole in the tent. That last night of storm and rain filled the cup, and there was no way of measuring the water that spilled over into the blankets. With the rain gauge out of business there was no longer any reason for remaining; so we broke camp in the wetgray of dawn and plunged eastward across the lava to the Kaupo Gap. East Maui is nothing more or less than the vast lava stream that flowed long ago through the Kaupo Gap; and down this stream we picked our way from an altitude of 6,500 feet to the sea. This was a day's work in itself for the horses; but never were there such horses. Safe in the bad places, never rushing, never losing their heads, as soon as they found a trail wide and smooth enough to run on, they ran. There was no stopping them until the trail became bad again, and then they stopped of themselves. Continuously, for days, they had performed the hardest kind of work, and fed most of the time on grass foraged by themselves at night while we slept, and yet that day they covered 28 leg-breaking miles and galloped into Hana like a bunch of colts. Also, there were several of them, reared in the dry region on the leeward side of Haleakala, that had never worn shoes in all their lives. Day after day, and all day long, unshod, they had traveled over the sharp lava, with the extra weight of a man on their backs, and their hoofs were in better condition than those of the shod horses.

THE SCENERY BETWEEN Vieiras's (where the Kaupo Gap empties into the sea) and Hana, which we covered in half a day, is well worth a week or a month; but, wildly beautiful as it is, it becomes pale and small in comparison with the wonderland that lies beyond the rubber plantations between Hana and the Honomanu Gulch. Two days were required to cover this marvelous stretch, which lies on the windward side of Haleakala. The people who dwell there call it "the ditch country," an unprepossessing name, but it has no sister. Nobody else ever comes there. Nobody else knows anything about it. With the exception of a handful of men, whom business has brought there, nobody has heard of the ditch country of Maui. Now a ditch is a ditch, assumably muddy, and usually traversing uninteresting and monotonous landscapes. But the Nahiku Ditch is not an ordinary ditch. The windward side of Haleakala is serried by a thousand precipitous gorges, down which rush as many torrents, each torrent of which achieves a score of cascades and waterfalls before it reaches the sea. More rain comes down here than in any other region in the world. In 1904 the

year's downpour was 420 inches. Water means sugar, and sugar is the backbone of the territory of Hawaii, wherefore the Nahiku Ditch, which is not a ditch, but a chain of tunnels. The water travels underground, appearing only at intervals to leap a gorge, traveling high in the air on a giddy flume and plunging into and through the opposing mountain. This magnificent waterway is called a "ditch," and with equal appropriateness can Cleopatra's barge be called a boxcar.

There are no carriage roads through the ditch country, and before the ditch was built, or bored, rather, there was no horse trail. Hundreds of inches of rain annually, on fertile soil, under a tropic sun, means a steaming jungle of vegetation. A man, on foot, cutting his way through, might advance a mile a day, but at the end of a week he would be a wreck, and he would have to crawl hastily back if he wanted to get out before the vegetation overran the passageway he had cut. O'Shaughnessy was the daring engineer who conquered the jungle and the gorges, ran the ditch, and made the horse trail. He built enduringly, in concrete and masonry, and made one of the most remarkable water farms in the world. Every little runlet and dribble is harvested and conveyed by subterranean channels to the main ditch. But so heavily does it rain at times that countless spillways let the surplus escape to the sea.

The horse trail is not very wide. Like the engineer who built it, it dares anything. Where the ditch plunges through the mountain, it climbs over; and where the ditch leaps a gorge on a flume, the horse trail takes advantage of the ditch and crosses on top of the flume. That careless trail thinks nothing of traveling up or down the faces of precipices. It gouges its narrow way out of the wall, dodging around waterfalls or passing under them where they thunder down in white fury; while straight overhead the wall rises hundreds of feet, and straight beneath it sinks a thousand. And those marvelous mountain horses are as unconcerned as the trail. They fox-trot along it as a matter of course, though the footing is slippery with rain, and they will gallop with their hind feet slipping over the edge if you let them. I advise only those with steady nerves and cool heads to tackle the Nahiku Ditch trail. One of our cowboys was noted as the strongest and bravest on the big ranch. He had ridden mountain horses all his life on the rugged western slopes of Haleakala. He was first in the horse breaking; and when the others hung back, as a matter of course, he would go in to meet a wild bull in the cattle pen. He had a reputation. But he had never ridden over the Nahiku Ditch. It was there he lost his reputation. When he faced the first flume, spanning a hair-raising gorge, narrow, without railings, with a bellowing waterfall above, another below, and directly beneath a wild cascade, the air filled with driving spray and rocking to the clamor and rush of sound and motion—well, that cowboy dismounted from his horse, explained briefly that he had a wife and two children, and crossed over on foot, leading the horse behind him.

THE ONLY RELIEF from the flumes was the precipices; and the only relief from the precipices was the flumes, except where the ditch was far underground, in which case we crossed one horse and rider at a time, on primitive log bridges that swayed and teetered and threatened to carry away. I confess that at first I rode such places with my feet loose in the stirrups, and that on the sheer walls I saw to it, by a definite, conscious act of will, that the foot in the outside stirrup, overhanging the thousand feet of fall, was exceedingly loose. I say "at first"; for, as in the crater itself we quickly lost our conception of magnitude, so, on the Nahiku Ditch, we quickly lost our apprehension of depth. The ceaseless iteration of height and depth produced a state of consciousness in which height and depth were accepted as the ordinary conditions of existence; and from the horse's back to look sheer down 400 or 500 feet became quite commonplace and nonproductive of thrills. And as carelessly as the trail and the horses, we swung along the dizzy heights and ducked around or through the waterfalls.

And such a ride! Falling water was everywhere. We rode above the clouds, under the clouds, and through the clouds! and every now and then a shaft of sunshine penetrated like a searchlight to the depths yawning beneath us, or flashed upon some pinnacle of the crater rim thousands of feet above. At every turn of the trail a water-

fall or a dozen waterfalls, leaping hundreds of feet through the air, burst upon our vision. At our first night's camp, in the Keanae Gulch, we counted 32 waterfalls from a single viewpoint. The vegetation ran riot over that wild land. There were forests of koa and kolea trees, and candlenut trees; and then there were the trees called ohia-ai, which bore red mountain apples, mellow and juicy and most excellent to eat. Wild bananas grew everywhere, clinging to the sides of the gorges, and, overborne by their great bunches of ripe fruit, falling across the trail and blocking the way. And over the forest surged a sea of green life, the climbers of a thousand varieties, some that floated airily, in lacelike filaments, from the tallest branches; others that coiled and wound about the trees like huge serpents; and one, the ieie, that was for all the world like a climbing palm, swinging on a thick stem from branch to branch and tree to tree and throttling the supports whereby it climbed. Through the sea of green, lofty tree ferns thrust their great delicate fronds, and the lehua flaunted its scarlet blossoms. Underneath the climbers, in no less profusion, grew the warm-colored, strangely marked plants that in the United States one is accustomed to seeing preciously conserved in hothouses. In fact, the ditch country of Maui is nothing more nor less than a huge conservatory. Every familiar variety of fern flourishes, and more varieties that are unfamiliar, from the tiniest maidenhair to the gross and voracious staghorn, the latter the terror of the woodsmen, interlacing with itself in tangled masses five or six feet deep and covering acres.

Never was there such a ride. For two days it lasted, when we emerged into rolling country, and, along an actual wagon road, came home to the ranch at a gallop. I know it was cruel to gallop the horses after such a long, hard journey; but we blistered our hands in a vain effort to hold them in. That's the sort of horses they grow on Haleakala. At the ranch there was a great festival of cattle driving, branding, and horse breaking. Overhead Ukiukiu and Naulu battled valiantly, and far above, in the sunshine, towered the mighty summit of Haleakala.

— Jack London

THESE VOLCANIC ISLES

DAWN AT THE CRATER ON horseback. It's cold at 10,023 ft above the warm Pacific—maybe 45°. The horses' breath condenses into a smoky cloud, and the riders cling against their saddles. It's eerily quiet except for the creak of straining leather and the crunch of volcanic cinders under foot, sounds that are absurdly magnified in the vast empty space that yawns below.

This is Haleakalā, the "house of the sun." It's the crown of east Maui and the largest dormant volcano crater in the world. Every year thousands of visitors shake themselves awake at three in the morning to board vans that take them from their comfortable hotels and up the world's most steeply ascending auto route to the summit of Haleakalā National Park. Sunrise is extraordinary here, colors from the palest pink to the most fiery red slowly spread across the lip of the summit. Mark Twain called it "the sublimest spectacle" he had ever witnessed.

But sunrise is only the beginning. The park encompasses 28,665 acres, and the valley itself is 21 mi in circumference and 19 square mi in area. At its deepest, it measures 3,000 ft from the summit. The two towers of Manhattan's World Trade Center could be placed one atop the other and still not reach the top. While Haleakalā is dormant, the vast, wondrous valley here isn't a single crater created by some devastating explosion. Misnamed by the first European explorers, Haleakalā's huge depression would be more properly called an "erosional valley," the result of eons of wind and rain wearing down what was likely a small crater at the mountain's original summit. The small hills within the valley are volcanic cinder cones, each the site of an eruption.

More than anything, entering Haleakalā is like descending to the moon. Trails for hiking and horseback riding crisscross the crater for some 32 mi. The way is strewn with volcanic rubble, crater cones, frozen lava flows, vents, and lava tubes. The colors you see on your descent are muted yet dramatic—black, yellow, russet, orange, lavender, browns, and grays, even a pinkish-blue. It seems as if nothing could live here, but in fact this is an ecosystem that sustains, among other, more humble life forms, the surefooted mountain goat, the rare nēnē goose (no webbing between its toes, the better to negotiate this rugged terrain with), and the strange and delicate silversword. The silversword, a spiny, metallic-leafed plant, once grew abundantly on Haleakalā's slopes. Today it survives in small numbers at Haleakalā and at high elevations on the Big Island of Hawai'i. The plants live up to 20 years, bloom only once, scatter their seeds, and die.

The valley's starkness is overwhelming. Even shadows cast in the thin mountain air are flinty and spare. It's easy to understand why in the early days of this nation's space program, moon-bound astronauts trained in this desolate place.

It is also not difficult to see this place as a bubbling, sulfurous cauldron, a direct connection not to the heavens but to the core of the Earth. Haleakalā's last—and probably final—eruption occurred in 1790, a few years after a Frenchman named La Perouse became the first European to set foot on Maui. That fiery outburst was only one of many in Hawai'i over the millennia, just as Maui and its now-cold crater are just one facet of the volcanic variety of the Aloha State.

Large and small, awake or sleeping, volcanoes are Hawai'i's history and its heritage; behind their beauty is the story of the flames that created this ethereal island chain. The tale began some 25 million years ago, yet it is still unfinished.

The islands in the Hawaiian archipelago are really only the very crests of immense mountains rising from the bottom of the sea. Formed by molten rock known as magma, the islands were slowly pushed up from the Earth's volatile, uneasy mantle, forced through cracks in the thin crust that is the ocean floor. The first ancient eruptions cooled and formed pools on the Pacific bottom. Then, as more and more magma spilled from the vents over millions of years, the pools became ridges and grew into crests; the latter built upon themselves over the eons, until finally, miles high, they at last towered above the surface of the sea.

AS THE ISLANDS COOLED in the Pacific waters, the stark lava slopes slowly bloomed, over centuries, with colorful flora—exotic, jewel-like species endemic only to these islands, with their generous washings of tropical rain and abundant sunshine. Gradually, as seeds, spores, or eggs of living creatures were carried by the winds and currents to these isolated volcanic isles more than 2,000 mi from the closest continental land mass, the bare and rocky atolls became a paradise of greenery.

This type of volcano, with its slowly formed, gently sloping sides, is known as a shield volcano, and each of the Hawaiian isles is composed of them. As long as the underwater vents spew the lifeblood lava out from the Earth's core and into the heart of the mountain, a shield volcano will continue to grow.

The Hawaiian Islands rest on an area called the Pacific Plate, and this vast shelf of land is making its way slowly to the northwest, creeping perhaps 2–3 inches every year. The result is that contact between the submarine vents and the volcanoes' conduits for magma is gradually disrupted and closed off. Slowly, the mountains stop growing, one by one. Surface eruptions slow down and finally halt completely, and these volcanoes ultimately become extinct.

That, at least, is one explanation. Another—centuries older and still revered in Hawaiian art and song—centers upon Pele, the beautiful and tempestuous daughter of Haumea, the Earth Mother, and Wakea, the Sky Father. Pele is the Hawaiian goddess of fire, the maker of mountains, melter of rocks, eater of forests, and burner of land—both creator and destroyer. Legend has it that Pele came to the Islands long ago to flee from her cruel older sister, Na Maka o Kahai, goddess of the sea. Pele ran first to the small island of Ni'ihau, making a crater home there with her digging stick. But Na Maka found her and destroyed her hideaway, so Pele again had to flee. On Kaua'i she delved deeper,

but Na Maka chased her from that home as well. Pele ran on—from O'ahu to Moloka'i, Lana'i to Kaho'olawe, Molokini to Maui—but always and ever Na Maka pursued her.

Pele came at last to Halema'uma'u, the vast firepit crater of Ki'lauea, and there, on the Big Island, she dug deepest of all. There she is said to remain, all-powerful, quick to rage, and often unpredictable; the mountain is her impenetrable fortress and domain—a safe refuge, at least for a time, from Na Maka o Kahai.

Interestingly, the chronology of the old tales of Pele's flight from isle to isle closely matches the reckonings of modern volcanologists regarding the ages of the various craters. Today, the Big Island's Ki'lauea and Mauna Loa retain the closest links with the Earth's superheated core and are active and volatile, though three other volcanoes that shaped the island are not. The remainder of the Hawaiian volcanoes have been carried beyond their magma supply by the movement of the Pacific Plate. Those farthest to the northwest in the island chain are completely extinct. Those at the southeasterly end of the island chain—Haleakalā, Mauna Kea, and Hualālai—are dormant and slipping away, so that the implacable process of volcanic death has begun.

Eventually, experts say, in another age or so, the same cooling and slow demise will overtake all of the burning rocks that are the Hawaiian Islands. Eventually, the sea will claim their bodies and, to Pele's rage, Na Maka o Kahai will win in the end. Or will she? Off the Big Island of Hawai'i a new island is forming. It's still ½ mi below the water's surface. Several thousand years more will be required for it to break into the sunlight. But it already has a name: Loihi.

By far the largest island of the archipelago, the Big Island of Hawai'i rises some 13,796 ft above sea level at the summit of Mauna Kea. Mauna Loa is nearly as high at 13,667 ft. From their bases on the ocean floor, these shield volcanoes are the largest mountain masses on the planet. Geologists believe it required more than 3 million years of steady volcanic activity to raise these peaks up above the waters of the Pacific.

Mauna Loa's little sister, Ki'lauea, at about 4,077 ft, is the most active volcano in the world. Between the two of them, they have covered nearly 200,000 acres of land with their red-hot lava flows over the past 200 years or so. In the process, they have ravished trees, fields, meadows, villages, and more than a few unlucky human witnesses. For generations, Ki'lauea, in a continually eruptive state, has pushed molten lava up from the Earth's magma at 1,800°F and more. But as active as she and Mauna Loa are, their eruptions are comparatively safe and gentle, producing continuous small and especially liquid lava flows rather than dangerous bursts of fire and ash. The exceptions were two violently explosive displays during recorded history—one in 1790, the other in 1924. During these eruptions, Pele came closest to destroying the Big Island's largest city, Hilo. She also gave residents another scare as recently as 1985.

IT IS AROUND THESE major volcanoes that the island's Hawai'i Volcanoes National Park was created. A sprawling natural preserve, the park attracts geology experts, volcanologists, and ordinary wide-eyed visitors from all over the world. They come for the park's unparalleled opportunity to view, up close and in person, the visual wonders of Pele's kingdom of fire and fantasy. They come to study and to improve methods for predicting the times and sites of eruptions. They have done so for a century or more.

Thomas Augustus Jaggar, the preeminent volcanologist and student of Ki'lauea, built his home on stilts wedged into cracks in the volcanic rock of the crater rim. Harvard-trained and universally respected, he was the driving force behind the establishment of the Hawaiian Volcano Observatory at Ki'lauea. When he couldn't raise research funds from donations, public and private, he raised pigs to keep the scientific work going. After his death, his wife scattered Jaggar's ashes over the great fiery abyss.

The park is on the Big Island's southeastern flank, about 30 minutes out of Hilo on the aptly named Volcano Highway. Wear sturdy walking shoes and carry a warm sweater. It can be a long hike across the lava flats to see Pele in action, and at 4,000 ft above sea level, temperatures can be brisk, however hot the volcanic activity. So much can be seen at close range along the road that circles the crater that Ki'lauea has been dubbed the "drive-in volcano."

At the park's visitor center sits a large display case. It contains dozens of lava-rock "souvenirs"—removed from Pele's grasp and then returned, accompanied by letters of apology. They are sent back by visitors who say they regret having broken the *kapu* (taboo) against removing even the smallest grain of native volcanic rock from Hawai'i. A typical letter might say: "I never thought Pele would miss just one little rock, but she did, and now I've wrecked two cars . . . I lost my job, my health is poor, and I know it's because I took this stone." The letters can be humorous, or poignant and remorseful, requesting Pele's forgiveness.

It is surprisingly safe at the crater's lip. Unlike Japan's Mount Fuji or Washington State's Mount St. Helens, Hawaii's shield volcanoes spew their lava downhill, along the sides of the mountain. Still, the clouds of sulfur gas and fumes produced during volcanic eruptions are noxious and heady and can make breathing unpleasant, if not difficult. It has been pointed out that the chemistry of volcanoes—sulfur, hydrogen, oxygen, carbon dioxide—closely resembles the chemistry of the egg.

It's an 11-mi drive around the Ki'lauea crater via the Crater Rim Road, and the trip takes about an hour. But it's better to walk a bit. There are at least eight major trails in the park, ranging from short 15-minute strolls to the three-day, 18-mi (one way) Mauna Loa Trail, which is, as you might expect, only for the seasoned hiker. A comfortable walk is Sulfur Banks, with its many vast, steaming vents creating halos of clouds around the rim of Ki'lauea. The route passes through a seemingly enchanted forest of sandalwood, flowers, and ferns.

Just ahead is the main attraction: the center of Pele's power, Halema'uma'u. This yawning pit of flame and burning rock measures some 3,000 ft wide and is a breathtaking sight. When Pele is in full fury, visitors come here in droves, on foot and by helicopter, to see her crimson expulsions coloring the dark earth and smoky sky. Recently, however, Ki'lauea's most violent activity has occurred along vents in the mountain's sides instead of at its summit crater. Known as rift zones, they are lateral conduits that often open in shield volcanoes.

KI'LAUEA HAS TWO RIFT zones, one extending from the summit crater toward the southwest, through Kau, the other to the east–northeast through Puna, past Cape Kumakahi, and into the sea. In the last two decades, repeated eruptions in the east rift zone have blocked off 12 mi of coastal road—some under more than 300 ft of rock—and have covered a total of 10,000 acres with lava. Where the flows entered the ocean, roughly 200 acres have been added to the Big Island.

Farther along the Crater Rim Road (about 4 mi from the visitor center) is the Thurston Lava Tube, an example of a strangely beautiful volcanic phenomenon common on the Islands. Lava tubes form when lava flows rapidly downhill; the sides and top of this river of molten rock cool, while the fluid center flows on. Most formations are short and shallow, but some measure 30 ft–50 ft high and hundreds of yards long. Dark, cavelike places, lava tubes were often used to store remains of the ancient Hawaiian royalty—the *ali'i*. Thurston Lava Tube sits in a beautiful prehistoric fern forest called Fern Jungle.

Throughout the park, new lava formations are continually being created. Starkly beautiful, these volcanic deposits exhibit the different types of lava produced by Hawaii's volcanoes: *a'ā*, the dark, rough lava that solidifies as cinders of rock; and the more common *pahoehoe*, the smooth, satiny lava that forms the vast plains of black rock in ropy swirls known as lava flats, which in some areas go on for miles. Other terms that help identify what may be seen in the park include *caldera*, which are the open, bowl-like lips of a volcano summit; *ejecta*, the cinders and ash that float through the air around an eruption; and *olivine*, the semiprecious chrysolite (greenish in color) found in volcanic ash.

But it isn't all fire and flash, cinders and devastation in this volcanic landscape. Hawai'i Volcanoes National Park is also the home of some of the most beautiful of the state's black-sand beaches; humid forest glens full of lacy butterflies and colorful birds like the dainty flycatcher, called the *'elepaio;* and exquisite grottoes sparked with bright wild orchid sprays and crashing waterfalls. Even as the lava cools, still bearing a golden, glassy skin, lush, green native ferns—the *ama'uma'u, kupukupu,* and *'ōkupukupu*—spring up in the midst of Pele's fallout, as if defying her destructiveness or simply confirming the fact that after fire, she brings life.

Some 12 centuries ago, in fact, Pele brought humans to her verdant islands: the fiery explosions that lit Ki'lauea and Mauna Loa like twin beacons in the night probably guided to Pele's side the first stout-hearted explorers to Hawai'i from the Marquesas Islands, some 2,400 mi away across the trackless, treacherous ocean.

Once summoned, they worshiped her from a discreet distance. Great numbers of religious *heiau* (temples) dot the landscapes near the many older and extinct craters scattered throughout Hawai'i, demonstrating the great reverence the native islanders have always held for Pele and her creations. But the ruins of only two heiau are to be found near the very active crater at Halema'uma'u. There, at the center of the capricious Pele's power, native Hawaiians caution one even today to "step lightly, for you are on holy ground."

For all the teeming tourism and bustle that is modern Hawai'i, no one today steps on the ground that Pele may one day claim for her own. In future ages, when mighty Ki'lauea is no more, this area will still be a volcanic isle. Beneath the blue Pacific waters, fiery magma flows, and new mountains form and grow. Just below the surface, Loihi waits.

— Gary Diedrichs

BOOKS AND VIDEOS

BEFORE YOUR TRIP, pick up a copy of James Michener's *Hawaii,* one of the best novels set in the Hawaiian Islands. Other excellent novels with a Hawaiian setting include James Jones's *From Here to Eternity* and John Dominis Holt's *Waimea Summer,* based on the author's experiences growing up in Hawai'i.

Hawaii: An Uncommon History, by Edward Joesting, gives a behind-the-scenes look at the factual side of some of the same events in the Michener novel. *A Voyage to the Pacific Ocean,* by Captain James Cook, ranks as one of the first guidebooks to the Islands and still contains many valid insights. Gavan Daws's definitive *Shoal of Time* will take you from Captain Cook's landing until statehood in 1959.

Maui, How It Came to Be, by Will Kyselka, will tell you more about Maui's origins. *Maui, Mischievous Hero,* by Barbara Lyons, illuminates the legends of the Valley Isle. Paul Wood's essays, collected in *Four Wheels, Five Corners: Facts of Life in Upcountry Maui,* offer insights into Island lifestyles through the use of pidgin prose and local settings and convey a real sense of place. Mary Kawena Pukui's *Place Names of Hawai'i* can tell you some of the interesting names in the state originated.

Rita Ariyoshi's *Maui on My Mind* is a beautiful collection of photographs in a coffee-table-book format, as is *A Day in the Life of Hawaii. Hawaiian Hiking Trails,* by Craig Chisholm, gives a good idea of the best paths to take around Maui. John R. K. Clark's *The Beaches of Maui County* offers a good overview of the island's surf and sand. *Surfing: The Ultimate Pleasure,* by Leonard Lueras, covers everything about the sport from its early history to the music and films of its later subculture. Those interested in the physical attractions of the Islands may want to read *A Guide to Tropical and Semitropical Flora,* by Loraine Kuck and Richard Tongg. The *Handbook of Hawaiian Fishes,* by W.

A. Gosline and Vernon Brock, is a must for snorkelers; *Hawaii's Birds,* by the Hawai'i Audubon Society, is perfect for the bird-watchers.

Albert J. Schütz's little souvenir-worthy paperback *All About Hawaiian* discusses the history, spelling, and pronunciation of Hawaiian words, as well as recent efforts to preserve the Islands' language. *Pidgin to Da Max,* by Douglas Simonson, explains the humorous creole language—known as Pidgin—which you'll no doubt hear all over the Hawaiian Islands.

IF YOU WANT TO PREPARE your palate for an upcoming Maui visit, or have returned from the Islands in love with haute Hawaiian cuisine, get *The New Cuisine of Hawaii,* by Janice Wald Henderson, published by Villard Books, Random House. This beautifully designed and photographed book features recipes from the 12 chefs who are credited with defining Hawai'i regional cuisine. If your interests run to the everyday, not-so-haute local diet of dishes inspired by Hawai'i's unique ethnic mix, try *The Foods of Paradise* by Rachel Laudan.

At Kahului Airport you'll find racks of free weekly visitor guides, including *Maui Gold, This Week Maui,* and *Maui Beach Press,* full of coupons, discount offers, and suggestions for what to see and do on the Valley Isle.

Movie buffs will enjoy *Made in Paradise: Hollywood's Films of Hawaii and the South Seas* by Luis Reyes; it points out movie locations and pokes gentle fun at some of the misinformation popularized by Tinseltown's version of island life. Most people automatically think of Elvis when the words "Hawai'i" and "movie" are mentioned in the same sentence. Elvis Presley's Hawaiian-filmed movies are *Girls! Girls! Girls!* (1962), *Paradise, Hawaiian Style* (1966), and *Blue Hawaii* (1962). Films with Maui locations include *Exit to Eden,* the 1994 sex-themed comedy starring Dan Akroyd and Rosie O'Donnell, which was filmed on Maui and Lāna'i; and *George of the Jungle* (1997), in which Brendan Fraser frolicked on Maui and Kaua'i. Other movies filmed in Hawai'i include *Six Days, Seven Nights* (1998), *Raiders of the Lost Ark* (1981), *Jurassic Park* (1993), and *From Here to Eternity* (1954).

Hawaiian Glossary and Menu Guide

HAWAIIAN GLOSSARY

ALTHOUGH an understanding of Hawaiian is by no means required on a trip to the Aloha State, a *malihini*, or newcomer, will find plenty of opportunities to pick up a few of the local words and phrases. Traditional names and expressions are widely used in the Islands, thanks in part to legislation enacted in the early '90s to encourage the use of the authentically spelled Hawaiian language. Visitors are likely to read or hear at least a few words each day of their stay. Such exposure enriches a trip to Hawai'i.

With a basic understanding and some uninhibited practice, anyone can have enough command of the local tongue to ask for directions and to order from a restaurant menu. One visitor announced she would not leave until she could pronounce the name of the state fish, the *humuhumunukunukuāpua'a*. Luckily, she had scheduled a nine-day stay.

Simplifying the learning process is the fact that the Hawaiian language contains only eight consonants—*H, K, L, M, N, P, W,* and the silent *'okina* or glottal stop, written '—plus the five vowels. All syllables, and therefore all words, end in a vowel. Each vowel, with the exception of a few diphthongized double vowels such as *au* (pronounced "ow") or *ai* (pronounced "eye"), is pronounced separately. Thus *'Iolani* is four syllables (ee-oh-la-nee), not three (yo-la-nee). Although some Hawaiian words have only vowels, most also contain some consonants, but consonants are never doubled.

Pronunciation is simple. Pronounce *A* "ah" as father; *E* "ay" as in weigh; *I* "ee" as in marine; *O* "oh" as in no; *U* "oo" as in true.

Consonants mirror their English equivalents, with the exception of *W*. When the letter begins any syllable other than the first one in a word, it is usually pronounced as a *V*. *'Awa*, the Polynesian drink, is pronounced "ava"; *'ewa* is pronounced "eva."

Nearly all long Hawaiian words are combinations of shorter words; they are not difficult to pronounce if you segment them into shorter words. *Kalaniana'ole,* the highway running east from Honolulu, is easily understood as *Kalani ana 'ole.* Apply the standard pronunciation rules—the stress falls on the next-to-last syllable of most two- or three-syllable Hawaiian words—and Kalaniana'ole Highway is as easy to say as Main Street.

Now about that fish. Try *humu-humu nuku-nuku āpu a'a.*

The other unusual element in Hawaiian language is the *kahakō* or macron, written as a short line (¯) placed over a vowel. Like the accent (´) in Spanish, the kahakō puts emphasis on a syllable that would normally not be stressed. The most familiar example is probably *Waikīkī.* With no macrons, the stress would fall on the middle syllable; with only one macron, on the last syllable, the stress would fall on the first and last syllables. Some words become plural with the addition of a macron, often on a syllable that would have been stressed anyway. No Hawaiian word becomes plural with the addition of an *S* since that letter does not exist in *'ōlelo Hawai'i* (which is Hawaiian for "Hawaiian language").

What follows is a glossary of some of the most commonly used Hawaiian words. Don't be afraid to give them a try. Hawaiian residents appreciate visitors who at least try to pick up the local language.

'a'ā: rough, crumbling lava, contrasting with *pāhoehoe*, which is smooth.

'ae: yes.

akamai: smart, clever, possessing savoir faire.

ala: a road, path, or trail.

ali'i: a Hawaiian chief, a member of the chiefly class.

aloha: love, affection, kindness. Also a salutation meaning both greetings and farewell.

'a'ole: no.

'auwai: a ditch.

auwē: alas, woe is me!

'ehu: a red-haired Hawaiian.

'ewa: in the direction of 'Ewa plantation, west of Honolulu.

hala: the pandanus tree, whose leaves (*lau hala*) are used to make baskets and plaited mats.

hale: a house.

hana: to work.

haole: originally a stranger or foreigner. Since the first foreigners were Caucasian, *haole* now means a Caucasian person.

hapa: a part, sometimes a half; often used as a short form of *hapa haole*, to mean a person who is part-Caucasian; thus, the name of a popular local band, whose members represent a variety of ethnicities.

hau'oli: to rejoice. *Hau'oli Makahiki Hou* means Happy New Year. *Hau'oli lā hānau* means Happy Birthday.

heiau: an outdoor stone platform; an ancient Hawaiian place of worship.

holo: to run.

holoholo: to go for a walk, ride, or sail.

holokū: a long Hawaiian dress, somewhat fitted, with a yoke and a train. Influenced by European fashion, it was worn at court, and at least one local translates the word as "expensive mu'umu'u."

holomū: a post–World War II cross between a *holokū* and a *mu'umu'u,* less fitted than the former but less voluminous than the latter, and having no train.

honi: to kiss, a kiss. A phrase that some tourists may find useful, quoted from a popular *hula,* is *Honi Ka'ua Wikiwiki:* Kiss me quick!

ho'omalimali: flattery, a deceptive "line," bunk, baloney, hooey.

huhū: angry.

hui: a group, club, or assembly. A church may refer to its congregation as a *hui* and a social club may be called a *hui.*

hukilau: a seine; a communal fishing party in which everyone helps to drive the fish into a huge net, pull it in, and divide the catch.

hula: the dance of Hawai'i.

iki: little.

ipo: sweetheart.

ka: the. This is the definite article for most singular words; for plural nouns, the definite article is usually *nā.* Since there is no S in Hawaiian, the article may be your only clue that a noun is plural.

kahuna: a priest, doctor, or other trained person of old Hawai'i, endowed with special professional skills that often included the gift of prophecy or other supernatural powers; plural: *kāhuna.*

kai: the sea, saltwater.

kalo: the taro plant from whose root poi is made.

kama'āina: literally, a child of the soil, it refers to people who were born in the Islands or have lived there for a long time.

kanaka: originally a man or humanity in general, it is now used to denote a male Hawaiian or part-Hawaiian, but is occasionally taken as a slur when used by non-Hawaiians. *Kanaka maoli,* originally a full-blooded Hawaiian person, is used by some native Hawaiian rights activists to embrace part-Hawaiians as well.

kāne: a man, a husband. If you see this word on a door, it's the men's room. If you see *kane* on a door, it's probably a misspelling; that is the Hawaiian name for the skin fungus, Tinea.

kapa: also called by its Tahitian name, *tapa,* a cloth made of beaten bark and usually dyed and stamped with a repeat design.

kapakahi: crooked, cockeyed, uneven. You've got your hat on *kapakahi.*

kapu: keep out, prohibited. This is the Hawaiian version of the more widely known Tongan word *tabu* (taboo).

keiki: a child; *keikikāne* is a boy, *keikiwahine* a girl.

kona: the leeward side of the Islands, the direction (south) from which the *kona* wind and *kona* rain come.

kuleana: a homestead or small plot of ground on which a family has been installed for some generations without necessarily owning it. By extension, *kuleana* is used to denote any area or department in which one has a special interest or prerogative. You'll hear it used this way: If you want to hire a surfboard, see Moki; that's his *kuleana.* And conversely: I can't help you with that; that's not my *kuleana.*

lamalama: to fish with a torch.

lānai: a porch, a balcony, an outdoor living room. Almost every house in Hawai'i has one. Don't confuse this two-syllable word with the three-syllable name of the island, Lāna'i.

lani: heaven, the sky.

lau hala: the leaf of the *hala* or pandanus tree, widely used in Hawaiian handcrafts.

lei: a garland of flowers.

luna: a plantation overseer or foreman.

mahalo: thank you.

makai: toward the ocean.

malihini: a newcomer to the Islands.

mana: the spiritual power that the Hawaiian believed inhabited all things and creatures.

manuwahi: free, gratis.

mauka: toward the mountains.

mauna: mountain.

mele: a Hawaiian song or chant, often of epic proportions.

Mele Kalikimaka: Merry Christmas (a transliteration from the English phrase).

Menehune: a Hawaiian pixie. The *Menehune* were a legendary race of little people who accomplished prodigious work, such as building fish-ponds and temples in the course of a single night.

moana: the ocean.

mu'umu'u: the voluminous dress in which the missionaries enveloped Hawaiian women. Now made in bright printed cottons and silks, it is an indispensable garment in a Hawaiian woman's wardrobe. Culturally sensitive locals have embraced the Hawaiian spelling, but often shorten the spoken word to "mu'u." Most English dictionaries include the spelling *muumuu*, and that version is a part of many apparel companies' names.

nani: beautiful.

nui: big.

Pākē: Chinese. This *Pākē* carver makes beautiful things.

palapala: document, printed matter.

pali: a cliff, precipice.

pānini: prickly pear cactus.

paniolo: a Hawaiian cowboy, a rough transliteration of *español*, the language of the Islands' earliest cowboys.

pau: finished, done.

pilikia: trouble. The Hawaiian word is much more widely used here than its English equivalent.

puka: a hole.

pupule: crazy, like the celebrated Princess Pupule. This word has replaced its English equivalent in local usage.

wahine: a female, a woman, a wife, and a sign on the ladies' room door; plural: *wāhine*.

wai: fresh water, as opposed to saltwater, which is *kai*.

wikiwiki: to hurry, hurry up. (Since this is a reduplication of *wiki*, quick, neither W is pronounced as a V.)

Note: Pidgin is the unofficial language of Hawai'i. It is a creole language, with its own grammar, evolved from the mixture of English, Hawaiian, Japanese, Portuguese, and other languages spoken in 19th century Hawai'i, and it is heard everywhere: on ranches, in warehouses, on beaches, and in the hallowed halls (and occasionally in the classrooms) of the University of Hawai'i.

MENU GUIDE

Much of the Hawaiian language encountered during a stay in the Islands will appear on restaurant menus and lists of lūʻau fare. Often these menus will also include terms from Japanese, Chinese, and other cultures. Here's a quick primer.

ʻahi: locally caught yellowfin tuna.

aku: skipjack, bonito tuna.

ʻamaʻama: mullet; it's hard to get, but tasty.

bento: a box lunch.

chicken lūʻau: a stew made from chicken, taro leaves, and coconut milk.

guava: This tasty fruit is most often used in juice and in jellies. As a juice, it's pink and quenches a thirst like nothing else.

haupia: a light, gelatinlike dessert made from coconut.

imu: the underground ovens in which pigs are roasted for lūʻau.

kālua: to bake underground. A *kālua* pig is the pièce de résistance of a Hawaiian feast.

kaukau: food. The word comes from Chinese, but it is widely used in the Islands.

kim chee: pickled Chinese cabbage made with garlic and hot peppers.

Kona coffee: coffee grown in the Kona district of the Big Island; prized for its rich flavor.

laulau: literally, a bundle. In everyday usage, *laulau* are morsels of pork, butterfish, or other ingredients wrapped along with young taro shoots in ti leaves for steaming.

likoʻi: (passion fruit) a tart, seedy yellow fruit that makes delicious desserts, jellies, and sherbet.

lomilomi: to rub or massage; also a massage. Lomilomi salmon is fish that has been rubbed with onions and herbs, commonly served with minced onions and tomatoes.

lūʻau: a Hawaiian feast, also the leaf of the taro plant used in preparing such a feast.

lūʻau leaves: cooked taro tops with a taste similar to spinach.

macadamia nuts: These little, round, buttery-tasting nuts are mostly grown on the Big Island, but are available throughout the Islands.

mahimahi: mild-flavored dolphin fish, not to be confused with the marine mammal.

mai tai: fruit punch with rum, from the Tahitian word for "good."

malasada: a Portuguese deep-fried doughnut without a hole, dipped in sugar.

manapua: dough wrapped around diced pork.

mango: a juicy sweet fruit, with a yellowish-red smooth skin and a yellow pulpy interior.

manō: shark.

niu: coconut.

ʻōkolehao: a liqueur distilled from the ti root.

onaga: pink or red snapper.

ono: (n.) a long, slender mackerel-like fish; also called a wahoo.

ʻono: (adj.) delicious; also hungry.

ʻōpakapaka: snapper.

ʻopihi: a tiny shellfish, or mollusk, found on rocks; also called limpets.

papaya: This green or yellow melonlike fruit will grow on you; it's high in vitamin C and is most often eaten at breakfast with a squeeze of lemon or lime.

pāpio: a young ulua or jack fish.

pohā: Cape gooseberry. Tasting a bit like honey, the pohā berry is often used in jams and desserts.

poi: a paste made from pounded taro root, a staple of the Hawaiian diet.

poke: chopped, pickled raw fish and seafood, tossed with herbs and seasonings.

pūpū: Hawaiian hors d'oeuvre.

saimin: long thin noodles and vegetables in a thin broth, often garnished with small pieces of fish cake, scrambled egg, luncheon meat, and green onion.

sashimi: raw fish sliced thin, usually eaten with soy sauce.

sushi: a variety of raw fish, served with vinegared rice and wasabi (Japanese horseradish).

ti leaves: leaves of a member of the agave family, used to wrap food in cooking; they are removed before eating.

uku: deep-sea snapper.

ulua: a member of the jack family that also includes pompano and amberjack. Also called crevalle, jack fish, and jack crevalle and can also refer to the giant trevally.

Index

INDEX

NOTES

parasailing   p. 69
Island cruises   p. 60
Nightlife   p. 59
Beaches   p. 65
Snorkeling   p. 72, 66
Art Night   p. 78

Howard's Recommendation
     Alii Nui catamaran
           808 242-5949
     Mama's Fish House
     David Paul's
     Waterfront
     Pacific Cafe
     Nick's (@ Kea Lani in Waikea)
     Outrigger Hotel Luau

NOTES

Top 10 Places to Visit

BEN	BOTH	AMI
~~JAPAN~~	- GREECE	SPAIN
	- GERMANY/ AUSTRIA	
	- SOUTH AMERICA	
	~~- EAST COAST~~	
	- AUSTRALIA	
	- S.E. ASIA	
	- TAHITI/BORA BORA	
	- INDIA	
	- CARIBBEAN	
	EGYPT	

NEXT 10:
    MEXICO
    AZI ARIZONA
    HAWAII
    RUSSIA
    JAPAN
    ITALY

NOTES

NOTES

NOTES

NOTES

NOTES

Fodor's Travel Publications

Available at bookstores everywhere. For descriptions of all our titles, a key to Fodor's guidebook series, and on-line ordering, visit www.fodors.com/books

Gold Guides

U.S.

Alaska	Florida	New Orleans	Santa Fe, Taos, Albuquerque
Arizona	Hawai'i	New York City	Seattle & Vancouver
Boston	Las Vegas, Reno, Tahoe	Oregon	The South
California		Pacific North Coast	U.S. & British Virgin Islands
Cape Cod, Martha's Vineyard, Nantucket	Los Angeles	Philadelphia & the Pennsylvania Dutch Country	Islands
The Carolinas & Georgia	Maine, Vermont, New Hampshire		USA
	Maui & Lāna'i	The Rockies	Virginia & Maryland
Chicago	Miami & the Keys	San Diego	Washington, D.C.
Colorado	New England	San Francisco	

Foreign

Australia	Europe	Montréal & Québec City	Scotland
Austria	Florence, Tuscany & Umbria	Moscow, St. Petersburg, Kiev	Singapore
The Bahamas			South Africa
Belize & Guatemala	France	The Netherlands, Belgium & Luxembourg	South America
Bermuda	Germany		Southeast Asia
Canada	Great Britain	New Zealand	Spain
Cancún, Cozumel, Yucatán Peninsula	Greece	Norway	Sweden
	Hong Kong	Nova Scotia, New Brunswick, Prince Edward Island	Switzerland
Caribbean	India		Thailand
China	Ireland		Toronto
Costa Rica	Israel	Paris	Turkey
Cuba	Italy	Portugal	Vienna & the Danube Valley
The Czech Republic & Slovakia	Japan	Provence & the Riviera	
	London	Scandinavia	Vietnam
Denmark	Madrid & Barcelona		
Eastern & Central Europe	Mexico		

Special-Interest Guides

Adventures to Imagine	Fodor's How to Pack	Kodak Guide to Shooting Great Travel Pictures	Rock & Roll Traveler USA
Alaska Ports of Call	Great American Learning Vacations		Sunday in San Francisco
Ballpark Vacations		National Parks and Seashores of the East	
The Best Cruises	Great American Sports & Adventure Vacations		Walt Disney World for Adults
Caribbean Ports of Call		National Parks of the West	
The Complete Guide to America's National Parks	Great American Vacations	Nights to Imagine	Weekends in New York
	Great American Vacations for Travelers with Disabilities	Orlando Like a Pro	Wendy Perrin's Secrets Every Smart Traveler Should Know
Europe Ports of Call		Rock & Roll Traveler Great Britain and Ireland	
Family Adventures	Halliday's New Orleans Food Explorer		Worlds to Imagine
Fodor's Gay Guide to the USA			
	Healthy Escapes		

Fodor's Special Series

Fodor's Best Bed & Breakfasts
America
California
The Mid-Atlantic
New England
The Pacific Northwest
The South
The Southwest
The Upper Great Lakes

Compass American Guides
Alaska
Arizona
Boston
Chicago
Coastal California
Colorado
Florida
Hawai'i
Hollywood
Idaho
Las Vegas
Maine
Manhattan
Minnesota
Montana
New Mexico
New Orleans
Oregon
Pacific Northwest
San Francisco
Santa Fe
South Carolina
South Dakota
Southwest
Texas
Underwater Wonders of the National Parks
Utah
Virginia
Washington
Wine Country
Wisconsin
Wyoming

Citypacks
Amsterdam
Atlanta
Berlin
Boston
Chicago
Florence
Hong Kong
London
Los Angeles
Miami
Montréal
New York City
Paris

Prague
Rome
San Francisco
Sydney
Tokyo
Toronto
Venice
Washington, D.C.

Exploring Guides
Australia
Boston & New England
Britain
California
Canada
Caribbean
China
Costa Rica
Cuba
Egypt
Florence & Tuscany
Florida
France
Germany
Greek Islands
Hawai'i
India
Ireland
Israel
Italy
Japan
London
Mexico
Moscow & St. Petersburg
New York City
Paris
Portugal
Prague
Provence
Rome
San Francisco
Scotland
Singapore & Malaysia
South Africa
Spain
Thailand
Turkey
Venice
Vietnam

Flashmaps
Boston
New York
San Francisco
Washington, D.C.

Fodor's Cityguides
Boston
New York
San Francisco

Fodor's Gay Guides
Amsterdam
Los Angeles & Southern California
New York City
Pacific Northwest
San Francisco and the Bay Area
South Florida
USA

Karen Brown Guides
Austria
California
England B&Bs
England, Wales & Scotland
France B&Bs
France Inns
Germany
Ireland
Italy B&Bs
Italy Inns
Portugal
Spain
Switzerland

Languages for Travelers (Cassette & Phrasebook)
French
German
Italian
Spanish

Mobil Travel Guides
America's Best Hotels & Restaurants
Arizona
California and the West
Florida
Great Lakes
Major Cities
Mid-Atlantic
Northeast
Northwest and Great Plains
Southeast
Southern California
Southwest and South Central

Pocket Guides
Acapulco
Aruba
Atlanta
Barbados
Beijing
Berlin
Budapest
Dublin
Honolulu
Jamaica
London

Mexico City
New York City
Paris
Prague
Puerto Rico
Rome
San Francisco
Savannah & Charleston
Shanghai
Sydney
Washington, D.C.

Rivages Guides
Bed and Breakfasts of Character and Charm in France
Hotels and Country Inns of Character and Charm in France
Hotels and Country Inns of Character and Charm in Italy
Hotels and Country Inns of Character and Charm in Paris
Hotels and Country Inns of Character and Charm in Portugal
Hotels and Country Inns of Character and Charm in Spain
Wines & Vineyards of Character and Charm in France

Short Escapes
Britain
France
Near New York City
New England

Fodor's Sports
Golf Digest's Places to Play (USA)
Golf Digest's Places to Play in the Southeast
Golf Digest's Places to Play in the Southwest
Skiing USA
USA Today The Complete Four Sport Stadium Guide

Fodor's upCLOSE Guides
California
Europe
France
Great Britain
Ireland
Italy
London
Los Angeles
Mexico
New York City
Paris
San Francisco

Looking for a different kind of vacation?

Fodor's makes it easy with a full line of guidebooks to suit a variety of interests—from sports and adventure to romance to family fun.

At bookstores everywhere.
www.fodors.com

You've read the book. Now book the trip.

For all the best deals on flights, hotels, rental cars, and vacation packages, book them online at www.previewtravel.com. Then click on our Destination Guides featuring content from Fodor's and more. You'll find hotels, restaurants, attractions, and things to do around the globe. There are even interactive maps, videos, and weather forecasts. You'll have everything you need to make your vacation exactly what you want it to be. All it takes is a trip online.

Travel on Your Terms™
www.previewtravel.com
aol keyword: previewtravel

preview travel℠

WHEREVER YOU TRAVEL, *H*ELP IS NEVER FAR AWAY.

From planning your trip to

providing travel assistance along

the way, American Express®

Travel Service Offices are

always there to help

you do more.